WEST FROM MONTEVIDEO

Uruguay by Bike

WEST FROM MONTEVIDEO

Uruguay by Bike

J. D. HOLZHAUER

CASSELL

Cassell Publishers Ltd
Artillery House, Artillery Row, London, SW1P 1RT

Copyright © J. D. Holzhauer

All rights reserved.
No part of this publication may be reproduced
or transmitted in any form or by any means,
electronic or mechanical including photocopying,
recording or any information storage or
retrieval system, without prior permission
in writing from the publishers.

First published 1989

Distributed in the United States by
Sterling Publishing Co. Inc.
2, Park Avenue, New York, NY 10016

Distributed in Australia by
Capricorn Link (Australia) Pty Ltd
PO Box 665, Lane Grove, NSW 2066

British Library Cataloguing in Publication Data
Holzhauer, J. D. (Jan D)
West from Montevideo: Uruguay by Bike
1. Uruguay. Description & travel
I. Title
918.95'0465

ISBN 0–304–31752–7

Typeset by Input Typesetting Ltd, London SW19 8DR
Printed in Great Britain by Richard Clay Ltd, Bungay, Suffolk

For Patricia,
without whom none of this
would have been possible.
Or worth it.

CONTENTS

ACKNOWLEDGEMENTS

There really is no way at all that we can adequately thank all the people who were so kind to us as we made our way around Uruguay. Their hospitality towards us stands as a tribute to the warmth and generosity of an entire nation. Apart from all of those whom you will meet in these pages, there are a few others we wish to thank: the staff of the Biblioteca Nacional, in Montevideo; the Servicio Geográfico Militar, for their help and excellent maps; Lufthansa in London and Montevideo; our family, for their support; and my old friend Bruce, who pointed us in the right direction.

We also want to thank all the people who supplied our excellent equipment, and did so on such desperately short notice.

The manuscript was written on an Apple Macintosh™ with software from Word Perfect®.

London

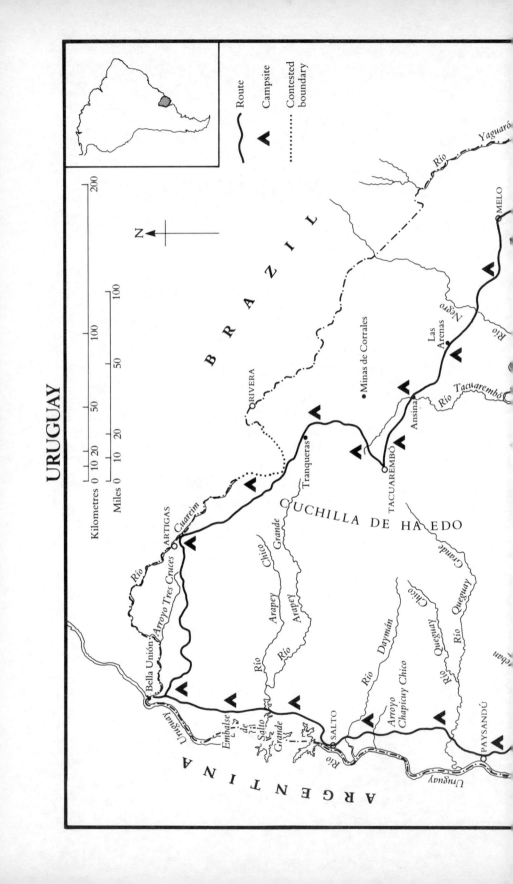

URUGUAY

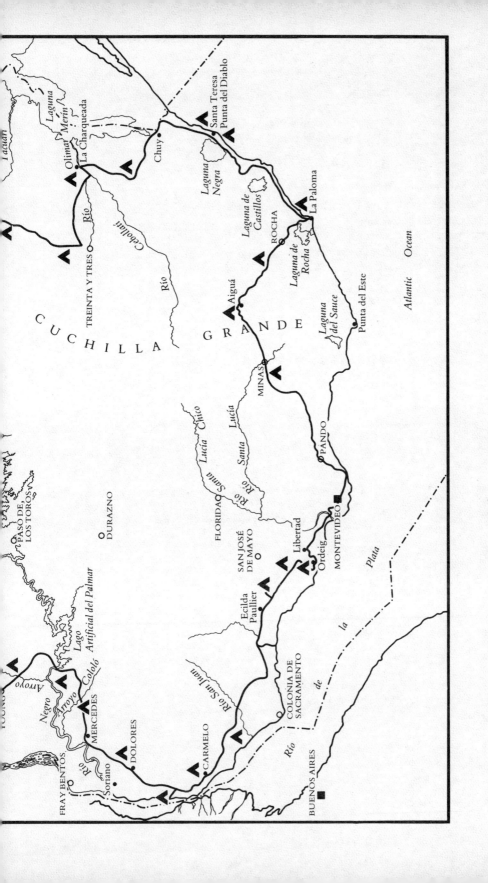

CHAPTER ONE

GO WEST . . .

'I need an adventure,' murmured Patricia, from somewhere beyond my newspaper.

'Don't we all!' I agreed, through a mouthful of toast.

'No no, I'm serious, I *mean* it,' she insisted.

I let the paper fall back onto the table, and followed her gaze out through the rain-spattered window at the grey November morning. The chestnut across the road was in an advanced state of yellow and practically naked. The garden was thick with wet, papery leaves.

'Any sort of adventure in particular?'

'Oh, I don't know. Anything, so long as it's different. How about that trip you were going to take before we got married?'

A couple of years before I'd bought a splendid bicycle, intending to cycle to Toulouse that August. Instead I'd stayed in London and used my holiday to look for another job, which I hadn't found. But that was in the far-off days when I *had* a job to change. I'd since given up on jobs, supposedly to write a thriller. I wasn't making much headway. After a hair-raising chase halfway around the globe in pursuit of the villains, my hero was now dangling from the undercarriage of a small aircraft somewhere in the vicinity of the Iguazú Falls. He was in what you might call a tight spot. Heck, we were both in a tight spot: *I* was having trouble getting *him* out of trouble.

'We could, I suppose,' I said. 'Can you get the time off?'

Patricia, you see, was gainfully employed. She was also engaged in a fight to the death with her employers, who were behaving rather shabbily. Of course, the men in shiny suits hadn't realized that, for all her gentle, decorative exterior, my wife is not the sort of woman you can push around for long.

'I can try. How much do you think we'll need?'

'Oh, I don't know. A few weeks,' I said. 'Maybe I could write about it,' I was warming to the subject, 'I could do with the change.'

'Excellent!' She banged her hands together and leaned across the debris of breakfast. 'Let's do it!'

'Of course,' I added gloomily, 'everybody and his brother has traipsed across France and written about it. Nothing new there. Plus the roads are probably so polluted and jammed with traffic that we'd be lucky to get beyond Boulogne in one piece.'

Patricia's shoulders sagged. Speculating aloud more than actually suggesting it, I went on, 'Of course, if we really want an adventure we should cycle around Uruguay instead. *That* would be new.'

Patricia's eyes glazed over. 'Yes,' she pondered, 'and more expensive.'

'And we'd need more than a couple of weeks for it, too.'

For some days the mundane business of living absorbed all our time and attention so we left the idea alone, although neither of us really stopped chewing on it. After years and years I was heartily fed up with people asking me, 'Where were you born?' – only to see the polite smile freeze on their faces when I said 'Uruguay', a reply which invariably led to something on the lines of 'Oh? How nice . . . er . . . I think. Where's Uruguay?' or perhaps 'Oh, really? What's it like there?' with the unspoken proviso that I trim my description to fit between the soup and the main course.

The subject came up again one evening, after a bellyful of wine. Patricia wanted to know exactly how much I thought it would cost and how long it would take.

'More than we can afford dear, in both cases.'

She scolded me roundly for giving up so easily. Just to keep the peace, I promised to look into it. I should point out that neither of us had ever been on a trip like this before: I could count on one hand the number of nights I'd spent in a tent and as for Patricia, well, she could count them with no hands at all. She only bought her first bicycle *ever* when we were, as they say, 'courting', so that we could go for picnics up the towpath beyond Kew Bridge. Nor was either of us particularly athletic. Oh, we put in a couple of 'keep fit' sessions a week at the local gym, but nothing too vigorous.

We started making lists of the things we might need. The Golden Rule was that everything had to be small and light. I thought we'd come unstuck at last on the day we did our arithmetic, but it coincided with Patricia completely losing her temper with her employers and threatening to take them to court. Someone from Head Office gave her a quiet cup of coffee, a bagful of money not to go through with the lawsuit, and sent her home to me. We now had the funds and the time. We pulled the trigger. From that moment on everything happened at once. It was like being on a runaway train.

We'd kicked out the idea of using the bicycles we already had. However good, they were both in need of an overhaul and even then we were unsure that they'd stand up to the trip. We toyed with the idea of getting trail bikes, but eliminated it in the end on the grounds that if the terrain were that rough we wouldn't be able to cycle anyhow, because of the weight of our equipment, and on open road the thick tyres and the weight of the vehicles themselves would only hold us back. Because we were familiar with them, we eventually decided on newer versions of what we already had.

From the 20 November until Christmas Eve panic was the order of the day as we raced all over London haggling with suppliers; weighing and measuring everything; arranging our flights; packing, unpacking and repacking our bags; galloping through Harrods; and assaulting the poor postman – already burdened with Christmas mail – with enquiries about where on earth this or that bit of still missing equipment might be. As though it played specially for us, wherever we went George Harrison's new single was thumping ominously from the public address system: *'and it's gonna take money, a whole lotta spending money . . .'*. Our telephone, needless to say, was practically red-hot from all the use it was getting. And, of course, we had to tell my mother – living in Uruguay – who had only the vaguest inkling of our plans. On the 29 December we were airborne, heading southwest, with 60 kilos excess baggage.

One of the smallest countries in South America, Uruguay is nonetheless as large as mainland Britain. It is famed for excellent beef, although its varied geography, benevolent climate and rich, alluvial soil also support vineyards, sugar-cane, rice paddies and orchards, together with the usual crop of cereals and vegetables. It remains, however, more pastoral than agricultural. In that green and pleasant land live less than three million souls, about two-thirds of whom are concentrated in Montevideo, the capital; most of the rest are spread amongst the towns scattered about the countryside.

The few days we spent in Montevideo passed in a blur of unpacking; visiting my family and showing off my new wife; assembling our bikes; recovering from jet leg; getting used to the heat; and setting up 'base camp' (at my mother's) which meant labelling all the spare parts so that she could send them on, if need be, and finding space in her refrigerator for 64 rolls of film. After some debate, we'd decided to ask Gómez, the neighbourhood factotum, to drive us to the bridge over the Río Santa Lucía at the western edge of the city, where we would start cycling. We arranged for him to come and pick us up at six o'clock on the morning of Monday 11 January.

Sunday night was absolute chaos. Too late we discovered that we had far too much stuff, and we spent several tense, highly emotional hours deciding what to discard and what to take with us. Tempers wore thin and nerves were stretched tight. It was two o'clock in the morning by the time we finally made it to bed, distraught and preoccupied. No sooner had we fallen asleep, than we were woken by a loud noise. Thinking it had been the alarm clock, we collided with each other in our haste to switch it off. The noise kept on going. It was a cricket. Somehow it had managed to get into our bedroom, where it had launched into a piercing serenade. When the alarm clock finally *did* go off we both ignored it, only to be woken by the doorbell. It was Gómez. With my underpants on back to front, I opened the door. Half-asleep himself, he glared at me with the sort of scalding contempt the habitually unpunctual reserve for the odd occasion when the tables are turned. I offered him a cup of tea but he preferred to sit bleary-eyed and scowling on the garden wall, sipping his *mate* and smoking a cigarette. I don't know how we did it, but we managed to get the show on the road only half an hour late.

Slowly we rattled and clanked our way across the sleeping city in Gómez's '51 Chevy pickup – probably due for the scrapheap in '52 – trying our best to wake up. Patricia sat dazed and oddly quiet, as the enormity of what she'd undertaken began to dawn on her.

Gómez trod hard on the brakes, raising a small cloud of dust as the van slid to a halt.

'Right,' he said, 'we're here.'

So this was it. Zero hour. The first coppery rays of the rising sun raced across the *matorrales* and fastened onto the wooden telephone poles, plucking the wires from a clear, cerulean sky. We had stopped near the bridge in a broad, bare earth clearing by the road, surrounded by scrub and low bushes. In the middle distance, the whitewashed wall of an *almacén* was lit rose by the dawn, silhouetting the few hardy souls waiting at the bus-stop. Nervously, we unloaded the bicycles. Festooned with equipment, they weighed a ton and a half.

'Well, this is it,' we said. 'We're on our way now.'

Wobbling unsteadily, we waved goodbye to Gómez and started pedalling. As we drew close to the bridge I decided I'd rather be in a different gear, so I moved the lever to make the change. With a loud twang the controlling wire snapped and went slack. Patricia and I exchanged a sombre look.

Juan Díaz de Solis, credited with discovering Uruguay, is said to have disembarked at the mouth of the Río Santa Lucía in 1516, where he was well received by the *Charrúa* Indians who had a large encampment here. He later sailed on up the Río de la Plata looking for the route to the coveted Spice Islands, and landed again further up the coast in the province of Colonia. That time the *Charrúas* weren't so hospitable. They killed him.

At first we found the bicycles difficult to handle, but we gradually grew accustomed to the bulky panniers. We carried four each: two large ones suspended like saddle-bags over the rear wheel and a smaller pair hung on either side of the front wheel at axle height by means of an ingenious, lightweight frame. The going was surprisingly easy. We cycled in silence, hardly daring to talk for fear of breaking the spell. My memories of that stretch of road are vague: straight black tarmac, eucalyptus trees, an occasional small, whitewashed house, wild flowers. *VIAJA O HUYE?* asked an enormous hoarding. Are you travelling or escaping? I wasn't sure. The air was fresh and clear, and a light breeze was blowing. Ahead of us the sun climbed steadily higher, warming up the morning. 'This is going to be a piece of cake,' I thought, pleased at our progress. Although we were on the main – nay, the *only* – road from Montevideo to Colonia, traffic was very light.

In London, in those mad, hectic days before departure, we'd said that we wouldn't be able to relax until all our equipment was safely on the aeroplane. Airborne, we'd said: 'We won't *really* be able to relax until we're through customs, and we know that everything's all right.' At my mother's house in Montevideo, we'd conceded that peace would only come once we were actually on our way. Well, here we were. I could feel the tension fade. I breathed deep, thinking how lucky we were. Looking around I saw Patricia grinning from ear to ear: she felt the same way.

'Okay?' I asked.

'Fine!' she replied.

'Tired yet?'

'No, but I'm thirsty. Can we stop a second?'

We pulled into a patch of shade on the verge amidst endless acres of green. While she had her drink, I waded into the grass for a much-needed pee.

'Ooh yes, me to!' said Patricia, 'Where can *I* go?'

'Same general area, I suppose. Not that you have a hell of a lot of choice.'

We had a moment's pause as we digested another of the realities we'd have to live with in the coming weeks.

No longer quite so flat, the terrain started taking on its characteristic roll. Hardly enough to worry us, but enough to make us perspire. We passed a tractor coming through a gate towing a large, hay-laden trailer. The driver and his companion, perched high on the mudguard, waved as we went by. Moments later, with a fierce, startling roar, they hurtled past us. For several kilometres we raced them up and down the gentle swell, our greetings becoming noisier and more elaborate each time one overtook the other. Eventually, on a rise that never seemed to end, they passed us for the last time, shouting encouragement, making pumping, pedalling movements with their arms and waving their caps in the air as they disappeared over the brow of the hill.

We reached the town of Libertad, where we would turn off the highway and head for the coast, a short while later. It was given its symbolic name

– meaning Freedom – by the original settlers, largely French refugees from Alsace-Lorraine who had fled their homeland when it came under German control in the 1870s. Now it is caught in that vacuum between being a 'true' country town or just another satellite in thrall to the nearby capital. The highway doubled as anonymous main street, flanked on either side by shops selling farming equipment, by mechanics' workshops and by several small, scruffy bars. Across the meadow in the distance to the south, standing in the middle of the fields, we saw what appeared to be a large and particularly ugly apartment building, very much like council flats in London. It was the infamous Libertad Prison. By one of those ironies of history, the military dictators of the 1970s and early 1980s had chosen *Cárcel Libertad* as a home away from home for their political opponents.

Our turning was a narrow, unpaved road that led off between modest homes with naked gardens and sun-bleached floral curtains hanging in doorways. We overheard a gaunt, brown-skinned woman scold her barefoot children, urging them indoors for lunch. Ploughed and planted earth stretched in every direction: the market gardens of Montevideo. Wild flowers choked the coarse verges with blues, yellows and white. A man on foot patiently followed a plough behind a single plodding horse. Parrots screamed from the telephone wires. Woodpeckers zipped back and forth amongst the stunted *espinillos*. We felt exhilarated: although the hand of man was everywhere, we were getting closer to the land. The only blight on this bucolic scene was the prison; its grim, brooding presence continued to dominate the skyline.

Horneros' nests, the shape and size of footballs, perched in the most improbable places: on fenceposts, on telephone poles – we even saw one, much later on, hung like a circus daredevil stunt between the wires of a fence. Working in shifts, the industrious oven-birds – about the size of thrushes – build a new mud nest every year, held together with dung, bits of grass, horsehair, wool, anything they can find, which the sun then bakes as hard as stone. The nests last for years, providing homes (once the *horneros* have vacated them, of course) for squatters such as swallows. Folklore has it that the first settlers who ventured into the countryside learned the technique for building their mud *ranchos* from the *hornero*.

Although we couldn't see it, we could smell the water. Expecting to reach the river at any minute, we grew increasingly disgruntled as every bend in the seemingly endless dusty road revealed yet more dusty road stretching out ahead. At a ford across a stream choked with purple flowers, we stopped for a rest. The going had become hard and heavy, and we were getting very hot and tired. There wasn't a patch of shade anywhere. Before we left Montevideo, everyone had told us never, but *never* to cycle in the midday heat. The sun would only burn our delicate, Europeanized skins and desiccate our brains. And yet here we were, frying. A plumber on a motorcycle towing a trailer crammed with the tools of his trade, even a white porcelain toilet bowl, came around the bend in front of us. We asked him whether it was very much further to the coast.

'Oh no,' he said cheerfully, 'it's not far at all. Just a little bit further, *pasando el repecho.*'

Pasando el repecho – just beyond the hill: it was a phrase which in time would become all too familiar, and which seldom meant what you thought it meant. Strictly speaking, it wasn't incorrect or untrue: in the Uruguayan countryside everything is, inevitably, just beyond the hill. The essential wisdom, however, so often omitted by the ever-helpful *paisanos*, is which particular hill one's destination lies just beyond.

Ordeig is a neat, unassuming cluster of small holiday chalets. We stopped to ask a tall, thin man in a bathing suit where we might buy some food and pitch our tent. He launched into a rapturous description of an excellent campsite, only 14 kilometres further along the coast, complete with showers and toilets and little stone *parrillas* and an *almacén* and heaven-knows-what other facilities, and he would have gone on for hours if we hadn't stopped him. Thank you, but we'd travelled 52 kilometres already, not bad at all for our very first day, and we wanted something closer; 14 *metres* sounded about right. He rubbed his jaw.

'Well,' he said, 'there's a little *almacén* around the corner, and the *alameda* over there is nice.'

Sold. We headed for the shop.

At the corner, Patricia stopped, got off her bicycle, leant it carefully against a fencepost and collapsed, spread-eagled, on somebody's lawn in the shade of a feather-leafed jacaranda.

'You go,' she said; 'I'm not moving.'

The shop was small, dark and not very clean. The enormously fat proprietor, wearing no shirt, stood with his porcine knuckles resting on the counter. There wasn't very much on offer. I bought a packet of *galletas*, a wedge of cheese, a dry – *very* dry – sausage, and a couple of bottles of *Salus*. He also recommended the *alameda*, and told me of a nearby stream, where the fishing was quite good.

Leaving the purchases with my already sleeping wife, I wandered off to explore. The road went past the poplars and ended on a high *barranca* overlooking a broad, sandy beach. The water was calm and very tempting. On the way back I stopped to talk to a couple of fishermen who were mending their nets in a small, shady garden. Oh yes, they knew the stream. It was a bit hard to get to though, unless you knew the way. As for the fish, well, they kept you busy but you would never be able to eat them. Full of bones. Mosquitoes were the problem. Millions of them. Very bad this year. If I'd had any lingering doubts, that killed them: Patricia is allergic to mosquito bites. So the *alameda* it was.

We wheeled our bikes across the grass and in amongst the trees near the beach. The moment we entered the shade we were set upon by hordes of mosquitoes.

'Quick, the insect repellent!'

Dancing about, we daubed ourselves with the bitter, strong-smelling oil, slapping it any-old-how onto each other's skin, hoping it would work. The insects retreated as if by magic. Mind you, the smell was such that we were sorely tempted to retreat ourselves.

We looked about at the place which was to be our first home, trying to select a suitable place for the tent. The copse suddenly seemed so exposed, and we felt awkward and shy. If through the branches we could see the people, it stood to reason that, although they were moderately far away, the people could see *us*, which we found vaguely disquieting. We were still very new at this camping lark.

We postponed our decision. In our luggage was a large nylon sheet, which we'd brought as a cover for our bicycles at night. We spread it out on the ground and sat down, planning to have a bite to eat, but before we could open our mouths we were both sound asleep. When we woke up again, an hour or so later, we were stiff and sweaty: the tarpaulin had joined forces with the weather, and made us perspire heavily. Changing into our bathing suits we slid down the bank to the Río de la Plata, so christened by Sebastian Cabot – another greedy, unscrupulous rogue looking for some easy money, who thought the river would lead him to the legendary Mountains of Silver and untold wealth, which it didn't. Of course, this 'river as big as the sea' isn't a river at all but an enormous estuary fed by the Río Uruguay and the Río Paraná. The water was mirror-calm and surprisingly warm and, no longer tainted by the Atlantic, not at all salty. We wallowed and soaked until our fingers wrinkled. Our swim, of course, washed off the repellent, so back at the *alameda* we had to go through our little application dance again.

Returning to the shop I found the proprietor and his wife relaxing in the yard at a rickety table in the shade, chickens scratching and pecking in the dust at their feet. Salted fish hung on the clothes-line, drying in the sun. I made some remark about the mosquitoes giving us a spot of bother. The woman suggested we burn some cow dung: the smoke it gave off was an excellent repellent.

Patricia was digging about in her bags when I got back.

'You know what the *almacenero*'s wife said?' I asked. 'She told me that cow dung makes the best mosquito repellent.'

'If you think I'm going to rub cowshit all over myself you've got another think coming!' she interrupted with a filthy look.

'No, no,' I went on, 'we have to *burn* it. It's the smoke that does the trick.'

Soon the *alameda* was veiled in choking clouds of acrid smoke, but as long as it kept away the bugs, we were happy. It was still early, but we were tired and wanted to turn in, so we put up the tent. We were very pleased with it. It had taken considerable effort to find. Dome-shaped,

like an igloo, it was double-skinned, with a porous inner envelope complete with waterproof groundsheet and zippered mosquito netting over
the 'door', supported on flexible metal rods which came apart into light
bundles about half a metre long. The outer, waterproof skin fitted tightly
over the inner shell and clipped into place. The advantage was that, once
it was assembled, you could move it around until you had it wherever
you wanted it, and only then fasten it to the ground with short aluminium
pegs. It took only minutes to put up and, according to the manufacturers,
it could withstand almost any weather. They had a long list of expeditions
that had carried it up Everest and into the Amazon to prove it. And,
wonder of wonders, it weighed less than four kilos. Although, true to
the manufacturer's claim, it happily survived all the stick we gave it for
nine long weeks on the road, here beneath the trees it didn't look as sturdy
as it had in our sitting room. It seemed thin and insubstantial, and we
could hear every leaf rustle and every fly hum through the fragile, eggshell
walls.

We soon got used to it, of course, but that first night wasn't easy.
Every sound startled us and once night had fallen even distant voices,
carrying on the still, warm air, seemed alarmingly near. Neither of us
could find a comfortable position, despite our inflatable mats which, until
we learned some days later to wrap them in a sheet, slipped and slid all
over the place. We dozed and woke, dozed and woke, worrying and
muttering about whether we'd done the right thing in coming on this
trip, swooning at the horrible expense, the uncertainty, the appalling
weight of luggage which had begun to make the cycling so difficult, our
hopeless lack of experience and preparation. Why, we hadn't even left
civilisation yet, and already we were having a tough time!

'We should have gone to Tahiti instead,' grumbled Patricia, 'and blown
all our money on a couple of weeks of unbridled luxury. Anything, rather
than *this*.'

As we were getting ready to leave, we noticed someone peering at us
through the branches. It was Manolín, one of the fishermen.

'*Buenos días*,' I called, waving.

'*Hola, qué tal?*' he replied, coming crab-like into the clearing, 'Leaving
already?'

A slight, small man, wearing only shorts and sandals, he had a leathery
skin tanned a deep, rich brown. In a quiet stammer, his dark eyes sparkling, he teased us for starting late. I'd told him that we would be on our
way at six. It was now half-past eight and we still weren't ready. He
wanted to know where we were going. He'd travelled the country too,
you see, when he was young. For some years he'd been part of the
support team in the annual *Vuelta Ciclista*, a marathon bicycle race around
Uruguay, very much like the *Tour de France* only more prestigious. He'd

been one of those people you see in the newsreels, festooned with wheels and mysterious spare parts, who follow on motorbikes behind the sweating, straining competitors.

With Manolín waving us on, we set off on our painful way west. Luckily the road followed the river fairly closely, so we didn't have to fight with any hills, which gave our stiff muscles a chance to warm up. Once we settled down, we found that our legs didn't ache nearly as much as we'd expected.

Kiyú was larger than Ordeig, but otherwise remarkably similar. Beneath the pines along the bank we saw the campsite and, for all our discomfort the previous night, we were glad we hadn't made it this far. Not that there was anything actually *wrong* with it: it was just a touch too public and organized for our taste. Beyond the campsite the road curved north, back towards the highway, and for quite a while we had it to ourselves, the only sound being the crackling of our tyres over the fine gravel. My friend Bruce had given us his nephew Jaime's address, and we were hoping to reach his *estancia* today. It had turned into a glorious morning: the few early skeins of cloud had tattered, unravelled and blown away, leaving the sky vivid and clear. The sun blazed down like applause onto fields of alfalfa.

A lone, antediluvian Dodge sedan, looking like a refugee from the pages of *The Grapes of Wrath*, thundered up and overtook us in a cloud of dust and a smell of burning oil. The car was loaded high with luggage and stuffed full of family, on their way home at the end of their holiday. Strapped onto the roof rack were mattresses, camp-beds, deck chairs, mangled suitcases and shapeless cardboard boxes. Improbably long bamboo fishing rods protruded from the mountain fore and aft. The boot, its lid held with string, bulged with blankets, parcels, even a birdcage complete with birds. Half a dozen shrieking, laughing children hung out of the windows and waved as the car went by, little brown arms going round like windmills, their liquid, running voices almost drowning out the explosive combustion of the ancient engine. From somewhere amongst them, an invisible dog was barking.

The lush, flat countryside began to get bumpy again. You couldn't call them hills, they weren't high enough, but they made up for their lack of stature by being long and tiresome, and following continuously, one after another. The real nuisance was the unpaved road: the fine, sandy gravel collected unexpectedly in loose, thick drifts which sucked at our wheels and made the bikes wobble and skid. Every so often we had to get off and push the paltry three or four paces it took to get clear. It sounds very silly now as I write, but at the time the relentless monotony wore our tempers thin. The countryside was lovely – clean, spacious and uncluttered – but wrestling with the road was ruining our enjoyment.

Although not much later than eleven o'clock, the sun was already high and slamming down its heat as though it bore a personal grudge. In addition, it was becoming ever more clear just how ludicrously overloaded we were. Hot, sweaty, in a towering rage and cursing fluently, we drew some satisfaction from listing, one by one, all those items we planned to get rid of as soon as we arrived at Jaime's. I kept thinking of those scenes in black-and-white films where Our Hero the Cowboy or the Foreign Legionnaire staggers across a wilderness, leaving behind a trail of discarded equipment. That had always struck me as wasteful and silly; but now, no longer watching from the comfort of a cinema seat, I began to sympathize more deeply than I ever had before. I was particularly keen to get rid of my shoes – a pair of 'garment leather' gym shoes purchased at considerable expense in London, especially for the trip. No matter what I did, the tongues kept slipping down inside the shoes and bunching up, cutting off the circulation to my toes, making my feet hotter and hotter and me madder and madder. Patricia was getting a glazed, out-to-lunch look on her face, her mouth hanging open, perspiration beading on her upper lip.

In the shade of some large old trees, their branches laden with clusters of glorious red and orange blossoms, we collapsed on our backs on the grass. The fire trees, we christened them, not knowing what they were. The meadows around us were carpeted in pale blue flowers, mimicking the sky. We realized then that we probably wouldn't make it all the way to Jaime's that day. Fortunately, we weren't far from the highway. At the crossing we found a cluster of houses and shops. Unerringly, my wife made a beeline for an *almacén* across the road, where she plonked herself down on an empty wooden fruit box in the shade.

'*Salus*,' she gasped, 'cold, please.'

I walked through the curtain hanging in the doorway into the cool, dark cavern beyond. The smell of coffee and *mate* teased at my nose, bringing on a rush of childhood memories. After the brilliant glare of the sunlight, it took my eyes a few moments to adjust to the deep, murky shadows. Tins of peas and jars of conserves were stacked in neat pyramids. Packets of pasta, biscuits and rice were laid out in rows on the shelves along the walls. Bathed in ghostly lights, hams and cheeses and bricks of red *membrillo* jam perspired like Amsterdam whores in glass-fronted cabinets. Salamis dangled on strings next to snorkels and saucepans. Bottles of soft drinks and beer stood rank upon rank all the way to the ceiling. Next to them, just what I needed: a case full of *alpargatas Rueda*!

I poured half the bottle of water into Patricia's enamel cup. She drained it almost in a single gulp, and held it out again. I busied myself with a triple ice-cream (chocolate, strawberry and vanilla), peeled off my gym shoes and socks and wiggled my ecstatically liberated toes before slipping on a new pair of *alpargatas*. They felt delicious.

The young postmistress brought a chair out of her office next door, and sat on the porch near us. By now the highway was quite busy. Most of the cars rushing past seemed to have Argentine licence plates.

'The ferry,' she said, 'between Colonia and Buenos Aires.'

She explained that we were in the middle of one of the day's rush hours, which coincided with the ferry's sailings.

In the *carnicería*, on the other side of the *almacén*, miscellaneous cuts of beef hung from the ceiling on hooks. We consulted the butcher.

'The *asado*,' he said, '*de novillo. Muy especial.*'

He brought down a couple of strips of short ribs. *Asado de tira* is a very popular cut in Uruguay, inexpensive, and rightfully highly prized for barbecueing. A *novillo* is a two-year-old heifer, and the cuts looked every bit as special as he claimed. Both strips, weighing about a kilo and a half all told, set us back the equivalent of 80 pence.

It was long gone midday and ferociously hot. After the Kiyú road it was bliss to be back on the smooth, hard tarmac, but our legs were now really beginning to beg for mercy. It felt as though our entire strength had slipped away, and it took all our willpower not to stop more often than we did. We were close to giving up for good when the open, rolling meadows gave way to a dense forest behind the wire fence on our right: row beyond orderly row of tall, stately pines, the ground beneath them cushioned with a thick, unbroken carpet of coppery needles. We'd found our campsite, all we had to do was find a way into it. Just there the road forked, Ruta 1 heading west on the left and, on the right, Ruta 3 heading north towards the city of San José and beyond. We turned right, following the forest.

We met two men coming out of a gate, one behind the other, balancing a long, freshly cut pole between them. They each carried a long-handled axe. Just the people we needed. Slowly and silently they lowered their cumbersome load to the ground.

'What was that you said?' asked one.

I repeated the question.

'Oh,' he said, giving me a long, quizzical look, 'you'll have to ask the *capataz* about that. He's in there.' He jerked a hitchhiker's thumb up the track.

Leaving our bikes at the fence, we trudged up the rutted path towards a whitewashed house at the edge of the clearing. Just within the first row of trees we could see a table at which a noisy family, consisting mainly of children, were having their lunch. The smell of woodsmoke and roasting meat wafted down to greet us. A dishevelled woman detached herself from the group, now fallen silent, and walked out to us. She listened quietly as I explained that we were looking for a place to pitch our tent for the night. Could we possibly camp in the woods, I asked.

'Nonono,' she said, '*de ninguna manera*. Not in the forest.' Against the rules, you see, this was government property and they couldn't take any chances, the risk of fire was too great.

A short, scruffy man, badly in need of a shave, his shirt unbuttoned and his toes sticking through holes in his *alpargatas*, sauntered up to join us, his hands thrust deep into the waistband of his faded blue shorts. This was her husband, the foreman.

'I told them they couldn't camp in the forest,' she rattled at him at once, 'because of fire. And they can't, can they?' she concluded, crossing her arms across her chest and rocking back solemnly on her heels.

'Nope,' said the man, studying us closely.

'Against the rules,' she repeated, 'dangerous. I told them.'

'Yup,' he said, with a shrug. He swallowed the mouthful he'd been chewing and took a deep breath. 'People come in here, you see, they have a bit of meat they want to cook, they light a fire and before you know i Poof! Bang! The whole forest is gone. Nothing left but ashes. Can't hav that, can we?'

I had to agree with him. For the third time I told our little story, saying that we did, indeed, have a bit of meat we wanted to cook, but that we were careful people and just as concerned as he was about protecting the trees. He thought about that for a while, his wife clucking and muttering in the background. Quietly at first but with mounting excitement, they discussed us and our plans to cycle around the country, explaining the idea to each other as though we weren't there to hear the conversation. We suddenly realized they were arguing about the merits of one potential campsite in comparison with another. That one has no shade, no, there's a wasp's nest over there, and so on. Still adamant that we couldn't camp in the forest, they finally reached an agreement.

'Come with me,' said the foreman.

From the gate he pointed across the road to another large clearing where a bulldozer, a tractor and a couple of trucks were parked in the yard in front of a long, low shed with a Highway Maintenance Department sign next to it. Behind the shed was a windmill.

'At the base of the windmill,' he said, 'there's a pump. You can get all the water you need from there. Now, look,' he pointed further up the road, 'you see beyond those trees there, on the left? Okay, just past there, you'll see a *camino* through the bushes. Follow that and you'll get to a clearing over there, beyond the windmill. You can camp there, cook whatever you like. There are some lovely pines, a very *especial* shade. Let me know if you need anything else. Be careful you don't miss the turning.'

Without his directions we never would have found it. The path led obliquely away from the highway, its mouth overgrown with tall grass and obscured by thick, tumbledown bushes. We wheeled our bikes across the deep but mercifully dry ditch and into the undergrowth. Ten paces later we could no longer see the road: we were in a broad, wild avenue cutting a curve through the woods. On our left were the pines, casting their deep, remedial shade. On the right, a towering forest of elegant eucalyptus, their silvery bark lit by the mottled sunlight that filtered through the high canopy. A herd of cows resting in a muddy patch of shade, pensively chewing the cud, curiously watched us go by. The breeze was rich with the perfume of cattle and tree resin. The silence was tasselled with the raucous call of parrots and the chatter of *horneros* and *pirinchos*. The satin sob of wood pigeons hung on the air like a transparent curtain. It was hard to believe we were only a few hundred metres from the Ruta 3.

There below us, from the glade, we could see the windmill. We leant our bikes against the fence, most of whose strands were broken or missing, and sank gratefully to the padded ground. We lay there and tended our discomfort, feeling it come away in layers like the skins of an onion, each revealing another beneath it in some sort of natural order. First went the fears about finding a campsite, then thirst, then our most immediate weariness, then the heat. I, at least, had been able to take my shirt off as we cycled, but Patricia had been denied that small blessing and her clothes were soaked with perspiration. She promptly stripped to her sandals and hung her damp, clammy things on the wire. We'd gone through the list and hunger was now in the Number One slot. While the *Señora* reluctantly pulled on her bathing suit and unpacked the food, I collected the firewood, cleared a patch of ground, dug a shallow, sloping trench and started the fire, feeding it until I had a nice heap of embers. Above this bed of glowing coals went our grille. We were particularly proud of it. Very light, marginally larger than an A4 sheet of paper, it fitted neatly into a pannier but, best of all, it hadn't cost us a penny. We'd scavenged it from Patricia's sister's rubbish. After a flood in her kitchen she'd been obliged to throw out everything and start again, hence the grille. Having carried the treasure halfway around the world, we were now about to inaugurate it.

While I minded the sputtering and totally bewitching *asado*, Patricia prepared a salad of tomatoes and sweet peppers with lemon juice and a pinch of herbs. The suspense nearly killed us, but in the end it was worth every minute of waiting. It was the best meal we'd had for years. So good, in fact, that it became the standard against which we judged everything we ate for the rest of our trip: the famous San José *Asado*. Even Patricia, whose morale had been flagging, perked up at once. After the peaches, which deserve a eulogy all to themselves, she was so revitalized and invigorated that she insisted we go off and find this pump and 'do the washing up', perhaps a spot of laundry and – who knows? – maybe even have a wash ourselves!

The pump stood over a slimy, moss-covered trough by the windmill. Blackened and greasy, it bore the scars of many a makeshift repair in the course of what must have been a long and very hard career. It was noisy, cumbersome and temperamental but, when properly treated and sworn at in Spanish, behaved very well. Every push of the rusty handle brought forth a crystalline jet of icy water, straight from the guts of the earth. Contesting the area with several large and dangerous-looking wasps, we finished our spurt of domesticity and then stood about in our bathing suits, neither quite daring to be the first to turn the chilling stream upon ourselves, regardless how hot the afternoon.

'There's only one way to do this,' I said, filling a saucepan Bruce had lent us; 'surprise me.'

I handed it to Patricia and, in an act of exemplary courage, turned my back. I could almost hear her grin stretch. Gleefully, she let me have it. Once the initial shock had worn off, it became great fun. We played about for ages, laughing and chucking cold water like children, working up masses of foam and lather, which became dangerously erotic as we helped each other soap inside the bathing suits. Having seen the *capataz* and his cronies gather to play *truco* in the tractor yard, we'd decided it was perhaps best not to strip.

We'd chosen a particularly spongy patch of ground under a pine for the tent, but had to reject it when we saw a large, heavy branch, long since severed from its parent, hanging by a thread above our heads. You never know. . . . The next tree held no such dangers. It was a spectacular spot, facing down the sloping meadow towards the windmill, with a stand of eucalyptus to one side reminiscent of a Cézanne ('*Sous-bois*') which I'd seen in an exhibition at the Royal Academy some years before.

In those early days, until we learned better, we used to bring all our panniers into the tent with us, and stand them in a row along the 'back wall'. Later, as we became more experienced, all we took into the tent was what we might need in the night, leaving the rest on the bikes under the tarpaulin. So, with Patricia once again cursing our excess baggage, wishing half of it would simply disappear, we turned in and collapsed. The last time I looked at my watch it was just eight o'clock and still daylight. One the second day of our expedition we'd advanced a mere 29 kilometres and, awake for barely twelve hours, couldn't keep our eyes open a moment longer.

We weren't asleep for very long. At midnight we both sat up with a jerk at the very same instant, our hearts in our mouths, as the atom bomb landed at our door. Flashes of lightning snaked across the sky from every corner of the vault, overlapping one another, bathing us in a flickering, ghostly light. The thunder was deafening and continuous, making nonsense of any boyscout ploy to count the seconds between flash and bang. We'd never heard such noise in our lives. The tent felt more frail than ever. As my brain caught up with my reflexes, I saw Patricia lit up in silhouette against the blue canvas, illuminated first from one side and then the other by the radiant, coruscating detonations. Without warning, like a locomotive already upon us, a wind came out of nowhere and started buffeting our home.

A different sort of crash brought me quickly out of my reverie. Something had fallen on the tent. I scrambled for the torch. Miraculously, nothing seemed to be broken. At first I thought it was the branch, until I remembered it was in the next tree, and then I recognized the flapping of the loose tarpaulin whipping in the wind. Our bicycles had been blown over.

'I'd better go and fix this,' I said, only too aware that I'd been too lazy to put in all sixteen of the tent pegs. I had a fleeting recollection of a friend of mine in Washington, whose waterbed came adrift one day and somehow tumbled down the stairs, taking with it half the house before exploding in the sitting room. I had no desire to be blown across the meadow like a large, pale blue beachball. I grabbed the rest of the pegs and got out, clad only in my flip-flops.

It wasn't yet raining, but it was blowing fit to bust. In the combined light of the torch and the lightning, I righted the bicycles and repositioned them against the tree, wrestling with acres of billowing nylon. Then I ran around the tent, driving home the pegs, looking up into the gloom at the branches overhead, feeling slightly ridiculous and very exposed, stark naked in a gale.

I was on my way back into the tent when a brilliant flash of lightning, accompanied by a simultaneous crash, revealed Patricia's face in the doorway. Behind her brand-new glasses I thought she looked like an owl, which for some reason I found hilariously funny. She was saying something I couldn't hear.

'What?' I asked, at the top of my lungs.

'My Barbour,' she said again, 'Where is it?'

Another crash heralded the start of rain. I felt the fat, cold drops falling onto my back.

'God knows,' I said, pushing past her, 'in one of the panniers, I expect. Why? Where are you going?'

'I want to put it on,' she said, 'it's lightning-proof.'

'It's what?'

I looked at her carefully. She didn't seem to be pulling my leg.

'I want to put it on,' she said quietly, 'it's lightning-proof. It says on the label.'

'Listen, Barbours are great, but I don't think they're *that* great. And however madly they advertise, I don't think that even *they* would go quite that far.'

'I want it. It's lightning-proof. Where is it?'

I took her in my arms and rocked her back and forth. Please Lord, if you're there don't let her lose her mind *now*, we've still got another 2,000 kilometres to go. . . .

'You don't need it anyway,' I said, 'not in here.'

'The tent poles,' she said solemnly; 'they're made of metal. The lightning will be attracted to them and then we'll fry like bugs in a trap.'

'Nonono dear, you've got it all wrong, there's no need to worry. They're metallic all right, but it's a special sort of anodized magnesium and titanium alloy, the sort of thing they use in the space shuttle, completely non-magnetic and all that. Completely safe. Perfectly all right here, nothing to worry about.' (Horse manure! I didn't have a clue *what* the blasted poles were made of.) 'Besides, we're not earthed. Any lightning will hit the windmill first.'

Just then the precarious branch in the tree next to ours came crashing to the ground, killing all conversation stone dead. Patricia lay motionless, flat on her back, with me alongside. As abruptly as they'd started, the fireworks moved away, and the storm settled into a calmer pattern. The rain beat down in a uniform, unbroken torrent, but the worst was past. The muted sounds around us mingled with the peaty, penetrating smell of wet earth and wrapped us in a comforting, primeval embrace. We put our arms around each other, and slowly fell asleep again.

CHAPTER TWO

LOS MACACHINES

By morning the storm had passed us by. Tiny drops of water jewelled every leaf and blade of grass, and glittered in the rising sun. Faint wisps of fast diffusing vapour rose from the sodden ground into the crisp forest air, threaded with the smells of pine and cows, ringing with the call of birds. Despite our midnight interruption we felt rested. As she dressed, Patricia nonchalantly picked a furry grey spider the size of squash ball out of her shoe and dropped it on the ground without a word. At home, any bug a fraction of its size would have had her screaming her lungs out and calling the police.

We nibbled at pears and left-over *asado* as we packed. Our troubles began almost immediately afterwards, on our hike back to the road. The sodden path through the wood was booby-trapped with puddles of syrupy mud. We managed to walk around the worst of them, although we failed to avoid them all. Relentlessly, the sticky stuff built up in cakes on our tyres and, by the turning of the wheels, it collected on the brakes, the dynamos, the inappropriately christened mudguards, and the bags. Whatever was left over found its way onto our legs. The worst was yet to come: yesterday's ditch by the side of the road was, of course, no longer dry. We waded across the muddy stream, carrying our bicycles onto the verge where the tightly packed pebbles at once stuck in clumps to the paste on our wheels and our shoes. It took us half an hour with a knife to scrape off the stony nougat.

We coasted down the slope back onto the Ruta 1 and pointed ourselves west. A small white van overtook us, made a U-turn in the middle of the road, and raced by again. A little while later it passed once more, to stop beneath a tree up ahead. Two men got out and waited in the shade. They made an improbable pair. The driver was fair-haired, carefully groomed, and fashionably dressed from top to toe in baggy white. His scruffy, unshaven companion, by contrast, had all the presence and poise of a village idiot. While he hovered in the background, grinning simply, the lad in white assaulted us with questions. In between the quizzing he told us of his ice-cream parlour in San José, giving us his business card with last year's calendar on the back. He'd been so consumed, he said, with curiosity about us, that he'd simply *had* to stop to see what we were doing.

'Rubbish!' snarled Patricia, full of venom, after they were gone. 'The blood fairy only wanted a closer look at your legs!'

According to our map, the countryside was flat. Or, at least, undulating no higher than 50 metres above sea level. Flat it decidedly was not. As for the undulation, well, there was plenty of that. Ridges and low hills rolled like ripples one after another in almost perfect symmetry. Our meagre reserves of energy quickly slipped away again. Patricia's thighs began to ache. My problem was in the knees: they didn't hurt, they just felt infinitely tired. For every climb there was a descent, of course; at least, there *must* have been, but for some reason the downhills never felt as long or as steep as the ups. We certainly drew little comfort from them. Whatever momentum we gained was cruelly dissipated long before we reached the next blunt crest. We had little appetite to appreciate the countryside around us, some of the most intensively farmed land in the country, as much for its fruitful soil as for its proximity to the markets of the capital. Much of it is pasture for the dairy herds, with the rest given over to crops. From time to time we passed isolated houses and once or twice a little hamlet. Unpaved roads, rarely more than rough earth tracks, led away to either side, soon to be lost amongst the folded meadows. Traffic was light. In the broad, seldom interrupted tangle of wild flowers and weeds along the verge, we saw here a single ear of corn, there a patch of stunted wheat and over there a lonely sunflower: all bastards, all brought here by the wind. Birds burst from the brush, calling out as we passed. Dark furry bundles darted undercover before we could see them well.

As we pedalled the hours and minutes slowly by, we felt the temperature climb. The sun stood almost directly overhead, shrivelling our shadows, its radiance tangible and hard like a soundless slap. If the horror stories about erosion of the ozone layer turn out to be true, this beautiful corner of the world will be one of the first to fry, just before it floods, due to the melting of the polar icecap caused by the greenhouse effect.

Bathed in perspiration, we made frequent stops to rest in patches of shade and drink our now warm water. Patricia, who had started the day in high spirits, was wilting fast. Every uphill became a personal issue, as though it existed to torment her. We'd known, before we started out, that the first few days would be the hardest. On the road, the knowledge was no longer enough. Her darkening mood excluded any chance of calm reason. Only with more care and tact than I normally have was I able to avoid being held responsible for every stage of her discomfort. Seeing her labour her way up a hill, falling behind, getting off her bicycle to push it the rest of the way, I began to feel increasingly guilty. Reaching the summit before her, I took to leaving my bike in the grass and walking back down to help. At first she welcomed my concern, accepting the proffered bottle of water and handing over her load, but it wasn't very long before even that began to annoy her. As the morning grew hotter and the going no easier, she began to resent my assistance, reading into it a criticism of her performance. I tried to cheer her up with banalities such as 'Come on, you can do it!' and 'Attagirl, that's great, not much further now!'

'Don't patronize me, you creep,' she grunted, her rage and frustration boiling over into a muttered stream of invective, as she listed one by one all the things that were making her miserable. First the countryside which, she crowed, was far from the 'mostly flat' that I had promised. Then the heat and the excess baggage. She even became angry with her own body, accusing it of unreliability, lack of co-operation and no team spirit at all. The downhill slopes were no longer exempt, and were indicted as mere refinements in an already exquisite torture.

'This is no reward, do you hear me?' She yelled as we glided down an echoing, tree-lined slope. 'No reward at all! See? There's *another* bloody uphill, straight ahead!'

Not that my progress was trouble-free, mind you. I kept wishing my knees were boxes so that I could lift the caps away like lids and fill the cavities with grease. My thumbs and wrists I just wanted to detach and throw away, thanks to the vibrating handlebars. So sore were my hands that it wasn't until several days after I'd exchanged the flimsy handlebar tape for more substantial foam-rubber grips that they returned to normal.

At the crest of a ridge we found what looked like a factory, which a large hoarding identified as the Kasdorf cheese and dairy products plant. The name resonated with memories. When I was a small boy in Montevideo, the men from Kasdorf were almost synonymous with the sluggish heat of summer afternoons. In their distinctive yellow uniforms and matching caps, the name embroidered in lilac around the crown, they walked the streets pushing yellow, two-wheeled carts. Those big square boxes were treasure chests full of ice-cream, stacked in layers atop a steaming slab of dry ice. Like medicine men, the *heladeros* were very conscious of the magic they wrought every time they lifted the lid, heavy as the door to Fort Knox, and then, hey presto, out of the billowing cloud drew forth the requested delight. They were much more sophisticated than their competitors, because their tubs were intriguingly cubic instead of merely round. In those days, only Kasdorf had the tantalizing *triple mixto* and, if you were lucky and caught the *heladero* at the start of his run: pineapple!

We turned into the driveway and coasted to the building. My worn-out associate leant her bike against the wall and collapsed in a semi-comatose heap on the steps, like some pitiful beggar at the cathedral door. I gathered our empty water bottles and approached a group of workmen in tall rubber boots and white plastic aprons who were stacking empty milk cans onto a waiting truck. With a smile, one of them led me into the dark, cool loading bay to a tap above a large, white basin.

'Help yourself,' he said, with a wave of his arm.

I gave the tap a vigorous twist. A powerful jet surged forth, and poured through the gaping plughole all over my feet. Unexpected, but far from unpleasant. Letting it wash around my toes, I splashed water on my face and head.

When I returned, the Celebrated Cyclist was still prostrate on the steps, snoring sonorously under the foreman's bemused and watchful eye. He rather spoiled my day by telling us that the ice-cream division had gone bust and closed down years ago. This particular plant only made processed cheese, never our favourite, but by now we were too hungry to care. No, he hurried to explain, they didn't sell any here. They didn't have the facilities for storage or for taking money. Just as well, really, he chuckled, as it would only mean more work for him, not an encouraging prospect at the best of times, what? He laughed at his own joke. Free samples? Don't be daft. In any case, today's production had already gone. On a truck, to Montevideo, we might even have crossed it on the road. Oh, yes, and they also made *Dulce de Leche*, he said, as he left.

Now, if ever there was a truly magical confection, *Dulce de Leche* is *it*. So much so, in fact, that I've often wondered why the Three Wise Kings of Araby didn't have some in their sacks. As a restorative for the young mum it would have been splendid. It's been described as sweetened condensed milk carried a stage further, but then bread has been described as flour, water and a little bit of yeast, and that doesn't do the result justice either. In Uruguay – where the finest is found – as indeed in most of South America, this treacly confection is consumed in vast quantities, in all sorts of ways, and on the most transparent of pretexts. Even chocolate doesn't have such fanatical devotees. Patricia, although a mere Peruvian, is not only an authority on the subject but also a champion consumer, not at all the sort of woman prepared to pass a *factory* of the stuff without at least getting her fingers sticky. While I returned for more water, she went on an expedition. Her sudden appearance on the factory floor so disturbed the few employees on the production line that for a moment there was a very real danger of something going horribly wrong. Over the din, struggling bravely not to lose their rhythm, they somehow made her understand that they could neither give her any of the caramel nectar in the vats, nor interrupt their tending of the obscene tubes through which it issued for long enough to explain why not. Despondent and empty-handed, we returned to the road with a vow never to touch the company's products again.

A kilometre or so further on, we turned off the highway onto a miserable, rutted, pot-holed travesty that made the Kiyú road seem like a miracle of modern engineering. To rub salt into the wound, there was more traffic on that track than there had been on the highway. Truck after truck thundered past, coming empty, going back full, laden with the choking discharge from the quarry up ahead. We might as well have been invisible for all the notice they took of us. On the way in they came like racers, foot to the floor, their wheels lifting the road into our faces. On the way back, unable to travel so fast, they compensated by pouring half their load onto our heads each time they hit a pot-hole which, invariably, happened to be right next to wherever we were. Since the coarse muck cascading down seemed just the same as the coarse muck being lifted up, I wondered out loud whether this might not be a new way of resurfacing the road which ensured that the stuff being delivered was dropped where it was needed the most.

'Yeah,' coughed Patricia, 'underneath my collar.'

Most of the cultivated fields arounds us were sown with winter feed. I tried to draw madame's attention to a shimmering field of lotus grass on our right. The tiny, brilliant yellow blossoms spread like a carpet up the slope.

'To hell with the damn things!' she growled. 'How much further?'

My wife had stopped again. I looked around to see her dismounted, standing astride her bicycle from which she'd been unseated by one of those treacherous drifts we'd come to know so well the day before. She was banging her fists rhythmically on the handlebars and, head down, was cursing softly in time. Tears glistened on her cheeks.

'Shit,' she said, as her fist struck.

'Shit, shit, shit, shit, **shit!**' she added, in gradual crescendo.

'*Shit!*' this time through clenched teeth.

More than her tears, her curses made it plain that she was having a pretty awful time. Patricia seldom, if ever, swears. I'm normally the one who gets accused of sounding like a stevedore. I thought my chest would crack. How could I ever have imagined that a trip like this would be a good idea? How could I ever have believed that I could take such a gentle, thoroughly urban girl out of her natural environment, where life was safe and predictable, to drag her across this wilderness in the scorching sun? I was still trying to find the right apology when a large white station wagon, engine howling, roared over the hummock behind us and skidded to a halt in a shower of gravel and sand. Like some latter-day Hollywood Flynn, a handsome young man, moustached and wearing the traditional gaucho get-up of *bombachas*, checked shirt and whiskered *alpargatas*, dropped casually out of the driver's seat, slammed the door with a crash and, taking off his sunglasses as he came, sauntered towards us through the settling dust.

'Need any help?' he drawled, grinning from ear to ear.

'*Jaime?*' I asked with some surprise. He'd been three years old the last time I'd seen him. He shook my hand firmly.

'*Hola che, qué tal?*' he said.

Patricia was transformed. With elegance and panache she let go of her bicycle and stepped nimbly out of the way as it clattered to the ground. As though he were her very own Blue Prince arrived at last, she bounded up to him, threw her arms around his neck, and planted a firm, noisy kiss on his cheek.

'Boyoboy, are *we* glad to see *you!*' she said, with feeling, 'My old man here was just about worn out.'

'C'mon,' he said, 'let's put the bikes in the back and I'll drive you the rest of the way.'

Good thinking, I thought to myself, this lad will go far. But my wife hadn't finished her surprises.

'Oh no,' she said disapprovingly, shaking her head, 'we can't do that. We're enjoying the ride, aren't we dear? Tell you what, though: we'll give you the bags. We'd like to cycle all the way to the house.'

It was all news to me but, coming as it did with one of her biggest and brightest smiles, I wasn't going to argue. Inwardly I promised never again to feel guilty. She is a grown-up, I explained to myself, she chose to come on this trip of her own free will, I added. Her idea, even. Jaime's brow furrowed and he grunted once or twice as I handed up the bags, but he was far too polite to say anything. Yet. He told us how to find the house and roared off ahead.

Relieved of their heavy loads, the bicycles were so unexpectedly light they felt positively skittish. Cackling like children on the last day of school, we raced each other the last few kilometres to Los Macachines. We seemed to fly.

'The first thing I'm going to do,' yelled Patricia, happiness bubbling in her voice, 'is to have a long, hot shower. And the second thing, a long, cold drink!'

'Hm,' I answered, busy with plans of my own. 'A beer would go down well. I wonder whether he has a swimming pool? I'd pay violent sums of money for a swim right now, wouldn't you?'

When we reached our destination, breathless but in high spirits, Jaime was carrying the last of our luggage into the house. Large and square, it stood amongst jacaranda, pines, palms and *timbó*. The walls were painted white. The woodwork and the high, steeply raked corrugated roof which projected out beyond the walls to form a broad veranda all the way around, were the same dark shade of green. The porch was tiled in chessboard black and white, and shielded in places by wooden lattices holding up wisteria, jasmine, honeysuckle and tiny roses. Two dogs, one large the other small, lay dozing on the cool tiles. Through the tall doors we caught glimpses of long halls shrouded in deep shadow. A few very peculiar chickens, scratching in the dust, scattered squalling as we approached. They were smaller than normal chickens and seemed to have something wrong with their feathers, as though they'd been caught in a lawnmower.

'Hungry?' asked Jaime.

My good impression of the lad was getting better by the minute.

'Or would you rather have a shower first?'

Patricia's face lit up.

'Or shall we just go for a swim in the pool and worry about everything else later?'

Oh, frabjous day . . .

'Yes.'

'Yes!'

'And *Yes!*' we burst out in unison.

The pool was not, in fact, a swimming pool at all. Known locally as a *tanque Australiano*, it was a large, concrete cylinder, shaped like a giant biscuit tin about three metres deep and comfortably twice that across, almost entirely above ground. A wobbly, rough-hewn wooden ladder led up to a flat platform attached to the lip at one side. Ingeniously drafted into service as a swimming pool, it was really a water storage tank, fed by a windmill and in turn feeding the drinking troughs for the cattle and horses. Water tanks like this are common throughout the country, and often serve this dual purpose. Our elbows resting on the rim, Patricia told Jaime how much we – and I in particular – had been ready to pay for something like this.

'Damn!' he said with a scowl. 'Wish I'd known. I'll have to find another way to get my hands on your money!'

After our swim we gathered in the cavernous kitchen and concentrated our attention on the cold beers that Jaime had laid out on the marble-topped table. While he rattled our steaks and fried eggs on the blackened cast-iron range, I suggested that it was only after the sort of morning we'd had that one could really appreciate the small pleasures in life, such as a swim, a beer and the prospect of lunch. The observation earned me a dark look from Patricia.

'If you think that I need to be flayed alive before I can enjoy this,' she said emphatically, taking another sip, 'you're wrong. I can enjoy it just fine without the hassle.'

After lunch we went for a lazy stroll around the farmyard to the dairy, where the last of the herd was still being milked, and from there to a paddock into which Emilio, the foreman, had herded a few dozen sheep. He vaulted the wooden fence and strode solemnly up to us. He was a tall, strongly built man, perhaps in his early thirties, wearing much the same outfit as Jaime, with the addition of a broad leather belt and a dark blue beret tilted slightly forwards. He greeted us gently, almost formally, brown eyes twinkling above a neat moustache. For Patricia's benefit the tips of his blunt fingers paused briefly at his *boina*.

Casting an expert eye over the small flock, he selected a ewe and, lifting it in his arms like a child, carried it into a small shed. It had no door, and three of the breeze-block walls were only chest-high. The thatched roof rested on the fourth, at the back, and on wooden posts set like pillars into the other two corners. The smooth floor was made of concrete, and sloped gently down to a gutter at one end of the small chamber. At its centre, strongly reminiscent of a Mayan altar stone, stood a solid concrete table. Its waist-high top was concave, rather like a cradle. The imagery grew stronger as Emilio carefully placed the unresisting animal on its back into the hollow, which had been carefully shaped to receive it.

With the gaucho's typical economy of movement, Emilio drew a knife and matching steel from the sheath thrust through his belt at the small of his back and brushed the long, razor-sharp blade once or twice. Using a knee to hold the lamb in place, with one smooth stroke he deftly plunged the *facón* through the chest straight into its heart. The animal jerked once and was still. It struck me that those familiar words about going to the slaughter as meek as a lamb, far from being poetic licence or mere biblical imagery, were based solidly in fact: sheep go to their death without complaint. I remember seeing the same thing done to pigs, and the noise they made was enough to bring the house down.

Without pausing or hardly changing his position, Emilio withdrew the lethal blade and, holding back the animal's chin, opened the veins in its neck. As the blood surged forth I understood the sloping floor. When the bleeding had stopped, the man repositioned the carcass and rinsed the blood down the drain with water before the flies could find it. For a few eerie seconds the exanimate body seemed to resuscitate, kicking and galloping violently before finally settling again. With the skill of long practice, Emilio skinned and gutted the carcass. The unwanted parts went into a bin, some of them to be fed later to the dogs. The rest he placed in a barrow and wheeled away to the storeroom. From start to finish he'd taken twenty minutes, at the most. The skin would be scraped and rinsed and stretched on a frame to dry in the sun. Then it would either be sold, for eventual use somewhere in the garment industry, or kept on the farm where, amongst other things, it could be used as padding on the *recado*, the gaucho's traditional saddle.

Although Uruguay is famed as a producer of fine beef, the staple diet in the countryside is lamb or, more often, mutton. Another product vital to the national economy is wool, although on some *estancias*, the flocks are kept only to feed the personnel. Beef is more costly and a greater source of revenue, so cows are seldom slaughtered for food nowadays. A far cry from colonial times, when an entire animal would be sacrificed for its hide and a steak, the rest being left there to rot.

Jaime invited us to join him on his daily tour of the estate.

'We can ride or drive,' he said accommodatingly, 'whichever you prefer.'

We were leaning against a fence at the time, admiring the horses.

Patricia, who had never been in a saddle in her life and was still feeling sore from the cycling, was reluctant to make today the first time.

'They're so enormous,' she whispered.

Instead, we piled into the station wagon, the two excited dogs in the back, and bumped and lurched our way across the fields. I was given the job of opening and closing the gates. The latches, intricate and baffling, were all different, and I had to pause before each one to work out how the systems of levers and tensors fitted together. At a brook we got out of the car and continued on foot. Jaime handed me the rifle which he'd brought along 'in case we see a hare or something'. The dogs raced ahead, scattering birds in every direction. With a flurry of wings, partridges exploded screaming from the grass and raced to safety. A couple of hares broke cover, gave us a taunting glimpse of their tails and were gone, the dogs in hot pursuit.

As we walked up a gentle slope, sparsely dotted with twisted, ancient trees, no sign of mankind's presence to be seen and not a single mechanical or human sound reaching our ears apart from our own muted voices, it was easy to believe that we had somehow found a hole in time and, stepping through it, had left behind the modern world. Even the stunted vegetation, wispy leaves and thorny branches, looked prehistoric to my eyes. So far as he knew, Jaime said, the fields we were in had never tasted the plough. All was much as it always had been, allowing perhaps for the changes wrought by grazing cattle.

We were talking of medicinal plants when Jaime, by way of reply, bent down and pulled an emerald stem from a tuft on the ground at his feet.

'This is one of the best,' he said, giving it to me, 'grows everywhere, as you can see,' he added, with a wave of his arm.

The leaf in my hand was long and slender, like a broad stem of grass, except that it grew from the central artery in a curious, 'triple-bladed' shape, the sort of thing that in cross section would look like the Mercedes Benz trademark.

'*Carqueja*,' he went on, '*Eupatorium Bonifolium* if you want the Latin name. You make a tea with it. If ever you have any stomach trouble, this will sort you out at once.'

I made a mental note, not realizing then just how vaulable the knowledge would prove.

The air around us echoed with the constant call of birds. *Teros* rose cawing from the ground; woodpeckers, oven-birds, thorn-birds, *dormilones* and parrots; partridges and pigeons all zoomed around us. Along the skyline Jaime pointed out perhaps the most impressive of the native birds, the flightless *ñandú*, the South American ostrich. Neither as large nor as brilliantly coloured as its African cousin, it is none the less an imposing creature. Looking closely, we soon saw through their camouflage: there were several of them grazing across the face of the hill, strutting like pompous, middle-aged dowagers on parade. That slightly ridiculous walk can, if necessary, be translated into quite astonishing bursts of speed. They watched us watching them as we drew near, but we were too far away to be a threat.

We followed Jaime into a hollow, where the grass was tall and matted and found a motionless ostrich sitting on its eggs, its shape and colour blending perfectly into the thicket. Had Jaime not known it was there, we would never have found it. Only when it realized we were coming straight towards it, did it move. It unfolded its impossible legs and stood up, a good five feet tall, watching us through enormous eyes. We approached with care, talking loudly. Ñandú have been known to attack if they feel cornered or threatened, and a single kick from those powerful legs can break thigh bones as though they were pencils. Fluttering its stubby, ineffective wings, it suddenly darted straight towards us, breaking away at the very last minute and then, seeming to stumble and fall, limped theatrically across our path. It was trying to draw us away from the nest. Seeing that we weren't yet in pursuit, it feigned another mortal injury and beckoned us again, dragging a wing like a toreador's cloak. By this time we were close enough to peer into the nest, a large messy bundle of tangled branches, and counted in it sixteen eggs the size of grapefruit. As we walked away again, watched by the jealous – and perhaps a little puzzled – bird, Jaime explained that there would, in fact, be seventeen eggs in all. One would have been buried underneath the nest and left to rot. When the baby chicks hatched out, the adult would unearth the seventeenth and smash it. In a matter of moments the smell would attract a horde of flies, and these would be the young ñandús' first meal.

I marvelled aloud at how she could have laid so many eggs at once. To begin with, Jaime said, it was a fairly average crop as these things went. He had, not long ago, found a nest in which he'd counted forty-two, although that was, perhaps, exceptional. In addition, not only was the adult not the mother but it was, in fact, a male, and even then not the father of a single egg. As the males in a flock reach maturity, he went on, the young pretenders fight, often violently, for supremacy. One by one they abandon the contest until the final confrontation, rather like a title bout, between two finalists. The victor, of course, wins all the usual privileges and fathers the next generation. The loser leaves the flock, but never strays very far. Instead, he follows at a safe distance until eventually the females, duly served by their champion, all lay their eggs, usually in the same place and within moments of each other, hence the numbers. Then, the business done, the flock seems to lose interest and moves away. All except the vanquished male, who now comes into his inheritance. He gathers the eggs neatly together and hatches them, bringing up the young, who grow up under his guidance into a new flock. Next year, when the mating season comes around again, this older, tougher, wiser bird is unlikely to lose out in the fisticuffs again, so he becomes the boss and gets the girls, while the job of nursemaid goes to someone else.

'That's where Emilio's parents used to live,' said Jaime, pointing to some grass-covered humps and depressions in the ground, overgrown with scrub. We could just see the outline of two single-roomed buildings. Those vague traces were all that remained of a mud *rancho*, until not very long ago somebody's home. Here they had lived out the seasons and sheltered from the cold. And then, when they had gone away, the elements had torn it down, returning it to the earth from whence it came. There was a sort of natural justice about it: no litter or pollution, and nothing left behind to clutter or deface the land. But life would have been hard and unforgiving here, with none of the comforts that we take so easily for granted: no plumbing, no electricity, no amenities of any sort. I tried to imagine how they might have passed the time in those rare, brief moments when they hadn't been working, as they say, 'from sun to sun'. Emilio's father had also been the foreman here, on the estate which even then had already been in Jaime's family for years.

At the top of a ridge we found another ruin. Large, irregular stones torn from the ground by the muscular roots of a spreading wild fig marked the site of an old inn. Over a century ago the road from Montevideo to Colonia had come this way, and on this spot the stagecoach used to stop for the night. Looking out across the rolling pastures we tried to find some traces of the trail, but the job needed more imagination than eyesight. The only other clue, which we came to later, was the broken remnant of a stone ford across the brook. Family tradition has it that a sack of gold coins lies buried very near that ford. Jaime's uncle used to tell of the day when a man approached him for permission to look for the gold, apparently hidden by his father. Tantalizingly, the story doesn't reveal where the bagful came from, nor on what dark and stormy night it had been buried there. The man and his companion searched by the brook for two days, but treasure found they none.

We were walking back towards the car when another hare appeared, but by the time Jaime had reminded me that I was carrying the gun and I had thought of loading it, Loba and Gypsy had chased the prey halfway to Bolivia. I don't normally hunt for 'sport'. It's not because I'm squeamish – or perhaps I should say it's not *only* because I'm squeamish – I simply can't see the point or find the thrill. On the other hand, we'd embarked on this trip believing we might have to hunt just to eat. Not that we were anywhere near such a need at the moment, but the thought was running through my mind.

'We'll eat it if I get one?'

It was a statement as much as a question. Jaime's eyes twinkled.

'Sure,' he drawled softly, 'if you want. And *if* you get one.'

Of course, he had no way of knowing that in my youth I'd roamed the neighbourhood with an airgun as Deadeye Dick, The Dreaded Lightbulb Killer, and cast many a suburban garden into darkness.

Soon enough, another pair of ears appeared out of the grass, in the middle distance to our left. Jaime whispered something to the dogs. They sensed that something was afoot, or perhaps they were afraid of being shot at by mistake, but they stayed as still as statues just behind me as I fired. The report was flat and disappointing, followed by a distant thud and the high-pitched whine of a ricochet. The hare fell over. I walked across the field to find it wounded but alive. It lay quite still there on its side, breathing quickly, eyes wide and staring. I noticed they were hazel, and inordinately large. Its fur looked very soft. Feeling no sense of triumph or achievement I reloaded and, at point-blank range, dispatched it with a second shot. Like the lamb only a few hours ago, it went into convulsions, hind legs pumping hard and fast a dozen times or more, as its ghost went galloping away to bunny heaven. It certainly put paid to any appetite I might have felt for hunting. Unless our survival depended on it – unlikely in *this* country – I wasn't going to test my marksmanship again.

Back at the farmhouse, under Jaime's expert guidance, we skinned and gutted the hare. Two or three cats, champion mousers, wrestled for the scraps. Jaime twisted off the tail and I kept it as a souvenir, hanging it from my handlebars with a piece of fishing line. The cleaned carcass we hung in the meat safe, next to the lamb. As on most *estancias*, the meat safe was a shed underneath the water-tower. The water overhead kept the chamber cool, at least by comparison with the air outdoors, and wire screens on the window and door kept out the flies.

We collapsed at the table on the veranda. It had been a long day. Jaime started a fire in the stone *parrilla* in the yard and, while an entire front quarter of lamb roasted slowly over the coals, we watched the sun come down over the remains of an ornamental garden. In 'the old days', gravel paths had wound around ornately patterned flowerbeds and carefully trimmed hedges. Nowadays, the budget didn't run to such diversions. The garden was trimmed and cleaned when time allowed, but no longer tended with such devotion. Jaime brought out bottles and glasses and a bucket of ice. In the deepening twilight, a large, pale owl swooped from its perch on the head of a stone statuette, hunting small squeaky things for its dinner. Fireflies winked on and off amongst the shrubs. Somewhere far away, near the distant barn, the protesting generator coughed into life, coaxing a wan orange glow from the few naked bulbs that hung inside the house. The sky was an almost solid curtain of stars. Come eleven o'clock, our bodies tingling with that delicious soreness that makes one feel alive, we fell gratefully into our beds.

It was still dark when a loud and unfamiliar noise from somewhere very near my head abruptly woke me up. In that drowsy, semi-conscious state, while I wondered where I was and what on earth I was doing there, it took me a moment or two to realize that what I could hear was a cock crowing just outside the bedroom window, which we had left open in the hope of seducing a breeze from the hot night air. It sounded more like the metallic grinding of a broken piece of machinery than anything a rooster's throat might produce. It turned out that the culprit was in the habit of sleeping there on the veranda, on top of a precarious tower of bricks and timber that leaned against the wall. As the bird had by this time settled into a steady rhythm that showed no sign of stopping, we did the proper thing and got out of bed, although I might have preferred to wring its fiendish neck instead. Jaime had, of course, been up for hours. The cock which we'd heard was only the backup system, being a late riser himself. The farm's official timekeeper – which luckily for him we hadn't heard – had crowed hours ago.

Since we had the morning to ourselves, I took advantage of the time to tinker with the bicycles and change the handlebar tape on mine. We'd left them in a shed, and during the night a small frog had managed to climb onto my rear mudguard. We took care not to disturb it and, curiously enough, it was still on the bike two days later, when we evicted it gently before continuing on our way.

Emilio cantered into the yard. A cow had fallen into a ditch where she lay, seemingly unable to stand. However hard he tried, Emilio hadn't managed to rescue her, and had come for the tractor in the hope that he might tow her out. When we met him again later, he told us that by the time he got back to the cow, she had died. He'd recovered the hide and left the carcass where it lay. Animals that die of so-called 'natural causes' are never destined for the table.

Towards the end of the morning Jaime returned. We had a *mate* together and debated what to do that afternoon. I'd mentioned that, since most of the cheese in Uruguay is manufactured in the region, we would like to visit a dairy. He offered a choice between a modern factory farm or what he called an *artesano*. Naturally enough we chose the latter.

Mate is an infusion brewed from the leaves of a tree, *Ilex Paraguariensis* or *Ilex Mate*, similar to the bay in appearance. The cured, broken leaf is placed into a dried gourd (*Lagenaria vulgaris*) to which hot water is added. The resultant liquor is drunk through the *bombilla*, a metal (usually silver) straw with a perforated bulb at the lower end, forming a filter, to prevent the leaf being taken up, too. The first settlers learnt the habit from the *Guaraní* Indians, who attributed various magical and religious properties to it. It is a mild stimulant, although the physiological effects are different – and less hazardous – than those of coffee or tea. It also aids digestion and contains a number of nourishing vitamins, notably vitamin C. It is significant that on their long marches in the wars of independence, the gaucho armies, whose diet consisted only of meat and *mate*, didn't suffer from the usual litany of gastrointestinal disorders that plagued other armies of the time, probably due in part to their custom of drinking this infusion, for which the water had been boiled. Nor did they suffer from scurvy and similar disorders, as their minimum vitamin requirements were also being catered for. Whereas at first its consumption was reserved to the rural population, it being frowned upon, even proscribed in polite society for several generations, now practically everyone in Uruguay drinks it; its social function and importance are equivalent to the use of tea in

Britain. The traditional way to serve it is *cimarrón* or *amargo*, meaning bitter, although a few – usually the ladies – prefer to add sugar. The leaf is so strong that it will tolerate several additional servings of boiling water before its flavour begins to fade. A certain amount of ceremony accompanies the drinking, and close friends or relatives will sometimes share the same gourd, each one drinking it empty before refilling it for his companion.

Patricia made the hare into a rich stew. We enjoyed it, although Jaime didn't seem to be tremendously impressed. He appeared to be sharing more than usual with the dogs.

As soon as we arrived, I understood why Jaime had described the artisan's farm as rustic and primitive. The overgrown track beyond the drooping gate was no more than a corridor of deep, parallel ruts in the mud, long since baked to brick by the unforgiving sun. It brought us to a cluster of low, untidy buildings around a tired and trodden patch of earth, strewn with farmyard litter of every description and from every age. Rusted shards of ancient machinery lay heaped in the brown dust with broken tools, twisted sheets of corrugated iron, buckled oil drums, tangled lengths of wire and assorted remnants of timber and masonry. What at first we took to be the abandoned ruins of a colourless pickup truck and a peeling, absurd American sedan several decades old, sagged pitifully in the tall weeds by the fence. Later we learned that both these improbable monsters were still in daily use. Tractor tyres, worn down almost to their canvas core, had been resourcefully split into circular halves which lay on the ground, serving as troughs for the livestock.

Amongst this disorder an aggressive parade of chickens, ducks, geese and turkeys competed for whatever they could scratch from the stingy earth. Columns of adolescent pigs snuffled and snorted in the wake of their cumbersome mothers. Several large, bony dogs lifted themselves dutifully to bark and bay as we descended from the car. They soon lost interest and returned, sluggish and shamefaced, to their scruffy patches of shade.

A small herd about thirty cows strong emerged from an adjoining field and plodded through the rabble, followed by two boys on horseback. Beneath their battered hats both lads had bright, carrot-coloured hair. Their bare arms and legs were covered in freckles. Barefoot, riding bareback, they nodded in shy greeting as they passed us on their way towards the milking shed, a low thatched building with mud-spattered walls. The cows ambled drowsily around it to a paddock at the back. To the left of the shed rose a tall, ramshackle wooden barn with only three walls, completely open to the weather where the fourth wall would have been. It was jammed full of bits of farming machinery, piled in no particular order. Beyond the barn, set in a wild and overgrown tangle of fruit trees and flowers, stood a small, single-storeyed house, its paint and plaster flaking.

One of the boys reappeared from behind the shed and strolled sheepishly towards us across the battered yard. He shook us diffidently by the hand, shifting his weight from one leg to the other as Jaime introduced us. His eyes were a startling sky blue. He mumbled that he'd told his father we were here, just as the farmer came to join us.

Darío Galarza was a dark, corpulent man. He wore a flat cap, neatly pressed blue trousers and a clean white shirt. Unlike his sons he also wore shoes, all of which he explained away dismissively as being his 'city' outfit. He'd just come back from seeing a seed merchant in the town. His jovial, almost obsequious manner and quick, ready smile did nothing to conceal a shrewd and practical mind. It didn't take much encouragement to get him telling us about his business and how he'd built it up. He'd grown up in the north of the province, one of several children born to a poor, itinerant dairy labourer. As soon as he'd been old enough he'd travelled south, unable to find work closer to home. He was lucky, and soon had a job on a large dairy farm near here, using the skills he'd learnt at his father's knee. In time his employer offered him a small piece of land (20 *cuadras*, about 35 acres) on very attractive terms, which Darío accepted. By dint of hard work, good luck and good judgement, he now owned 600 *cuadras*, (over 1,000 acres) and his own dairy herd, which varied in number, according to season, between 30 and 50 cows. He was planning to build a larger, more modern dairy on another part of his land very soon. For the time being, he had all the farming equipment he needed and, although some of it was perhaps a little old, at least it belonged to him and still could do the work it had been designed for so many moons ago. Life had been hard at first, but now he was doing very well. He had no employees but there again, he didn't need any. He had another two sons, older than these, and together they could handle all the work. And after all, why does a man have sons if not to help him?

We followed him through the small room where the cheese was made, to the main part of the milking shed. His red-headed sons had already lined the cows up side by side in two rows, facing the walls. The only light to penetrate the gloom came in through the large open doorway at the far end. It cast the cattle into sharp silhouette and made the wet floor shine. In the dark, aromatic shed the boys were milking by hand into galvanized buckets, walking barefoot through the luminous sludge from one animal to the next. The eldest was fourteen and had already finished school. Which was really just as well, he explained, overcoming his shyness, since with all the work there was to be done on the farm, he hadn't always been able to attend his classes. His brother, one year younger, still had a year to go and, as he was facing the same sort of difficulty, was impatient to get all his schooling over and done with. Since the enlightened Public Education Act passed in the 1870s, schooling is free and compulsory for all children.

The milk rattled into the metal pails with a soothing, comforting sound. Patricia, watching the boys at work, asked whether they might let her try her hand at it. Enormously amused, the youngest tried to teach her but, pull and squeeze at the teat as she might, she was unable to coax forth more than a droplet or two, a far cry from the sonorous jets the boys were sending into their buckets with such ease. As these filled they took them to the next room, where they poured the frothing white through a funnel, lined with a makeshift filter of tattered cheesecloth, into a large, stainless steel cauldron which hung by a chain from a bracket on the wall. The air was thick with flies and so was the milk in the urn, where those that had fallen in were making last desperate efforts to learn how to swim.

Once all the milk is in the cauldron, a fire is lit in a shallow pit in the floor and, above its glowing embers, the milk is heated. Any impurities – including, I presume, the unsuccessful swimmers – are scooped out with a special ladle, and the rennet is added. The warmed milk is stirred until it separates, and the whey is drawn off (and fed to the pigs). The curds are scooped into cylindrical moulds and compressed with heavy weights. Twelve hours later the new cheeses, weighing about seven kilos each, are taken out of the moulds and submerged in basins of highly salted water, where they remain for several days. When they reach the required consistency they come back out of the water, to be placed on wooden racks in the dark storeroom to harden and dry. Then they are sold to one of the large dairy plants in the region to be melted down for use in the preparation of processed cheese. Wondering idly about the enormous variety of cheeses made in the world, I asked Darío whether he'd ever tried his hand at any other sort.

'Well, no . . . ' he answered hesitantly, taking off his cap and scratching the back of his head, 'only cheese.'

His wife, with two little girls peering out from behind her skirt, came out to join us. Mrs Galarza was fifty-two and as dark as, if not darker than, her husband. Time, childbirth and work had all left their indelible marks, but she was still a lively, handsome woman. With blunted hands she toyed delicately with her daughter's hair as the three of them, huddled close together, reclined against a wall. María, the eldest, had inherited her mother's colouring in a lighter shade but her sister, a small pugnacious three-year-old, was as bright and as freckled a redhead as her brothers. We couldn't help commenting on it, such colouring being so rare in a largely Hispanic community. For an awful moment, while she clicked her tongue and thought of a reply, I was afraid I might have made a dreadful blunder, but then Mrs Galarza chuckled richly and said it might come from her side of the family. Her maiden name, you see, was Shannon. And, to heap wonder upon wonder, her mother's maiden name had been MacKenzie. I wanted to know more, but she had no more to tell. She couldn't remember ever having heard a word of English spoken in her home. I wondered who the original Messrs Shannon and MacKenzie might have been, what brought them to these shores and when, what they found here and what they left behind. The past was shut like a tomb.

From what little we could see of its interior through the windows, the house was far from plush. Spartanly furnished, it was also far too small for a family of eight with two grown-up sons. Patricia, urban to the core, had graduated from worrying about their lack of shoes to worrying about the state of the bedlinen. Mrs Galarza explained that the two elder sons had their own place in the barn, and only slept in the house on exceptionally cold winter nights. We'd already seen the barn and I certainly hadn't noticed any separate enclosure or indeed seen anything else there that looked as though it might serve as a bedroom. I could only assume the arrangement was extremely primitive, a fact later confirmed by Jaime. As far as bedlinen was concerned, some cowhides probably did the job. But they all looked remarkably healthy, happy and strong, and none of them looked hungry or remotely underfed. Like most people in the countryside, their staple diet was mutton but when they had none of that, 'well,' said Mrs Galarza with an eloquent shrug and a wave of her arm that encompassed the jostle in the yard, 'we still have plenty to eat.' If anything, they were walking advertisements for the virtues of the rustic life. No doubt they could all have done with a bit of hot water and plenty of soap, but then again so would so many. Try taking a trip on the London Underground in the rush hour on a midsummer's afternoon.

That evening at Los Macachines, Patrica took great pleasure in emptying our panniers all over Jaime's dining room, where they overflowed the vast table onto the chairs and part of the floor. It was an impressive display. Jaime stood in the doorway, eyes wide, trying to find the right words.

'*Pajarito!*' he said at last. 'What a lot of stuff, *che.*'

As ruthlessly as possible we jettisoned everything that wasn't obviously essential, even though much of it had been bought expressly for this trip. First to go were two pairs of expensive Italian hiking boots, lightweight by comparison with others we'd seen but still far too heavy to carry, followed closely by one and a half kilos of Patricia's cosmetics. Out too went assorted items of clothing, half our supply of spare parts, Bruce's saucepan, extra soap and salt and spices and Lord-knows-what-else. Trowel? Out. Gloves? Out. We argued about the fishing tackle and in the end we kept it, but out went my prized Webley air pistol and two tins of pellets. Had it not been for Patricia's adamant objection, out too would have gone the photographic equipment. By the time we'd finished, our luggage was lighter by a stunning 12 kilos, roughly a third of what we'd had at the start. Had it not seemed foolhardy, we would have discarded even more.

In the dark hall, Jaime was shouting down the elderly, hand-cranked telephone. Given the loudness of his yells, I was surprised he needed the machine at all. It might have been easier to stand on the porch, facing in the right direction, and simply cup his hands to his mouth. He eventually hung up in disgust and we retired outdoors to our favourite table, where we sat sipping our drinks and taking potshots with the pistol at the seed pods on the wisteria, until one of the little roosters and his untidy wife struggled into its branches to perch for the night. We saw a *dormilón*, the 'sleepy head', a large brown bird which only appears at twilight. It builds no nest, but simply lays its eggs straight onto the ground, choosing a spot where its excellent camouflage will allow it to blend with the bracken around it. It has a curious, erratic way of flying, clumsy and with frequent crash landings which make it seem wounded; obviously a defence mechanism like that of the ostrich. As a method it must have its virtues, even taking into consideration the fact that in Uruguay there are very few predators, since not only does the species thrive, but it also is not the only one to use such ruses. Our friend the owl appeared again, gliding menacingly through the shadows. The fireflies were winking on and off – miniature, flickering stars – while overhead the real ones spread across the sky like a luminous spray. I could sit here forever, I thought.

Munching sardines from a tin, we sampled the contents of several bottles. There was *grappa*, into which Jaime had dropped the peel of a lemon – a traditional drink – and two sorts of *caña*, one with an orange peel in place of the lemon and the other with a handful of crushed *pitanga* berries (*Stenocalix pitanga*) in the bottom of the bottle. By the time we'd tasted them all, the three of us were floating several feet above the ground.

I couldn't help noticing the contrast between the fortunes of our twenty-four-year-old host and the Galarzas. Jaime was born into a fortunate family, grew up in the capital and went to the best school in town. He spent his holidays on the family estates (both his parents had property) and came to feel such a deep affinity with the countryside that he took a degree in agronomy. His mother then put him in charge of Los Macachines, the estate she'd inherited from her father: 1,600 *cuadras* – almost 3,000 acres – of prime, beautiful, rolling countryside. And yet there was nothing ostentatious or affected about him, quite the contrary: he was refreshingly straightforward and uncomplicated.

We'd decided to stay another day, so that we could visit Colonia de Sacramento, one of the oldest cities in the country, and one that played a crucial role in the history of the Río de la Plata. Jaime announced his intention to take the entire next day 'off,' so we stayed up until midnight, and solved all the world's problems. It's easy, if you know how. Much to Patricia's disgust, I had a cigarette.

Colonia de Sacramento was founded in 1680 by the Portuguese, and for the next hundred years it became a bitter bone of contention between

Portugal and Spain and later, Buenos Aires. In a manoeuvre typical of Spanish greed, her colonies in America were not allowed to trade independently. Since Spain was none the less unable to supply the growing demand for goods, and there was never a shortage of traders who would gladly fill the gap, this inevitably created a situation in which the smuggler was king. Colonia, controlling not only the Río de la Plata but the routes upriver to Paraguay, Brazil, Bolivia and Peru, was in a privileged position to exploit the situation. In addition to earning the odium of the Spanish Monarch and his Viceroy in Lima for their sanction busting, the Portuguese were also reprehended by the Inquisition, which suspected them of being of Jewish descent. This led to invasion after invasion, with devolution treaties being signed with alarming regularity in practically all the major cities in Europe (only to be broken soon afterwards); at one point, even the Pope became involved.

In one of the treaties, Spain made a *leetle* mistake, granting 'Colonia and all the surrounding area' to Portugal, instead of the intended 'within the range of a cannonball'. They had to go to war to correct that little clerical error. In another treaty, signed in Madrid, Spain was to have Colonia in exchange for the Misiones Jesuíticas, which would go to Portugal. Only too late Spain realized that she'd been sold a pig in a poke and, for a small colonial town, had given away a piece of land the size of England. In a particularly ludicrous episode, Spain decided to *take* Colonia instead, and sent in Cevallos (then Governor of Buenos Aires) and his army, only to return the city with apologies a year later, in a treaty signed in Paris. In the meantime, Portugal had reciprocated Spain's aggression by taking Misiones, which she *didn't* give back.

Then, in 1776, Cevallos (now Viceroy) took advantage of the fact that Britain, Portugal's ally, had her hands full trying to quash a little uprising of her own in North America. He marched on Colonia once more, this time with 7,000 men and, to save himself the trouble of having to invade it again, he flattened the city. This, quite naturally, delighted the merchants of Buenos Aires (not averse to a bit of contraband themselves), whose position of supremacy in the Río de la Plata was strengthened by the disappearance of their greatest rival. But now, with Colonia gone, the stage was set for the growth of Montevideo in its stead.

As we left Colonia behind us, we had to slow down for a man walking boldly down the middle of the road, carrying aloft a full-sized Uruguayan flag. He was dressed in the blue and white national colours and, escorted by a carload of *Policía Caminera*, was causing quite a stir. Intrigued, we craned our necks to get a better look, but the police impatiently waved us on. Our curiosity unsatisfied, we drove away, little knowing that soon our paths would cross again.

Home at last – for that is how Los Macachines had begun to feel – we made our farewell *asado* in the stone *parrilla* and settled on the porch. There was a melancholy flavour to the evening: we knew that we would miss this new friend we'd found. So much had happened here, and so much of it new. It struck me, halfway through our dinner, that it was the second time in as many days that we were eating the flesh of an animal we'd seen die. It was a reminder of things we tended to forget in our city lives, and made us feel primitive and somehow connected to the land.

CHAPTER THREE

HOW LONG THE ROAD . . .

The tattered remnants of a thin haze still hung in the brisk morning air as we hoisted our bicycles onto the back of the station wagon. With a last fond look at the house, we clattered off down the driveway back to the dusty road. We'd decided to modify our route and travel along a secondary road to our next destination, the vineyards on the outskirts of Carmelo. This short cut would take us inland through the town of Tarariras. Our plan was to camp about 10 kilometres beyond it where, according to our map, we would find the valley of the Río San Juan, a convenient halfway point. Jaime took us a short distance along the highway where, with warm embraces and promises to meet again, we slid off down the hill.

Our three days of rest had done us a world of good: we were bursting with energy and keen to get some cycling done. The terrain was far less arduous than the last piece we'd pedalled and, for the first few kilometres, the road was deliciously shaded by long lines of tall eucalyptus. Thanks to all the baggage we'd shed, our bikes were noticeably lighter and we made good progress, twisting through the cornfields from one emerald pocket to another.

We'd been travelling for about an hour, the shelter of the trees behind us, when, as we glided down a slope into a valley full of cattle, we spotted a lone figure in the distance. It was the man with the flag although, unlike yesterday, he no longer had his police escort. Carrying himself stiffly erect he crossed the deserted road to where we'd stopped on the verge. He was wearing the same outfit: jogging shoes, pale blue tracksuit trousers with a matching cap, and a white cotton T-shirt with a colourful inscription on his chest. It was his name, and he'd had the design specially printed in honour of his mission. His skin was dark and tanned, and his black hair escaped in thick, matted curls from under his cap. He wore a harness with a special pocket, level with his hip, in which nested the base of the cumbersome flagpole. He carried nothing else, not even water. We offered him a drink of ours, which he solemnly declined. He'd refreshed himself a while ago, he said. His colleague, who carried the supplies, had gone on ahead and they'd be meeting again soon.

Florentino Rezende was Brazilian, from Río de Janeiro. He described himself as a schoolteacher and a poet. It was his second day on the road, he explained gravely. He'd started out in Buenos Aires, where a cluster of diplomats and politicians and *gente importante* had given him a big sendoff. The Uruguayan Minister of the Interior himself had donated the flag. Florentino had crossed by ferry to Colonia, and was overflowing with indignation because his police escort, after depositing him in a *pensión* in Tarariras, had abandoned him, obviously failing to appreciate the importance of his mission and treating him as though he we were *un loco*, which he most certainly was *not*. His was a serious undertaking, he said. No daft little exercise. His destination was Brasilia, roughly 6,000 kilometres to the north, and his walk was for world peace. He was vague about precisely what effect he expected his long trek to have, but he was genuine enough in his concern. We wished him good luck and a pleasant trip, and watched his figure dwindle into nothing as he marched solemnly on towards the horizon.

'Oh, dear,' muttered Patricia, invisible beyond the tall yellow grass, 'it's started.'

'Started? What's started?' I asked, looking left and right along the empty road for clues, even up towards the sky in case she meant rain. 'Can't see a thing.'

'My period,' she sighed, pausing briefly, indicating fluently by elision that the word 'silly' would fit neatly into the gap. 'I thought it might be due. Oh, well . . . could you hand me my bag, please?'

'Which bag?'

'You know, the little red one. With hearts on it. And a zipper.'

'Okay. Where is it?'

'It's in the first-aid pannier.'

'Ah. And which is the first-aid pannier?'

'I've got it. On the front.'

I walked over to her bicycle. There was a pannier on either side of the front wheel.

'Yeah, okay. Which front?'

'Oh, I don't know . . . left, I think.'

'Right.'

'No, *left*.'

'Yeah, right, I heard you the first time, don't panic.'

'Left! I said **left**! Oh God.'

'I *know* you said left! I was just saying right as in "correct" or "I get it." Geddit?'

'Yeah, I geddit,' she groaned. 'Now, have *you* got it?'

'Yes, I've got it. Where are you?'

'Over here.'

'Right,' I said with a chuckle.

'Oferchrissake don't start *that* again!' she wailed, standing up.

At the bottom of a golden, wheat-covered fold we came to our turning. A squad of surveyors was fooling about with theodolites and bits of string at the intersection. They waved and cheered as we passed. Ruta 22 was narrower than the highway and, bordered with hedges and low bushy trees, it felt somehow intimate and close, giving us the confidence to cycle side by side instead of in single file as we'd being doing until then. The day was warming up and the sun was promising to make it even warmer. We chattered as we went, pointing out splashes of colour in the never-ending green. We spotted our first *cardenal*, a small grey bird with a white collar and a brilliant red-crested head. There was a lot of movement on the ground, as furry little *apereá*, tailless rodents very much like guinea-pigs, darted in and out of the weeds that tasselled the edges of the road.

The featureless, untidy countryside beyond Tarariras was in complete contrast to the orderly farms before it. The road, too, was broken and unkempt. A thin haze had drawn an opaque veil across the sky, transforming its previous blue glory into a flat, grey void without blocking out the sun's increasing heat. We reached the Río San Juan in good time only to find that the river, lined with trailing willows, was also infested with mosquitoes. As a campsite, it was out. In addition, thanks to our exertions over the last ten kilometres, through air now palpably thick and clammy, we were running out of water once again. That settled it: we'd have to travel on.

A signpost by a gate identified the land as belonging to the Highway Maintenance Department, like our last campsite in San José. We turned into the driveway and rode through a dense thicket. As soon as we were clear of the bushes we were greeted by the acrid reek of burnt forest and an ashen landscape of charred stubble and blackened stumps. Fire had stripped the area bare. Someone had been less than careful. With the bitter smell still in our noses and the bitter thought in our hearts, we turned away and cycled on.

The rolling plain was bleak and deserted. We searched the grim horizon for some sign of human habitation but couldn't find a thing until, emerging from between the high clay banks of a cutting, we saw some buildings in the distance with a windmill sprouting in the yard amongst them. The sight was a great relief, especially for Patricia who, as well as thirst and general exhaustion, was suffering rather badly from menstrual cramps. We wondered whether other women travellers, whose accounts we'd heard, didn't suffer from them or simply didn't mention them.

Letting the wooden gate creak shut behind us, we walked up the rutted incline to the small, neat house. A woman's head, grey-haired, appeared at the kitchen door in answer to our call. She beckoned us in and came to meet us as we entered the garden. Of course we could have some water, she said, leading me to a tap outside the kitchen. While I refilled our bottles, Doña Marisol settled Patricia into a canvas deck chair in the shade of a peach tree, and scurried back into the house. She returned a moment later with a tray, balancing a jug of iced water and a bowl of peaches straight from the fridge. She clucked like an old mother hen around my wife, giving me a look that asked how I could have done this to the girl, at such a time as this. Patricia, after several glasses of water and a couple of peaches, promptly fell asleep.

The L-shaped house was painted a rich, buttery yellow with a red, corrugated roof which extended over a gallery. The posts holding up the roof were festooned with honeysuckle. While Patricia dozed I looked around for a suitable place to put up the tent. Our requirements were fairly straightforward: clean ground, shade and some privacy, as we were still a little shy.

We asked Doña Marisol whether she could suggest a place nearby for us to spend the night. Inviting us to follow, she walked to the hedge and pointed across the treeless, sun-bleached scrubland at a distant ribbon of green. '*La cañada*,' she said, 'over there. It's lovely. Plenty of shade, nice and clean . . . we often go there ourselves, with a picnic, for the afternoon. You can fish in the stream, too.'

The veil of cloud had broken up, and there were only a few rags and patches of it left. The mid-afternoon sun, waiting in ambush just beyond the shelter of the shaded yard, slammed down on us with renewed intensity the moment we stepped through the gate. By the time we reached the *cañada*, a couple of kilometres away, we were hot and sweaty again. A stone bridge spanned the tiny brook. Downstream the thicket was impenetrable and, from what little we could see, the banks were crumbling and tangled with roots. Leaving my bike on the verge, I picked my way through the matted, razor-sharp reeds upstream, along the eastern bank, to be confronted by a taut, seven-stranded wire fence. We could have climbed it, but the bicycles couldn't, so I returned to the road, my legs criss-crossed with cuts from the saw-toothed grass.

'There's a path over here,' said Patricia, who'd wandered over the bridge.

I followed it through the thicket: tall, thistle-like plants towered over my head and caught at my clothes. Ten paces later the road had disappeared. I was in a different world: a sweltering, clammy world where the air was thick and hot and laden with unfamiliar smells. Dripping with perspiration, I ducked under a single drooping strand of barbed wire that crossed the narrow corridor at waist height. Beyond it the dense walls of vegetation gradually thinned and soon I was standing in an open, sloping meadow, the brook on my left. The field was full of cows and twice as many calves, which gazed at me curiously before bolting away. They huddled in groups in the shade of the stunted trees along the bank. The air was heavy with the smell of cattle and fermenting dung and, just behind it, something else, something strong and sickly. I followed the line of the stream. It trickled weakly along at the foot of the cluttered gully, barely wetting its bed. Whatever fish it held, I thought, must have had legs as well as fins: the water wasn't deep enough for anything to swim in. As the cows lurched out of my way I had a look at the few patches of shade big enough to accommodate the tent. Unsurprisingly, they were carpeted with a thick layer of moist, trampled dung. And then I found the reason for the smell, which by now was overpowering: in a clearing, in the full glare of the sun, covered with flies, lay the exploded carcass of a cow. A short way beyond it, I thought I'd found the perfect spot: a luminous, emerald meadow beneath a spreading, solitary *paraíso*. What the heck, we'll get used to the smell, I thought as I approached, only to find that the ground was marshy and wet. From somewhere in the distance I could hear Patricia blowing her policeman's whistle, so I went back to the road. She was full of questions, the where-have-you-beens and what-took-you-so-longs tumbling out thick and fast.

'I didn't really find a place,' I explained, 'but there may be one a little further in. Would you like to come and help me have a look?' Muttering darkly, she agreed to come along.

This time wheeling the bikes we retraced the claustrophobic path, fighting off the flies, past the wire and past the rotting carcass, getting dirtier with every step as our skins grew ever more plastered with bits of leaf and dust and tatters of spiders' webs. Startled calves galloped bleating from the thicket as we passed. My sweaty companion stopped in her tracks.

'Come on,' I said, 'perhaps a little further . . . '

'You go,' she said flatly, 'I'm not going another step. This is ridiculous.'

We were standing at a wide bend in the brook, closed off by a wire fence that crossed the gully. On the opposite bank, through the overhanging branches, we could see a man approaching us on horseback along a rough earth track.

'Look,' I said, pointing, 'we can ask him.'

'*You* ask him,' answered Patricia, casting her eyes to the heavens.

As I climbed over the fence to get closer to the man, I realized that the ground there, like the patch under the *paraíso*, was marshy and soft, but the man had already seen me, so it was too late to turn back. He was in his early twenties and rode bareback, using a length of tattered rope in the place of reins. He wore battered tennis shoes without any laces, a pair of faded blue shorts and the wreckage of an old straw hat. He was chewing on a long stem of grass.

'*Buenas tardes!*' I called.

'*Buenas,*' he replied, with a lazy grin.

'Tell me,' I said, trundling out our story and, for some reason, mentioning that we hoped to write a book about our trip. The broad smile never leaving his lips, he draped himself languorously forward onto the horse's neck, hitching his ankles together across its broad rump.

'A book, eh?' he answered, deep in thought. 'I'm honoured.'

I could feel my feet sinking slowly into the mud. Perhaps in part because of that, my reaction was a bit delayed.

'To have you on my land,' he went on.

'Oh no, of course not, not at all,' I answered, understanding him at last, 'quite the contrary: the honour is all mine.'

Which I shouldn't have said either, as it triggered a lengthy diplomatic tussle as we debated which of us was most honoured by our meeting. Eventually I manoeuvred him back to campsites, my wife and I, for the use of.

'A tent, eh?' he paused. 'Don't see many of those around here. Nice one, is it?'

I bent over to rescue one of my shoes from the slime, wishing he'd hurry up and answer the bloody question.

'Well . . . I don't know. Let me think, now . . . ' he said pensively. 'There might be a place . . . ' his voice tailed off as he paused again to rub his chin.

'There is a place, now that I think of it. Quite nice, too. Shady. Soft. Yes, I think you'd like it there. Of course, it's a little hard to get to from where you are, especially on bicycles. It's on *this* side of the stream, you see. This track leads straight to it,' he pointed at the ground. 'If you get back on the road, you can come up through my farm.'

With mud up to my ankles I scrambled through the undergrowth back to Patricia. Hot, tired and heartily fed up, she'd been through more than enough for one day. Since getting onto the man's farm meant going all the way back to Doña Marisol's, I knew that I would have to explain it as subtly as I could.

'Well, here I am, darling,' I said, trying to sound cheerful and nonchalant. 'Tell me, how adventurous are you feeling?'

Not subtle enough, I realized at once as she went purple with rage and burst into tears.

Having wasted over an hour on this unsuccessful hunt, we plodded back to the road, Patricia ranting on about the heat and the dust and the flies and the stink and the why on-earth two people like us ever got caught up in something like this in the first place; we should have known better, why in God's name hadn't we gone to Tahiti or Paris or even bloody Brighton and heaven knows what else. I brought up the rear, making ineffective consoling noises.

'Don't worry, dear,' I murmured, 'the first few days are bound to be the hardest.'

This only precipitated the caustic enquiry as to how many hardest days would have to pass before they ceased to qualify as the first few.

We pedalled back to the gate which led to Doña Marisol's and the young horseman's farm. One look at the track was enough to convince

Patricia that she wanted no part of it. Since we were there anyway, we went to the windmill for some water. A light breeze had come up, hot like a dragon's breath but strong enough to turn the creaking vanes, drawing a crystal stream from a pipe suspended over a trough. We stuck our heads under the jet, soaking our faces and necks, splashing it onto our skin with our hands, feeling it penetrate our pores, cleaning and renewing. Hoping it would cheer her up, I rummaged in my bag for the bread and cheese.

'Have a sandwich,' I said, 'it'll cheer you up.'

'Don't want a sandwich,' she scowled; 'I'm not hungry.'

But she took it just the same, and wolfed it down. From the next paddock a grizzled, twisted, toothless old man was yelling at us. Only after he'd repeated himself several times were we able to understand what he was saying. It was this: 'Are you enjoying the fresh air?'

I thought Patricia was going to throw something at him.

'Yes thank you, lovely,' I said in a hurry.

He strolled across to join us, and we explained what had happened.

'Did my sister say you could camp there?' he asked, plainly amazed. 'The old goat! What does *she* know about camping? Imagine! Over *there*? How *could* she? These women . . . ' he clicked his tongue. '*I'll* show you a place . . . Right *there*,' he said, pointing, 'underneath that tree. See? That's where you should have gone, right there, not that dreadful *cañada*, but there. See? Under the tree. Women! Bah!' He shook his head, 'What do *they* know? *There*. Lovely spot. Shady, none of those weeds or anything. Bit of water, even.'

We looked out across the colourless plain in the direction he was pointing. Almost directly across the road, standing alone in the middle of the field, was a large, leafy tree. We'd noticed it before but, for some reason, had ignored it.

'Easy to get to, too,' he went on, 'just follow the path. Takes you straight to it. Easy. *That's* the place you want,' he finished emphatically. 'Over there,' he added, as an afterthought.

We should have known better, of course, but neither of us wanted to cycle any further, and the prospect of a close, convenient campsite was too tempting to resist. We crossed the road, entered the gate and followed the footpath through the yellow grass. The water the old man had mentioned was a trickle even more meagre than the stream, which we crossed in one stride. But we really should have guessed. There had to be a catch. Not that there was anything wrong with the tree: it had a broad, generous crown and cast a large pool of shade. But it was the only patch of shade in the middle of the prairie, the only place where the cows could shelter from the summer sun or the winter rain, and every inch of it was knee deep in several seasons' supply of rich, macerated cowshit. For a few moments we waded through the turds, raising clouds of flies, in the hope that we might find a spot which, if not clear, at least would not be so clogged.

'We can't stay here either, you know,' I said to Patricia.

'I know,' she said without complaint. 'Let's go.'

Roundly cursing all the well-intentioned but cruelly misguided advice we'd been following all afternoon, we got back on the road and started pedalling again. Ahead of us the sinking sun was shining in our eyes. Although it was already early evening, its rays were still surprisingly fierce. The hot headwind unrolled itself towards us as though the sun itself were pushing it. For a while we looked for places on the verge but in the end decided against them. We didn't like the thought of camping in such plain view of the road even though, with the solitary exception of a greyhound bus, we seemed to have it to ourselves.

Crossing a suspension bridge, we considered settling on the banks of the *arroyo* that it spanned, but a family of scruffy gypsies had settled there before us, surrounded by their litter and their dogs. Hard eyes watched us as we passed, and two small children ran up to the road in silence holding up wicker baskets which they wanted us to buy. Nobody returned our waves or answered our hello.

It was getting close to nightfall, the sun a golden ball in front of us, about to disappear, when we rounded a bend in the pot-holed road to find ourselves in front of the 'Almacén y Bar La Humildad'. The sort of building one would normally expect to find in the colonial heart of a town, it seemed odd and out of place here in the middle of nowhere. As we leaned our bikes against the wall, we knew that this time nothing could persuade us to advance another step. The few locals gathered in the tiny bar fell silent as we walked in, waiting to see what we would do.

'*Buenas tardes*,' I said, including them all.

The pair playing billiards nodded in reply and returned to their game. A small boy leapt up from a chair and rushed outdoors for a look at our bicycles. The landlady, a stout, buxom woman with dishevelled hair and rosy cheeks, wearing a bilious green tank top, fussed about behind the counter, ready to take our order. Did she know, I asked her as she poured out our mineral water, whether we could put up our tent in the woods behind the *almacén*? Well it wasn't her land, she said shyly, she didn't really know.

She was probably about to tell us more when one of the customers, a tall, fibrous old man, dressed in shorts and sandals and a grubby cap, worked his way into the conversation. Propping himself on the bar, flies floating in his beer, he gazed fixedly at me with the rheumy eyes of the perennial drunk. He knew the foreman, he slurred, 'a sterling chap. He'll let you in, of course he will. I'll go and get 'im. You wait here,' he instructed, and tottered off. Patricia and I wondered what would happen next.

'Come here, come here,' beckoned the old man, from the doorway. 'Over there,' he said, pointing at the *capataz* who was skinning a sheep, using a wheelbarrow in much the same way that Emilio, at Los Macach-ines, had used his concrete table. Soon everything was settled and, with the foreman's blessing, we rode up the track to the woods. Quickly, in the fading light, we set up the tent under the trees, and then I hurried back to the *almacén* to collect the bottles of *Salus* the landlady had put in the chiller for us. While I was there, I had her pour a very large *Espinillar* into my canteen. I wanted something a little stronger than water. She very kindly offered her shower, should my wife want to refresh herself. With no one around to interrupt her, she also told me that Darío, the foreman, was her husband.

It was completely dark by the time I returned to my wife. We sat on the trunk of a fallen tree and had some bread and cheese, and the by now bruised and flattened peaches we'd bought in Tarariras.

'It was sweet of her to offer,' said Patricia, 'but I'd rather we wash together. Solidarity and all that.'

We stripped and somehow rinsed ourselves with water from a bottle. Someone, walking home perhaps along the track, had stopped to watch. In the dark he couldn't have seen very much at all; we only knew he was there by the glow of his cigarette. It was eerie, but it didn't stop us from finishing our bath.

It was a gloriously starry night when at last we retired. We'd been travelling for almost twelve hours, and had covered a mere 72 kilometres. I say 'mere' now, but at the time it seemed a monumental odyssey. I lay back on the mat, next to my softly snoring companion, clutching my treasured canteen of *Espinillar*. I'd been saving it as a nightcap, but I was sound asleep long before I finished it.

We woke on Sunday morning as though we hadn't slept at all. Stiff and aching, under the watchful eye of a pair of large-rumped mares, we stowed away our belongings. Perhaps because of their colour, the horses reminded me of a semi-girlfriend I had in my mid-teens. I had joined the intimidatingly posh Polo Club, of which she was a member, just so that we could go out riding together. Trotting about behind her, I used to find the symmetry of seeing her astride her horse the zenith of eroticism. But her heart belonged to someone else (sigh) and I eventually got thrown out of the club anyway for galloping through a ladies' tea party on the north lawn. It wasn't so much the trouble I caused which upset the membership committee, but my messy, plebeian horsemanship. Feet and elbows sticking out, shouting 'Yahoo', that sort of thing.

As we passed the closed *almacén* we met Darío once again. He was sitting amongst the chickens with his feet up, contentedly sipping at his *mate*. He told us, curiously enough, that only a small part of the *estancia* was actively farmed – and even much of *that* almost for the hell of it – the rest being given over to the estate's main purpose: a talcum mine. He invited us to see the works, but we were keen to reach the vineyards before noon, so we declined.

The road was very poor, possibly thanks to the trucks from the mine. We had to pay constant attention to the cracks and pot-holes, which robbed us of any joy we might have found in the few downhill slopes. It was cloudy once again, although fortunately not too hot. Closer to Carmelo the landscape became a fresher green as we passed through the irrigated patchwork of cultivated farmland. On the outskirts of town we stopped at a milk bottling plant and asked directions from a team of men loading up a horse-drawn cart.

'The vineyards?' mused one of them. 'Easy. Just follow this road all the way through town, take a right at the end of the cobblestones and keep on going. You can't miss them.'

Traffic grew heavier (heavier? Traffic *appeared*) as we came amongst the first scattering of houses on either side of the broad, tree-lined avenue. Many of the cars were antiques straight out of *The Untouchables*, often in remarkably good condition. Underneath the bonnet, of course, many had been 'modified' but none the less, seeing them clatter back and forth along that dappled, elegant road made us feel that once again we'd slipped back in time. We were soon at the red iron bridge across the Arroyo de las Vacas, on whose banks lies the town of Carmelo.

The stream takes its name from an event early in the seventeenth century which determined the country's history. Hernando Arias de Saavedra, then Governor of Asunción, and the first man to reconsider the role of these Spanish colonies as more than merely an alternative route to the plunder of Peruvian gold, brought 'a hundred cows and two herds of horses' into Uruguay from neighbouring Argentina, landing them here and letting them loose. Thriving on the rich, natural pastures, multiplying prodigiously, and with no predators or competitors worthy of the name, they wandered to the far corners of the territory. By the time Montevideo was founded, in 1726, it was estimated by a party of French freebooters busily harvesting cowhides up near the Laguna Merín that over 15 million head of this *cimarrón* cattle roamed the land.

Stopping to consult a Carmelite perched on a garden wall at the far end of the bridge, we confirmed the dairyman's directions and, pausing only for an ice-cream at a corner shop, jarred and jolted our way along the cobbled street to the other side of town.

The day had become steamy and close, the temperature was rising, and storm clouds were gathering overhead by the time we reached the vineyards. It was a family holding; they have a notable reputation in Uruguay for fine table wines. We were hoping for a tour and perhaps some heavy-duty sampling but, thanks to our less than brilliant planning, our visit was not a success. It was still several weeks before the harvest and, being Sunday, there was nobody about. We walked around the warehouses yelling ourselves hoarse, but were unable to raise even a watchman. The family's home – a sprawling, sumptuous house – was near the entrance to the estate. We rang the doorbell several times, but there was no one in. We were debating whether or not to go for an illicit swim in the magnificent pool, when the heavens opened up in a truly spectacular way, leaving us stranded on the porch in the company of an enormous, sleeping Alsatian. We were eventually rescued by the arrival of two men in a car, who told us that the family was out of town and not expected back for days. As soon as the rain stopped we retreated back into Carmelo and checked into a hotel.

We installed ourselves at a pavement table outside a café on the main square to watch the world go by. A gormless-looking lad struggled past us on a cumbersome delivery bicycle. Heavy public-address system horns were mounted facing fore and aft, attached to a small cassette player and powered by two large car batteries nesting in the basket at the front. From this set-up issued a remarkably loud, frenzied torrent of local advertising, extolling the virtues of this shop and that restaurant. A substantial red placard identified the contraption as the vanguard of a company calling itself 'Publicidad Laser'. In christening the enterprise, the owners had the right idea, we thought, even though the technology perhaps lagged a bit behind the concept.

The young waiter quickly recognised us as out-of-towners, and hovered a few paces away from our table, patently longing to talk to us; soon enough, he plucked up the courage to do so. He was close to twenty, lean and mildly scruffy, mousy hair combed carefully forwards in a dank Beatles fringe. As soon as he discovered that we'd come from London, he wanted to know all about Europe: how people there lived, what they did, what sorts of jobs there were to be had and how good the chances of getting them. He were restless and frustrated; small-town life was getting him down. There were no opportunities here. He and a couple of friends were making plans to leave the country. He was immovable in his conviction that roads in Europe above all others were paved with gold, and all the grass there greener. It was a disturbing encounter. Here we were, revelling in the open spaces, on a journey we had undertaken at least in part as a respite from the pollution, the noise, the crowds, the rat-race and the chemically reconstituted, hormone-injected 'food', and there *he* was, visibly yearning for the hustle and the bustle and the bright city lights, as though Life In Europe were one big, extended Martini advert. It made me terribly sad, not least by reminding me of my own teenage years when, feeling oppressed and confined by Montevideo, I longed to travel to exotic places and conquer the world with an electric guitar. The years since then weighed heavy on my shoulders. I couldn't think of anything to say to this eager, discontented lad which would have made any sense at all to him. Utterly depressed, we paid our bill and left, wishing him the best of luck. He was going to need it.

We found our way to a small *Parrillada*, which the manager of the hotel had recommended. Passing through the dingy, smoke-filled dining room, a giant grille over the coals at one end, Formica-topped tables set haphazardly on the bare concrete floor, we went outdoors to the patio at the back. The anaemic remnant of a once-lush canopy, a scrawny vine trailed across the wires about our heads. A small, tin-voiced transistor radio hung lopsidedly from a hook on the wall, blaring scratchy recordings by the long-dead heroes of the Tango. Our table, as did all the others, commanded an excellent view of the rubbish bins and stacked wooden crates of empty bottles awaiting collection by the gate. In contrast with his comrade-in-arms at the café, our waiter here was a walking antique, although his progress could perhaps better be described as shuffling. He attended us at his own, leisurely pace, pausing frequently for pulls at his *mate* which he kept on a trolley with the cutlery and plates. We ordered a mixed grill and, having missed our taste of wine that afternoon, a bottle from that very vineyard. Despite our hunger the meal was a severe disappointment and, I am sorry to say, so was the wine. That's the sad thing about the local wines: they vary wildly in quality from one year to the next, even from one bottle to another. When good, they can be excellent. When bad, on the other hand, they can be truly appalling.

Having decided to stay another day, on Monday morning we followed the Arroyo de las Vacas to where it flows into the upper reaches of the Río de la Plata. Power boats and yachts, most of them flying the Argentine flag, were moored along the near bank of the tree-lined stream. On the promontory of land formed by the meeting of the two rivers was a carefully landscaped park. By the roadside, in the shade beneath the trees, a scattering of brightly coloured booths were doing brisk business hiring bicycles and motor scooters to the tourists. There was a peaceful, almost festive air to the place, with pretty girls wandering about in bathing suits and executive-type men looking earnest in sunglasses. It was odd to think that in the early part of the eighteenth century a large estate here had belonged to wealthy British slave-traders.

In 1700 Europe was plunged into war, ostensibly over the succession to the Spanish throne. The costly, drawn-out squabble was only resolved by the treaties of Utrecht in 1713. The negotiations addressed themselves primarily to European and territorial matters, but were unique in their commercial implications. One of the agreements granted Britain the exclusive right to import African slaves to Spanish America. Queen Anne conferred those rights on the South Sea Company which, in turn, signed a covenant with the Royal African Company for the supply of those slaves. The British and Spanish Monarchies each held 25 per cent of the shares in the South Sea Company. The agreement was exceptional primarily because until that point Spain had forbidden free trade in its American colonies. It even went so far as to stipulate a price range, payable in cow hides, (a healthy buck could fetch anything up to 300 hides) and a sales tax (collected by the *Cabildo*, the colonial government) calculated at one-third of the retail value of the *hides*. With its signature, Britain had legitimate access to the River Plate, so the South Sea Company promptly set up a warehouse in Buenos Aires, in which to store the merchandise and, with the excuse of clothing the slaves and catering for their requirements, began importing such things as textiles by the boatload. Since there was considerable demand for such commodities, they soon began to trickle into the city's markets. The trickle quickly became a flood, and in no time at all Buenos Aires had become the centre of what, according to Spanish law, was British contraband. Portugal, of course, was already doing a roaring trade smuggling goods into the region via Colonia de Sacramento.

There was a thatched restaurant on the promontory and, it being about that time of day, a coffee sounded like a good idea. With so many people about, we were reluctant to leave our bikes unattended (which says more about us than it says about them) so we retraced our steps to the *Prefectura*, the Port Authority, which was housed in a large, opulent mansion overlooking the river. We were hoping to leave our bikes in the Navy's care.

I had scarcely put my front wheel through the gate when somebody barked 'Out! Out!' in an angry, intemperate voice. It was the guard at the head of the ornate marble staircase. Having lived abroad during most of the worst excesses perpetrated by the military regime of the 1970s and early 80s, I was confused by the peremptory command, somehow concluding that it wasn't meant for *me*. Indeed, so unaccustomed was I to the shoebox mentality which engendered it, that I was more conscious of its rudeness than its possible implications. Being innocent of anything which I could identify as criminal, I simply kept on going. That, of course, infuriated the sailor even more, and he accompanied further yells by ominously brandishing his gun.

'Okay, okay, I get the point. Relax,' I said in a conciliatory tone. I laid my bike on its side by the path and prepared to walk on.

'No, no, **no**!' he bellowed, 'No bicycles!'

Now this, I thought, was carrying Duty and Concern For National Security a little too far. After all, even James Bond would have trouble concealing a bomb in our light summer clothing, and a Trojan horse my bicycle decidedly was not. I considered forgetting the whole idea and going somewhere else, but something in Patricia's eyes said 'don't let him get away with it'. She was right. Why should I let this overbearing, jumped-up little creep push us around? The days when the military could treat the citizenry that way were long gone. I was feeling far less friendly as I walked back up the path and up the steps. The guard quickly stepped aside and let me pass into the front hall, where a uniformed gang had been idly milling about, watching the proceedings. I was surprised to hear, as though it came from someone else, the anger in my voice as I demanded to speak to the commanding officer. I was also secretly amused to see the men, caught off balance by my sudden entry, snap momentarily to attention. One stepped forward, he was in command, what did I want. Something in his insolent tone only made me angrier. I explained that I had come to make a simple enquiry which, as a law-abiding citizen I was fully entitled to do, although I might have preferred a more courteous reception. But perhaps it had escaped these gentlemen's attention that Uruguay was a democracy once again? Knowing just as well as he did that the Armed Forces are saddled forever with a severe public relations problem thanks to their recent shenanigans, I added pointedly that my wife and I were collecting material for a *book*, heavily underlining the word, and had only stopped to ask for help. Their reaction was the most surprising event of the day as, suddenly meek, the men tripped over each other competing for the privilege of wheeling our bikes into the shade, all except for the guard at the gate who was summarily ordered to shut up and stand to attention. For all I cared, they could cart him off and bastinado him all afternoon. Which probably is what they would have done to me a few years ago, had I behaved the same way. I'll never understand what it was that made the military believe they had the right to brutalise their fellow men and women.

'You bully,' murmured Patricia as we left.

That evening, back at the hotel, we settled in the lobby for a drink. Patricia had found a laundry in the town, and we'd had our washing done. César, the landlord, was moaning about being swamped in dirty linen, so she suggested he try the place she'd found.

'Oh no, I can't do that,' he said. He had a young girl who did all his washing. She might be a bit slow, but she needed the work. If he were to use the laundry, she'd be out of a job. He couldn't let her down.

The television was tuned to an Argentine station, churning out an endless succession of soap operas so turgid and relentlessly unredeeming that even the most discerning viewer would retreat gratefully for aesthetic reward and intellectual stimulation to 'Dallas' or 'Neighbours'. It seemed to be a military day. The broadcast was constantly interrupted by breathless news flashes detailing the death throes of a bizarre attempted coup. It seems that some absurd, ridiculous Argentine officer had persuaded his troops to mutiny and, bristling with guns and ammunition, they'd holed themselves up in their barracks in Monte Caseros, from where they were ready to take on the world. The whole pathetic episode would have been laughable had it not been conducted with such utter, lethal seriousness by a gang of grossly over-armed and just as grossly under-educated thugs. Presumably they were yearning for a return to the comforts and simple certainties of power. The military in Argentina – as, indeed, in most of South America – has a long, unhappy tradition of meddling in politics, an infection which Uruguay had honourably escaped for generations. The country's recent eleven-year taste of the tragicomedy of military rule was the first in living memory. Although one hopes that it was also the last, the sombre precedent has already been set. With this news from the neighbouring shore, and my own brush with the Navy that afternoon, I couldn't help reflecting on how precious and how fragile is democracy, and how long the road to civic and ethical maturity.

CHAPTER FOUR

BUG CITY

By the time we eventually left Carmelo it was almost noon. The day was lightly overcast and we had a stiff breeze behind us, which was a blessing. As we raced over the wooded folds we could already tell that we were much stronger and fitter than we'd been . . . was it really just a week ago? It felt like a lifetime. On the green, rolling slopes all around us the dairy herds of the south had given way to beef cattle. For a short stretch we rode amongst pine-covered dunes, brought inland by the *pamperos* from the west. We had occasional glimpses of the massive Río Uruguay, from which the country takes its name. The word Uruguay comes from Guaraní, the melodious and very beautiful language spoken by most of the now extinct indigenous tribes. There is still some academic debate about its exact meaning. Prevailing opinion translates it as River of the Birds, although some pundits maintain it means River of the Snails.

The two small shops on the highway were shut, so we turned towards the river, hoping we'd be able to buy some food somewhere down there. On the way we saw the carcass of a *mulita* (armadillo), killed by a passing car. Sad to say, in all our weeks of travelling, we saw a number of road casualties like this. Although we once came very close to it, we never saw a live *mulita*. By all accounts they're quite common, although perhaps not as much as they used to be. Their flesh is considered a delicacy and they're hunted without restraint, even though it's against the law.

We were headed for the Playa Agraciada. On the beach a stone obelisk, studded with brass plaques and inscriptions, commemorates the landing of Lavalleja and the *Treinta y Tres Orientales* in April 1825. Uruguay, having shaken off Spain and Buenos Aires, was then in its ninth year of Portuguese occupation. The Federalist troops had been dispersed and General Artigas, betrayed, had been pursued into exile in Paraguay. Lavalleja, who had served under Artigas, and a group of his compatriots who had fled to Buenos Aires, plotted the overthrow of the Portuguese invaders and crossed the Río Uruguay in rowboats to lead the revolution and fight the good fight. The government of Buenos Aires, which had fought Uruguay for so long, now came to its aid in the face of a greater threat, the continued Portuguese presence in the Río de la Plata, supplying financial and military aid to the revolt. Of course, the aim of the centralist Buenos Aires government was never the independence of the Province, but always that Uruguay should come under its sway once again. Nonetheless, Uruguay *did* achieve independence five years later, almost by accident. Argentina and Brazil, tired of their corrosive war of attrition, accepted the establishment of a buffer state between them, if only to deny each other possession of it. The prolonged conflict was also impinging upon Britain's commercial interests in the region. As a result, the British government, through Lord Ponsonby (Foreign Secretary Canning's special envoy) played a vital and decisive role in the negotiations which led to the birth of the new nation.

Not at all the deserted, starlit beach which greeted the liberating patriots, there was now a teeming city of tents beneath the trees. Torpid families slumped in deck chairs in the shade, the last tantalizing traces of countless *asados* still lingering in the air. Here a dog lay contentedly asleep, one paw guarding an enormous bone and there, hanging from a branch, some birds twittered softly in a cage. On a clothes-line with the laundry, hung fillets of salted fish. From one of the tents came the muted sound of snoring and, from another, a baby's fitful cries. Somewhere a radio played. In the clearing a group of barefoot boys in bathing suits expertly kicked a football about. The Uruguayan people have many virtues, but we were beginning to discern one which stood out practically above all others: when it comes to picnicking or camping, they simply have no match. The campers around us had brought everything they might conceivably need – tables, chairs, even a sofa – and spread it anarchically out all over the place. By comparison we felt distinctly under-equipped.

To one side of the site there was a bar and restaurant, the only building there. The barman told us he had no food he could sell us apart from what was on the menu. The only shops in the neighbourhood were those we'd passed on the highway. We didn't really want to camp amongst this throng, nor eat in the restaurant. We'd seen a track leading off the road just before the site so we set off to explore it. Almost at once we were in a different world. Gone were the tents and the campers and the rest of their paraphernalia, and in their place all we could hear was the soft, melodic fluting of wood pigeons and the occasional, fleeting voices of other invisible birds, underlined by the hum of the cicadas. Sunlight filtered through gaps in the canopy, dappling the thick, lush undergrowth. This was far more the sort of thing we'd been looking for. Our only problem now was how to get to the bank through all this vegetation. Eventually we found a place where the bushes thinned and, for a short distance, completely disappeared as if by magic. We walked our bicycles over the spongy ground through the pines almost to the river's edge, where a thick, impenetrable wall of *espinillos*, cacti and vines brought us to a halt. It took us a few minutes, but at last we found a gap through the tangled branches. Weeping willows and flowering *ceibos* stood on a beach so perfect and deserted it looked stolen from a calendar. The river's opposite bank, 9 kilometres away, was a thin green ribbon on the horizon. Worn and weathered tree trunks, the giant driftwood of a giant river, lay at the tideline. Our decision was instant: straight to the shops, kick down the doors if need be, and come back here.

We wandered barefoot back and forth along the clean white sand, letting the river ripple in between our toes. The water was soft and warm. The peace was so absolute we could feel it soaking into our skins. We splashed and stamped in the shallows as we went in, making as much disturbance as we could. When the sun is hot, a type of ray which lives in the river comes to bask at the edge: these fish bury themselves under a layer of sand, which makes them practically invisible. They have a very strong poison in their sharp, spiky tails, which can inflict an extremely painful wound if trodden on. When I was a boy one of my schoolteachers, an arrogant man fresh out from England who thought he knew it all and disdained all good advice, put himself in hospital for several unhappy days thanks to just such an accident. We had no desire to emulate him.

In our hurry to go for a swim, we'd overlooked another of the hazards of bathing in rivers: the *tábanos* which infest the banks. They look like large, dun-coloured houseflies, but there the similarity ends. Like mosquitoes, horseflies feed on blood but, unlike mosquitoes, their bite is sharp and surprisingly painful. It really makes you jump. For some reason they're more attracted to wet skin than dry and, although they hadn't disturbed us until then, the moment we stepped out of the water, they pounced. Luckily they're very slow and – provided you can resist the natural reflex to twitch or jump or scream the minute they appear – easy to kill. There is an art to it, of course. First you have to let them settle on your skin, which takes some nerve, especially if you've just been bitten. They don't bite immediately, perhaps because they're unpacking the cutlery or honking on you to tenderise the meat. Wait a second, let the villain relax. Only then do you strike. If you slap too soon, the *tábano* gets away. If you wait too long, well, you usually end up slapping an already sore but by then sadly vacant spot, only making it more painful. The good news is that they don't appear to carry any diseases and, once the initial surprise wears off, the bite doesn't itch. I have to admit, though, that as good news goes, this isn't up to much.

After a brisk and bracing battle with the horseflies, we drenched ourselves in insect repellent and spread out on the sand, thrilling in the beauty of our surroundings, to wait for our *asado*. Any minute now, I thought, Telly Savalas is going to pop out from behind a tree and offer me a daiquiri.

'What they never show you in the brochures,' said Patricia, 'are the bugs.'

They were, indeed, everywhere. Although they respectfully left us alone, the air was alive with humming, buzzing, clicking things. They tended to tarnish the idyllic beauty of the spot if you paid too much attention to them, and Patricia was definitely paying attention.

The afternoon passed quickly. We chose a spot above the tideline and put up the tent. As dusk began to fall, I raced back to the campsite for some water, returning just in time to see the sun dipping into the smooth, glassy river. Hot and sweaty from the dash, an evening swim seemed an excellent idea. Patricia, ever house-proud, was tidying up inside the tent. I persuaded her to join me and, as naked as the day we were born, we raced each other down to the shore and dived in. Only at the very last minute, just before my head went under, did I realise the enormity of my mistake. Hovering just above the surface like a fiendish grey mist, silhouetted against the glowing western sky, was a seething cloud of mosquitoes. Patricia hit the water just behind me. As I surfaced again I heard her gasp in horror, and turned to see her sprint yelping back to the tent, kicking up a shower of sand as she went. Unable to stand still, she was slapping her body and batting at the air in a futile attempt to ward off the voracious swarm.

'Oh, God . . . ' she moaned, 'oh, help. . . . '

'Get in!' I called, wading out after her. 'Into the tent! Go on, get in!'

'I can't,' she whimpered, running back towards me, 'I'm covered in sand!' She dived into the water for a rinse and headed back towards the tent again.

'Here, get in,' I said, unzipping the flap, 'come on!' She just sat in the doorway with her legs poking out, slapping at her arms, and burst into tears.

'My feet are all sandy,' she sobbed, 'I can't . . . I'll make a mess.'

I didn't know whether to burst out laughing or scream in her face, but knowing that nothing I could say would persuade my stubborn wife to ignore the mess and just get in, I didn't even try and simply ran to the river to fill one of our empty canteens. By this time, feeding several battalions myself, I rinsed Patricia's feet as quickly as I could, shoved her into the tent and zipped it shut. Now *I* was covered in sand and, knowing that I'd probably be murdered if I tried to get in with her, I went back to the water yet again, rinsed off, refilled the canteen, and hobbled back.

'Okay, move over, I'm coming in.'

Inside Patricia was bawling disconsolately, slapping and tearing at her skin as though she wanted to pull it off. Outside, my head was surrounded by a humming, noxious cloud.

'Darling? Could you please move over?'

'Nonono . . . ' she wailed, 'you'll bring more in!'

Life was becoming more and more like a stupid comedy sketch.

'But Patricia . . . ' I pleaded, doing the twist and the beebop and the boogaloo, 'It's okay, we can *kill* them.'

I was beginning to get pretty agitated myself. I don't share my wife's allergy to mosquito bites, nor her indiscriminate hatred of the entire insect kingdom, but I was beginning to understand what she was going through. I'd never seen the bastards in such numbers before.

'Nonono . . . ' she began again. Oh to hell with this . . .

'Move over!' I undid the zip, pushed her unceremoniously out of the way and plonked myself down. Quick rinse of the feet, legs in, zip shut, success. Right. Patricia lay curled on the mat in a foetal position.

'It's okay,' I said, 'it's okay. If any got in we can kill them. Don't worry. Now: where's the torch?'

She neither knew nor cared. She was caught in a nightmare come to grim, vicious life. I found the torch and switched it on. It seemed as though a thousand mosquitoes had managed to get in with us. The air was thick with their maddening, high-pitched whine. Pleading, comforting, joking and cursing, I tried to cajole my wife back to normality while I started the hunt. It took her another minute or two, but eventually she pulled herself together and joined in, slapping, squashing and squeezing with gusto.

The Great Mosquito Massacre took a good twenty minutes, and we made a gory, bloody mess of the tent in the process, but in the end we won and the last one was dead. Patricia, still sniffling and whimpering, daubed the spattered corpses off the canvas with a wet tissue. Looking for any stragglers that might have escaped, I shone the torch on the fine netting stretched taut across the entrance and for a moment my companion almost went off into orbit again. The outside of the net was covered in a thin grey film of twitching, anxious mosquitoes. They knew we were in there, and were desperately keen to join us. Alfred Hitchcock, where are you now? I thought, as I checked the seal. I pulled the plug out of our medicinal bottle of *Espinillar* and took a large gulp before handing it across. Patricia took it quietly. Her eyes were puffed up from crying, and her cheeks were smudged with tears. Her skin, especially on her legs, was covered with angry red bumps where the bites were already beginning to swell. We broke out the TCP and the Germolene and the Lord-knows-what-else and I daubed it onto her.

'Nature is so *hostile*,' she whispered, 'so aggressive.'

Aye lass, and red in tooth and claw. And proboscis.

The heat of the early morning sun shining on the tent woke us from a fitful, uneasy sleep. The river flowed serenely by in front of us beneath a mackerel sky. Bits of broken insect and smudges of blood scarred the tent, memorials to yesterday's battle. In her sleep Patricia had been scratching at her legs, and several of the bites were now open, ugly sores. We basted ourselves with the foetid repellent and clambered out for a closer look at the world. Sighing waves lapped at the sand. Brilliantly coloured butterflies, yellow, red and blue, fluttered lazily over the beach. It all looked so tame and innocent that it seemed a shame to simply up stumps and push off, as we'd sworn to do the night before. If we stayed, I suggested, Patricia could 'even up' her tan, patchy as a result of all the different shirts she wore whilst cycling. I could try my hand at fishin'. I described the magnificent beast I was certain to land and how it would taste, roasted over a fire. She let me talk her into it.

We strolled along the shore, paddling in the shallows and poking about for treasure in the debris washed up on the beach. Amongst the yellowed band of rushes and broken splinters of bamboo we found the decomposing carcasses of three rays, one with a 'wingspan' the size of a newspaper. Encouraged, we unpacked the fishing tackle we'd brought all the way from Harrods and set about assembling it. I wasn't a keen fisherman, in fact, I've never even been interested in fishing, always believing that if I needed to waste some time, I could easily find more entertaining ways to do so. I'd only been fishing 'properly' twice in my life, on both occasions at sea, from boats, with people who knew what they were doing. On one of those trips I caught a blue shark, and on the other several tuna. Which was 'easy peasy', because we were drifting right above a shoal.

In the course of a lifetime of fairly indiscriminate reading, I'd come across the inevitable percentage of angling stories, I'd seen people 'doing it' in films, and once I caught the tail-end of an angling programme on the BBC. So far as I was concerned, that was all I needed to know. The fish in the Río Uruguay are probably still laughing and passing on the story about the day the fair-haired halfwit (meaning me) tried to catch one of their number. All I can say is that I'm very glad we weren't depending on my skills for our next meal. An unexpected consequence of my failure was a determination to catch something, anything, so long as it was recognizably a fish, before the end of this trip.

While I struggled fruitlessly, bringing in tonnes of aquatic flora in the process, Patricia had settled on the sand and covered herself with suntan oil. It had mingled with the insect repellent and made her smell like a rancid tropical cocktail. ('Penis colada,' as I once overheard a rat-faced high-heeled typist order in a London bar.)

Slowly but inexorably the sky clouded over. The brisk, changeable breeze did nothing to dispel the thick, clinging soupiness of the air. Sooner or later, it was going to rain. We cycled over to the campsite to refill our canteens and, when we came back, waded into the river with our soaps and shampoos. Although it was only mid-afternoon the gathering storm had brought the bugs out in force, so we retired to the safety of the tent for a little cocktail party. Patricia chopped up the leftovers from yesterday's asado and interspersed them with slices of peach, while I poured out

a dose of medicine. We rested back against our piled-up bags and watched
the sky build up and gather strength. Gradually the featureless grey boiled
and ruptured into thick metallic towers. The river started getting choppy.
It was as though a giant bowstring were being drawn back, tighter and
tighter. In our shelter we, too, were getting tighter and tighter, not to
say boisterously drunk, toasting anything and everything that came to
mind.

'Looks like there's a storm cookin' up.'

'Yeah, great, thunner an' lightnin', cheers!' (bang the mugs together.)

Lounging naked in our teepee in that wild and unknown solitude, for
the first time we felt a million miles from home. Whatever the truth,
nothing we could see made us think that this landscape had changed since
the days when it belonged only to the Indians. We felt exposed and
adrift. Far from unpleasant, it made us feel invigorated and renewed. We
interspersed our ponderous debates with noisy, chaotic romance. We'd
got the hang of our mats by now, but although they were excellent for
sleeping on, they were slippery and smooth and obviously not designed
with making love in mind. The temperature inside the tent soared to
42°C, and we thought that we would burst. It wasn't long before the
combined effects of the heat and our celebrations put us both to sleep. By
the time we woke up again, feeling hot and clammy, it was late evening.
Patricia declined my invitation to come for a swim, so I went on my
own. The insects had gone. I sat in the shallows, the water lapping at my
chin. The breeze had stiffened into a wind, lifting white caps on top of
the waves. The sky crackled faintly and there were wan, distant flickers
of light behind the purple anvil clouds on the horizon. As I left the water,
I planted a line of sticks leading from the edge up to the mouth of our
tent, more out of curiosity than anything else.

We'd been asleep again for quite a while when that bowstring, drawn
back to its limit, let fly its gathered strength. With a triumphant, deafening
fanfare of tearing thunder and incandescent, varicose bolts of lightning,
the heavens opened up. The brilliant, excoriating power of raw, untamed
electricity ripped the last shadows from the darkened world. The crashes
of thunder followed one another so closely they became as one extended
rending, as though the sky were being torn up and cast upon us, stone
by monstrous stone. It made me think of Fabián, a friend of mine at
school, whose vision of the universe defined the stars as lightbulbs set
into a distant roof. And what lay beyond that roof? Earth. And stones.
And beyond the earth and stones? More earth. And more stones. It
sounded as though the whole lot were about to fall onto our heads. The
wind became a sudden gale, snatching at the fragile tent, pelting it with
sand and leaves and bits of litter. And then the rain began. Wide awake
and crouching on all fours, I peered out through the netting at the holo-
caust outside. The storm in San José was but a drizzle by comparison.
Patricia grunted in her sleep and, no longer the skittish virgin when it

came to storms, rolled over and nested deeper underneath the covers. The first of my four sticks had already disappeared.

When the water started peeling away the tideline strip by strip, I began to think of moving camp. Luckily we'd already chosen a secondary site, just in case. I went to check on it. In the torchlight the ground was seething with ants, which I hadn't expected to see in the middle of the night, and large transparent spiders. Better not tell my wife about them, I thought. In the few moments I'd been away the river had retrieved all the litter and appeared to be still rising. Patricia had already packed, and she handed out the bags. The water was no more than a metre away. We raced around the tent, pulling up the pegs, then lifted it – almost getting blown away by the wind – and carried it to the new spot. No sooner were we in again, than the rain returned in earnest. But we were safe now, and soon fell into a deep, untroubled sleep.

Unsurprisingly, we weren't feeling very rested when we rose again next morning. The river had receded, but we could see from the traces it had left behind that we were lucky to have moved when we did. We loaded up our bikes, and hit the road.

We reached Dolores in the early afternoon. I can't remember anything about the trip, except for a cheese sandwich we shared at the *almacén* on the highway as we were leaving Agraciada. From a distance the town in the middle of the plain, all church spires and rooftops, looked at its best. Close up it was flat and uninspiring. It lies at the heart of a wheat-growing area, the breadbasket of Uruguay. One of its claims to historical fame is that on this site the Spanish army of occupation at last won their first battle against the fierce *Charrúas*, killing three of their most venerated chiefs, Zapicán, Abayubá and Tabobá.

However much one may deplore the way the Spaniards treated the Indians, the *Charrúas* were a pretty rough bunch too. At the time of the conquest they lived all along the Uruguayan coast of the Río de la Plata, spreading inland along rivers and streams as far as the Cuchilla Grande. Hunter-gatherers, they planted no crops and kept no animals. Most of the time they ran about naked, only draping themselves with an animal skin if the weather was cold. They sheltered in rough teepees made of branches and hides, and moved whenever game grew scarce. They had no metals and only very primitive pottery, making all their tools and weapons of wood, bone, leather or stone. Turbulent and fierce, their idea of having a good time was bashing the hell out of all the other tribes and, eventually, the white man, who they fought off and on for 300 years. Although from time to time they did some trading – hides for tobacco, horses for rum, that sort of thing – their relationship with the settlers was never any better than uneasy, and usually a great deal worse.

In a busy, grubby café facing onto the pallid main square, we lunched on stringy steak and greasy gnocchi that frankly could only be described as bad. We pushed them around our plates and puzzled half-heartedly about how, with such an abundance of fine and toothsome produce, every restaurant we'd tried managed to serve such indifferent fare.

We stopped at a fork in the road amongst acres of nodding sunflowers just outside town and consulted the map. The left fork led to Soriano, the oldest settlement in the country, close to the mouth of the Río Negro. It was the site of the first Indian mission, run by Franciscan monks with the *Chaná*. Part of the loose family of tribes that made up the *Guaraní* nation, they were far more tractable than the *Charrúas*. In *Guaraní* the name *Chana* means 'my parent' or 'my family'. They were a friendly, peaceful, almost timid tribe who, pursued by their enemies the *Charrúas* and the *Bohanes*, lived by fishing, hunting and gathering on the islands in the Río Uruguay and on the northern banks of the Río Negro. They had canoes, were adept at pottery, weaving and other manual work, and were the most receptive to the Christianization programmes introduced by the Spanish missionaries. At the time of the conquest, there were about 100 *Chaná* families in the country, but by the early nineteenth century they had all been assimilated into the European communities and no longer existed as a tribe.

We took the right fork towards Mercedes, the provincial capital. It was late afternoon and we were getting tired when, up on a ridge to our left, we saw a cluster of farm buildings. '*Estancia La Itala*', said a hand-painted sign by the gate. We turned into the tree-lined, steeply climbing track and followed it up to the top. It was so badly rutted that we had to walk the last half of the way. As we drew near the houses, a strong, handsome gaucho cantered up across the cornfield to a gate in the fence on our left. Wheeling and turning his horse with casual, easy grace, he leaned down from the saddle, unlatched the gate, nudged his mount through and latched it shut again behind him. He stopped next to us and fluidly slipped to the ground. His manner was gruff but not unfriendly as he shook me firmly by the hand and tipped his broad-brimmed black hat to Patricia. Alcides Pinto was his name and, after listening to our story, he invited us to follow him up to the kitchen where the cook, he said, would make us feel at home. As we walked together along the track, Patricia and I wheeling our bicycles and Alcides leading his honey-coloured mare, two rough-and-ready farmhands, covered in muck, sauntered out of the milking shed. They spoke such a broken, dense patois that we had trouble understanding what they said, but they said it with a smile so we knew it was okay.

Two low, whitewashed sheds faced each other across a gravel yard. A scrawny cat, surrounded by her mewling young, attended to her toilet on the veranda. Several large dogs lifted themselves off the ground and, tails wagging, came to investigate the new arrivals. Irma, the cook, a fair-haired woman of indeterminate age, gentle and soft spoken, came to the kitchen door and invited us in. She put a kettle on to boil so that we could have some *mate*, and settled us at a table covered with a brightly coloured cloth. The kitchen was small but very tidy, and the fittings ranged across the wall under the window were surprisingly modern. Irma was making *tortas fritas* (fried cakes) rolling the pastry-like dough and cutting it into small, triangular pieces. She filled a pan with filtered sheep's fat, white and clean, and put it on the range to melt. As she kneaded the dough, Irma explained that this wasn't their farm, they were all employees. The *estanciero* lived in Montevideo and didn't visit very often. Their main source of revenue was milk, they had a dairy herd of about 50 cows, although they also grew some crops. Alcides was leaning on the doorpost, cracking jokes, when two small boys – one of them his son – raced into the yard carrying an airgun and a dead woodpecker. The boys tried to persuade Irma to clean and cook the bird for their dinner (roasted, please) but she wasn't having 'any of that nonsense'. Crestfallen, they went off to try their luck somewhere else.

Through the west-facing window, the setting sun flooded the kitchen with a glorious golden light as we sat at the table contentedly chewing our way through a mountain of hot *tortas fritas*, and sipping our *mate*. Frying had inflated the cakes to several times their original size. Irma reminded Alcides that they were almost out of meat, so he left apologetically to slaughter a sheep. She chattered happily about her childhood. She'd grown up not very far from here – 'Over there,' she said pointing through the open door towards a distant hill. Out there too, in one of those verdant folds, was the birth of the nation. The Spanish Viceroy, chased out of Buenos Aires, had established his headquarters in Montevideo. Initially welcomed, his rule soon became so obnoxious to the population that they joined with Buenos Aires – already confronting Spain – and rose up in the first stirrings of the long war for independence. A declaration of intent, made by a handful of rebels who gathered on the banks of the Arroyo Ascencio in early 1811, is revered in Uruguay as the first step towards nationhood.

Irma invited us to join them for dinner – very tempting mutton stew which we'd watched her prepare – but it was late and we were feeling very sleepy, finding it difficult to stay awake. We'd also stuffed ourselves on *tortas fritas*. We made our excuses and retired to our tent, which we'd put up on the grass near the house. As we drifted off to sleep, one of the dogs came and mounted guard across our doorway.

CHAPTER FIVE

JEREMÍAS

It was just after midday when we came up off the plains into the outskirts of Mercedes. Since its foundation in the late eighteenth century, the bustling provincial capital has changed hands from one occupying army to another, being variously Spanish, Portuguese and Argentine before becoming properly Uruguayan, although even then the warring political factions seeking control of the country swapped it back and forth several times before the nation attained some measure of stability. Even the city's foundation was the consequence of discord. The residents of nearby Soriano had banded together to build a chapel, but that unity was quickly dissolved when they failed to reach agreement with the Church as to exactly where in town the chapel was to be built. A handful of those early dissidents packed up in disgust and moved 'some ten leagues' away where they established a new town, with the chapel where they jolly well wanted it. They rather prosaically christened the settlement *Nueva Capilla*, and consecrated it to *Nuestra Señora de las Mercedes*.

There seemed to be a fruit and vegetable shop on every other corner; wares spilling out in colourful profusion onto the broad pavements. So tempting were they that we stopped at one and, much to the entertainment of the passers-by, settled onto the kerbstone to eat our way through a juicy, glorious melon, slicing it into half-moon wedges with our hunting knives.

We were heading for an *estancia* about 30 kilometres beyond Mercedes, which we wanted to reach in good time, so we preferred to push on rather than dally too long in the town. The road out led us along the bank of the Río Negro, through carefully tended public gardens across which a row of sumptuous houses faced the river. Moored at a short, wooden pier, a handful of yachts and launches nodded gently in the current. Spread out on the sandy beach, a few families took advantage of the summer sun.

Our hearts sank when we reached the junction with Ruta 14. Our destination lay 30 kilometres down it, but the road was so ruined and broken that it promised to rip our tyres to ribbons before we'd travelled even 30 metres. For a moment we stood there in silence. Patricia, who'd been feeling brittle since her brush with the bugs, was crestfallen.

'You promised!' she sighed. 'We agreed that we wouldn't go on any more bad roads. Just *look* at it.' I looked at it.

'Well, we'll just have to walk, I suppose, and hope for the best. Lucky we didn't hang about in Mercedes, this may take a while.'

'Nonononono,' she said, stamping her foot. A cloud of reddish brown dust lifted around her ankles and settled gently onto her socks. Stabbing an accusing finger at me, she went on: '*You* said that there weren't going to be any more bad roads. That's what you said. What's *this*, then?' she demanded belligerently, her hand now on her hip.

'Well, okay, it's not so hot, but I never *promised* . . . '

'Yes you did.'

'No, I didn't.'

'Did.' She crossed her arms.

'What I said was that we should try to *avoid* bad roads, because they'd be bad for the bikes.'

For some reason I couldn't fully believe that Patricia was being serious. Her behaviour was so dramatic and exaggerated that it looked more like a caricature than the real thing. I started to giggle foolishly, not at all the sort of response that was required. It only spurred her on to even greater heights of indignation.

'It's like that rubbish of yours about Uruguay being *flat*.'

'Compared to Peru, I said . . . '

'You see? You're always *lying* to me! I don't know why I even bother to listen any more.' Hand on brow, she was getting well stuck into her soap opera. You know what these Latin women are like.

'But Patricia,' I pleaded, trying – but not entirely succeeding – to suppress my laughter, 'if we want to get to the place that we want to get to, the only way we're going to get to it is along this road. Good, bad or indifferent, it's the only one there is.'

I had started to walk, Patricia following stubbornly behind.

'What?' she hesitated, trying to digest this pearl. 'But it's *awful*!'

'Yes, you're right, it is, but . . . '

'You promised.'

'Oh, come on, be reasonable! We have no choice. Unless you want to start changing our route.'

'But we agreed . . . '

'*Patricia*!' I counted my irrefutable arguments off on my fingers. 'I didn't design the road, I didn't build the road, I'm not responsible for the maintenance of the road, I didn't print the map of the road and until five minutes ago I'd never even *seen* the bloody road! Now be fair.'

We were mercifully rescued from further debate by the sudden appearance of a small, open-backed delivery van heading in our direction. I signalled hastily as it approached. The driver, a portly, balding business-man in middle age, got out of the cab. He wasn't going as far as we were, he apologized, but he'd be happy to give us a lift part of the way. I clambered into the back with the bicycles, and Patricia went in front. This ruin we were on, he told her, was the temporarily abandoned remnant of the 'new' road. Work had stopped when the new bridge spanning one of the streams flowing into the Río Negro had been washed away in a flood. As we crossed the old bridge he stopped to point out the wreckage of its fallen replacement a short way downstream.

Cycling was still out of the question, but now she'd let off steam Patricia had cheered up and we bantered gaily as we plodded on, feasting our eyes on the splendid, atmospheric countryside around us, so much wilder and untamed than the land futher south. We'd been walking for about an hour when a shiny black station wagon, kicking up a pillar of dust as it came, appeared behind us. We moved to one side and waited in hitchhiking position. There was something distinctly odd about the driver. All we could see of him was the top of his head and a small pair of eyes peering through the gap between the steering wheel and the top of the dashboard. We had a bit of a shock when the car skidded to a halt in the gravel, and a small boy dropped out of the cab. A very small boy: he was seven years old. His father, who slipped out of the passenger seat a second later, was taking advantage of the deserted road to give his son a driving lesson. Both of them were called Fernando. Until Fernando major assured us with a grin that he would take the wheel, we were a little hesitant to get on board. Then I wondered, as we juddered and jolted along, whether there really was any advantage after all in not having Fernando minor at the wheel.

The ripe, shimmering fields flew past. The air was so remarkably clear that it fooled my eyes into misjudging the distances, which I didn't realize until shortly after we'd clattered through the gate of La Sirená, where a herd was grazing across a nearby slope. Only as an afterthought did I register that 'nearby' was so far away that I couldn't even see the animals' legs. It took an educated guess to identify as sheep the small white tufts amongst the cows. We stopped for a moment at a second cattle grate to allow a very large lizard which lay basking in the sun to move out of our way. The *casero* came out of the house to meet us. The *Señor* and the *Señora* hadn't yet returned from town, he said, but he was expecting them at any minute. Fernando said that he and his son would stay and wait with us for a while so, unloading our belongings, we settled onto the thick, soft grass in the shade of a large *timbó*. His family's estate was only a short distance further along Ruta 14. He explained that, like his own ancestors, a fair proportion of the early settlers in Soriano were French Basques. In those days, he said, people seemed to settle in groups; another example was the province of Río Negro, on the opposite bank of that great river, where many of the early farmers had been British. All the region contained some of the richest and most fruitful farmland in the country. Lamentably, he said with a shrug, it was also taxed accordingly.

As we talked about farming he told us that in the days of military rule there was a brief 'Indian summer' during which farmers achieved good prices for their produce and prospects for export were good. Farmers were encouraged to modernize and increase their production, and enticed to invest in new equipment and reforms with the promise of cheap dollar loans. The government guaranteed that interest rates would remain low and the repayment terms long by the simple expedient of freezing the exchange rate. Like sleazy loan sharks on street corners, representatives of the international banking community tripped over one another in their haste and eagerness to lend, lend, lend. Overwhelmed by all this sudden attention, the farmers borrowed and borrowed, and spent, spent, spent. Then the bottom fell out. The military junta, riddled with corruption, its financial incompetence becoming daily more evident, its power steadily waning, was unable to maintain the artificial exchange rates any longer. Having promised a gradual and relatively painless 'stabilization', (mainly in order to prevent panic in the currency markets) the government instead simply released its grip from one day to the next. The dollar soared, returns plummeted and fortunes were lost (or made, for the few who by luck or inside information happened to be on the right side of the line when the hammer fell).

Fernando had escaped the worst of the débâcle although, like everybody else, he was suffering from its spreading consequences. It seemed ironical, he said, that in a country whose entire economy is dependent upon agriculture, the farmers always were the hardest hit.

Very much a family man, he was determined not to allow the pressures of the economic climate or any of the verities which determined rural life, to break up his home. Most of his peers were caught up in the age-old problem of their children's education. There are state schools throughout the country but, he pointed out pragmatically, they were seldom up to the academic standards he wanted for his boys. They were better in the larger towns, of course, and in some there were even reasonable private schools, but then the problem became one of getting the children there and back every day for only a marginal improvement in their schooling. In fact, if the sole objective was a good education, one really had no choice but to turn to the capital. Faced with this situation, many *estancieros* over the years had been compelled either to break up their families by sending wife and children to Montevideo and seeing them only on occasional weekends, or to neglect their businesses by moving lock, stock and barrel to the capital and, having left it in the hands of an overseer, only visiting the *estancia* from time to time. (There are no boarding schools in Uruguay: the very concept is anathema to the tradition of the close-knit family.)

In Fernando's opinion both alternatives were recipes for disaster, resulting only in a man becoming a lousy husband and father or a lousy farmer or, heaven forbid, both! His solution had been to build a schoolhouse on his *estancia*, and hire a teacher to run it to suit both his high expectations and the curriculum required by the State. He'd even arranged with the Ministry of Education to have the school officially recognized so that, in years to come, the children would have no difficulty entering the academic mainstream. Some years since its inception, not only his children but also those of some of his neighbours attended classes there daily, the parents sharing the costs. He conceded readily that, in effect, he was only postponing rather than solving the problem, as soon it would be time for secondary education and, ultimately, university, but for the time being his family remained united and his kids went to a decent school which, so far as he was concerned, was all that mattered.

It was a universe away from that dairy farm in Colonia.

Although Roddy and his wife hadn't yet arrived, the Fernandos were expected home for lunch so, urging us to visit whenever we liked, they rattled off down the driveway. The *casero*, who'd been trying to get us into the house ever since we arrived, led us into the sitting room and settled us into the leather sofa with a large jug of cold lemonade.

The old house was large and L-shaped, with an iron railing completing the square to enclose a gravel courtyard at its heart, a design dating back to the times when it provided a defence against the *matreros*, the marauding bands of rustlers and cattle thieves who roamed the countryside in those early days. The layout enabled the householders to direct a withering crossfire on anyone trying to enter uninvited. Along the entire inside length of the elbow ran a covered gallery, with flowering vines climbing up the pillars to the red tiled roof.

The whitewashed walls around us were hung with photographs of prize bulls and polo ponies. A profusion of trophies and cups vied for space in glass-fronted cabinets and on top of the baby grand which stood in one corner. A couple of steps led down into a small, cluttered study, festooned with armadillo shells, birds' nests, braided leather whips and a collection of relics gathered over the years. A short-wave radio crackled and spat from a corner of the paper-strewn desk. We hadn't been there for long when a car raced past the window and, moments later, Roddy erupted into the room, his wife Lucía trailing patiently behind him. We stood up to introduce ourselves, but Roddy had other things on his mind and was not about to be interrupted in midstream. With a perfunctory nod in our direction he launched himself into a long tirade against bankers and taxes and auctioneers and the government. Only when he paused for breath a little while later did he seem to notice we were there. Blinking mildly like a teddy bear just woken from its hibernation, he shook us by the hand. 'Yes,' he said dreamily, 'my sister told me about you, said you might turn up.' (His sister is Jaime's mother.)

Not very tall, stocky, balding on top, Roddy is a mad keen sportsman.

Most of the trophies were his, although Lucía had won a few at tennis. She was once in the first round at Wimbledon. They shouldn't have been here at all, they said, they should have been on holiday, but they'd had to interrupt it because of a cattle auction.

Lucía showed us to a spacious bedroom at one end of the 'L'. One of Roddy's daughters had decorated it with an old cartwheel, colourful tapestries and various bits of tooled leatherwork. As in the sitting room, the ceiling was spanned by dark, heavy wooden beams. Roddy came in behind us and sniffed at the musky, vaguely familiar scent that hung in the air.

'Bloody fools!' he snorted, peering through the back window towards the *casero*'s quarters. 'Skunk got into their bedroom a couple of weeks ago. Instead of leaving the door open so that it could get out again, the idiots set the dogs on it. No wonder it pissed all over the place. Now they've moved into the guest room, which is why you've got this one. Hope you don't mind?' he added with an apologetic smile.

We had gathered on the veranda for a little pick-me-up when we were joined by Falcón, the foreman, a stocky, powerful man about Roddy's age, almost as broad as he was tall. They had been together for longer than either of them cared to remember, and treated each other more as friends than as boss and employee. Roddy spoke of the *capataz* almost reverentially as one of the few remaining old-fashioned gauchos. They were going out later for a ride around the estate, and invited us along. Patricia let slip that I'd been pulling her leg about refusing Jaime's invitation a few days ago, so, with much laughter and dark threats to give me an unbroken stallion with a handful of burrs under the saddle as punishment for teasing my wife, the issue was decided.

Roddy's energy and indignation seemed inexhaustible. Over lunch he grew very heated about wildlife preservation, insisting fiercely that the protection of nature was everyone's duty. For all our wholehearted agreement we didn't realize until much later that, of all the people we met in our travels, he was almost unique in his concern. It's not that people were wilfully destructive: they just seemed to take nature's bounty for granted and seldom, if ever, stopped to consider the consequences of their behaviour.

In the late afternoon, once the day had cooled, we gathered at the stables. Six horses, already saddled, stood tethered in the shade beneath the palms. They snorted and stamped, harnesses creaking, their wonderful, salty smell peppering the air. Despite Roddy's threats and our forebodings, the mares they'd chosen for us were placid and good-natured. Patricia's was a lazy, half-asleep chestnut mare called Grillo – meaning 'Cricket' – whose favourite speed was standing still and from which she could only be urged with considerable effort into a leisurely plod. Mine was nameless, shaped like a barrel and very dark brown, nearly black. She'd started her career herding cattle, but lately had been relegated to more mundane duties, such as drawing a cart. I soon found out that she, too, had a two-speed gearbox, although the alternatives in her case were slow and flat out.

We set off at a slow walk down the gradual slope into a broad, shallow bowl and up the grassy swell on the other side. It seemed we'd only been riding for a moment, but when I turned in the saddle to look around, the farmhouse was nowhere to be seen, hidden in the grassy folds. As we skirted a field sown with red clover, Roddy and Falcón cantered off for a closer look at some bulls in a far-off pasture, arranging to meet us further ahead. Lucía chatted with Jeremías, another of the old-fashioned gauchos, who was softly bringing her up to date on what had happened in her absence. He and Falcón had practically grown up together and, as young tearaway bucks twenty-five years ago, had cut quite a swathe across the countryside. Slim and sinewy, tanned and weatherworn to the colour of an old saddle, he swayed in such easy harmony with his horse that he seemed to be part of the animal. Dark eyes, set deep in a creased, leathery face, spoke eloquently of a lifetime searching the horizon in blistering sunlight.

The gaucho, the quintessential symbol of rural manhood, was born in the days of the colonization when Europeans began to leave the safety of the coastal settlements and headed inland, spreading through the region that is now Uruguay, northern Argentina and southern Brazil. Those first coarse pioneers, often deserters from navies and armies or refugees of one sort or another, even escaped slaves, mixed and mated with the Indians, absorbing much of their errant, nomadic ways. The cattle and horses which had so successfully spread across the open prairie provided food, transport and leather for their equipment, defining their lifestyle and character. Rough, long-haired and bearded, they were gaudy and osten-tatious in their dress and habits. Their lives dictated by the movements of the herds, theirs was a mobile, equestrian society in which a gaucho's horse was often more highly regarded than his woman, whose function was entirely secondary. The gaucho's main weapon and most precious tool was his knife, an extension of his hand with which he slaughtered, skinned, ate, worked the leather for his boots, saddles, harnesses and lassoes and, when the need arose, fought. Those wild, semi-barbarian men had scant regard for Spanish law, and often formed marauding, predatory bands. They were to become the heart and arm of the fight for independence. The passage of the centuries has modified and tamed that raw, primitive breed but the traditions of virility and independence linger. Today's gaucho, hemmed in by fences and modernity, still a sublime horseman and a rugged individualist, is the 'civilized' version of his ancestors.

We came almost without warning to a sudden, secret crease in the infinite carpet of greens and tans. At its foot raced a shallow brook. Long accustomed to it, our horses slithered down the stony embankment and waded happily across to the other side, oblivious to the water flooding into our shoes. Roddy and Falcón caught up with us as we approached a moody, stunted forest: tall fibrous grass and untidy thorn bushes growing haphazardly in the gaps amongst the twisted, windswept trees. A heavy, primeval atmosphere enveloped us as we went deeper and deeper into the woods, ducking the overhanging branches and dodging the lichen-encrusted fallen trunks. Some of these trees, said Roddy, were here before Columbus sailed. Just then the dogs that had come with us, ranging wide, tore in a pack across our path, barking furiously in hot pursuit of a bulky, indistinct something that quickly disappeared into a burrow in the tangled undergrowth. An armadillo, said Falcón, cantering up to the torn soil where it had hidden from our prying eyes.

At the top of the forest the trees thinned and we found ourselves on a bluff overlooking the black, glassy stillness of the Arroyo Cololó. General Artigas, at the head of the epic Exodus of the Uruguayan people in 1811, had passed somewhere along the banks of this stream. Ordered by his commanding officer to abandon the siege of Montevideo, he'd repudiated the terms of the armistice Buenos Aires had signed with Spain (the latter backed up by the muscle of the Portuguese army) and had headed north with his gaucho troops to continue the struggle. In an unprecedented demonstration of loyalty and commitment to their chief, fully four-fifths of the rural population packed up their belongings onto ox-carts and wagons, closed up their farms and followed Artigas in their thousands on that long march. One of the most remarkable things about that journey was the stoicism, solidarity and good nature with which they bore what couldn't have been anything but constant hardship.

In its bends and twists, the stream was clogged with *camalotes*, floating islands of lily-like plants. The tips of tall, nodding bullrushes glowed in the last coppery rays of the sinking sun. Herons scooped and rummaged in the shallows for something to eat. The tranquillity was dense, almost palpable. As we emerged from the protection of the forest, back towards the house, Roddy pointed out some trees standing like an island in the middle of a distant meadow. That was once part of this forest too, he said. His neighbour's father – or possibly grandfather, I can't remember well – had felled the rest to make way for pasture and crops, but had left those few standing in honour of the Indians. Apparently a local chieftain had thrashed the Spanish army here, and hung the officers in those very trees that now stood alone as a living monument to his victory. Perhaps inevitably, the legend also tells of a chestful of gemstones and gold which the Spaniards had been carrying and which the Indians buried somewhere in these secretive hills. Later that evening, back at the house, Roddy showed us a collection of arrowheads, tips of spears, stone tools and bits of rusted, unidentifiable metal gathered from the ground over the years.

Whilst not confirming the tale, they lent a new dimension to its telling. Along all the fences stood a single line of trees: *talas*, *algarrobos* and *espinillos*.'

'How clever,' I said to Roddy, 'to plant them that way as a windbreak.'

He had to refuse the credit. 'Birds,' he said, 'they eat the seeds and then come and sit on the wire. Every time they shit they plant a tree.'

It was nearly dark when, after three hours in the saddle, we dismounted once again at the stable. The limpid, January moon was rising behind the trees. After dinner, as we strolled in the garden with Roddy and Lucía, more fireflies than we even knew existed in the world flickered simultaneously alight, carpeting the soft hills with glittering sparks, echoing the Milky Way above our heads.

'This is how the world used to be,' I thought aloud, 'everything at peace and in its place.'

'Not always peace,' corrected Roddy, taking us to see the remnants of the damage wrought by a hailstorm in December.

'Stones the size of hens' eggs,' said Lucía, 'like this they were.'

All the windows in the sitting room and the study had been broken. By the light of the moon we could see that there were still some roofing tiles that needed replacing.

'You should see the car! All bumpy, it is. I'd left it here. I came out in my nightshirt to move it and had to go back indoors. They can give you a hell of a headache, those stones. Killed sheep and chickens, stampeded the cattle. We lost a couple of calves. One of the mares, a beautiful animal, was so frightened she tore herself open on the wire. For a while we were afraid she'd have to be put down. Made a complete mess of the wheat and the cornfields. Didn't Fernando tell you? He lost God-knows-how-much wheat.'

Next morning, while we waited for the cattle trucks to arrive, Lucía grumbled about her infanticidal hen. She'd fallen into the habit of laying her eggs on the sloping corrugated roof over the woodpile. Quite naturally, but to the hen's constant confusion, the eggs rolled like Humpty Dumpties down the slope to a sticky end on the ground below.

Falcón, Jeremías and the farmhands, with much hallooing and cracking of whips in the air, were cutting their horses back and forth through the herd assembled in a grassy hollow, separating out the calves and driving them into a funnel-shaped corral by the loading bay. Dogs darted after the stragglers, barking excitedly and nipping at their heels, chasing them towards the pen. It was fascinating to watch them work since nobody seemed to be telling them what to do and yet, somehow understanding that only calves were wanted, they left the cows alone.

An articulated lorry, its cargo section an enormous metal cage, had backed up against the stone and wooden ramp. Perched high up on the cage, a man was opening the portcullis. There should have been an inscription on it: Abandon Hope, All Ye Who Enter Here.

I eat meat. I've always eaten meat, and I've always enjoyed it. I've never had any illusion about how my steaks are obtained, nor any qualms about eating them. I know that every day I live I cause the death of the animal whose flesh has fed me but, somehow, watching all those nervous calves, those huddled masses, wide-eyed and so tangibly afraid, I was compelled to stop and reconsider, even though I don't believe that eating meat is a moral issue. Although it might assuage my conscience – should it ever bother me enough to make me take the step – I can't see that I would change a thing by becoming a vegetarian. Being a purely intellectual condition anyway, vegetarianism doesn't alter our fundamental physiology as omnivores. Having said that, I *do* believe that fattening animals and 'enhancing' meats destined to be eaten by people, using artificial means such as hormones, chemicals, and unnatural confinement in the way that has become so prevalent in the industrialized world, *is* immoral, although the offence there is not only against the animal but also against the farmer's fellow man, whose body has to take up the residue of his tinkering. Living in cities and buying food in convenient parcels tend to dull one's awareness to the point that one often forgets where that food comes from. For days now, living close to the earth and to the roots of life, questions which demanded my attention had kept cropping up. I couldn't find any clear, easy answers, but by then I already knew that I could never look at a steak or a drumstick in quite the same way again. I understood, in a way that perhaps I never had, that food is worthy of respect.

The cage full, the portcullis was brought down with a crash and the truck pulled away from the loading ramp to make way for another. This one took aboard the *vacas gordas*, the heifers. Whereas the calves would probably go to another farmer, who would fatten them up to sell again, the heifers were almost certainly destined for the abattoir. The loading done, we raced to another pen closer to the house, behind a brown stone barn shaded by ranks of *paraísos*, their shining leaves a vibrant, impossible green. In the pen an old handyman moved amongst the sheep, clicking his tongue and murmuring softly, checking that they all were well. The air was laced with their sharp, pungent smell. Jeremías galloped up, tethered his horse to a post in the shade, and vaulted over the fence. A truck was parked by the loading ramp. The driver and his mate were busy laying planks across the cage, halfway up, to form a second storey: the flock would travel in two tiers. When the truck was ready, one of the men opened the gate from the pen and the animals poured down the funnel, urged along by whoops and whistles. Jeremías was shaking a rattle made of dozens of perforated tin disks threaded onto a large wire hoop, like a jailer's key-ring. Bleating and pushing, their hooves scraping as they scrambled up the wooden gangplank into the truck, the woolly stream flowed along the corridor. As the upper storey filled, one of the ewes fell through a gap which opened up between two boards, falling, much to her surprise, to the floor below. She kicked and stamped against the sides of the truck in a final demonstration of bravado.

That afternoon we went out again with Jeremías and Lucía on a ride around another part of the *estancia*, across fields lying fallow after last year's harvest, now choked with weeds and thistles and the stunted remnants of past crops. The ever-present dogs, circling wide around us, flushed a constant stream of partridges and hares from the brush. A large pool had built up behind a low stone dam across a small creek, in which *Lobitos de río*, mammals similar to otters, splashed and played. The water overflowed the dam like a rolling sheet of glass, cascading musically into a second pool and then away across the meadows.

At this time of year the cattle suffer very badly from a sort of hay fever. Camomile, which grows wild everywhere and makes the fields so pretty when they're clad in the tiny white and yellow blossoms, produces a very fine, light pollen. As the cows graze this dust gets into their eyes and, being a strong irritant, reddens and inflames them. Left untended, the inflammation can lead to infection, so the herds are regularly treated with a medicated eye-wash. Another serious threat to the livestock are the flies, which are quick to lay their eggs in any cuts or grazes, however small. Once the eggs are laid in a wound the voracious maggots advance at an alarming rate, and can do truly frightful damage in practically no time at all.

Falcón and the men were at work in the 'hospital', a grassy paddock surrounded by a tall, dense hedge. The cows entered from one end, through a corral which narrowed to a corridor the width of a single animal. This corridor ended in an ingenious wooden gate, shaped very much like the business end of a giant pair of pliers. As the cow comes through, the calipers are closed around its neck, holding it in place so that it can be treated. Every now and then the men weren't quick enough and a cow escaped the trap without its medicine. In then had to be chased around the paddock, lassoed, and brought to the ground. Falcón, being so broad and strong, was particularly good at this. Dispensing with the rope, he'd simply lunge at the steer, grab it by the horns, twist its head to one side and wrestle it down. Then everybody else would jump on board to hold it still, while whatever it had wrong with it was tended.

It's surprising how strong and resilient cows are, and what sort of punishment they can endure and still survive. One was having a routine checkup after having injured itself with a piece of fence wire which had become lodged in its mouth as it grazed. It was given the all clear: what had been a horrifying wound had healed completely. Another was checked to see how it was recovering from emergency surgery. The red clover which is cultivated so extensively for winter feed can, if eaten green and in too large a quantity, inflate the cows like beachballs. It ferments in the stomach, producing so much gas that it can temporarily cripple or sometimes even kill the animal. As a cow which is suffering from that amount of wind simply falls over, it can't be brought to the farmhouse, so treatment has to be done on the spot. There is a special tool, like a very large hypodermic needle, which can be used to lance the distended stomach and release the gas, but if that's not to hand, the gaucho's trusty knife will do. Find the spot, quick stab, hey presto: lots of noise, lots of stink, cow's okay. Far from causing it any distress, the relief is usually so great that the animal springs to its feet and immediately starts eating again.

That afternoon Jeremías had to ride out with Jorge, one of the farmhands, to bring a herd in from a distant pasture for their checkup next morning, so he invited us along. Patricia, her backside a little sore from two days in the saddle, politely declined. All his working life, Jeremías had been famous in the parish as a *domador*, a horse tamer. Even the most recalcitrant steed was as gentle as a puppy in his hands, as though it knew that it wasn't going to get away with any nonsense. He wasn't a showy rider: he simply sat astride, looking mild and supremely comfortable in the sheepskin saddle, stirrups set long, rolling a cigarette with one hand as we trotted along. His shoulder was troubling him, he said. Just over a year ago a mustang he'd been given to tame had thrown him rather badly, and put him into hospital for several days suffering from sprains and concussion.

'Damn near killed me, he did,' he murmured, 'that *pingo* was mean. He'd been spoiled, badly treated. I couldn't think straight for months. Doctor gave me pills. I was taking them for ages. "Don't drink," he said. I didn't, either. Until the patron's daughter had a party here. From his first wife. Lovely girl, always been very good to me. She sat me down and gave me a glass of whisky. Drank it in one gulp, just like that. Couldn't stand up again. She laughed . . . you should have heard her! She used to bake cakes. We'd sit in the kitchen and talk. Loves horses. Best rider of the lot. Out in the fields all day. When I came back here last year, she was the first to come and say hello. I used to work here before. I was working on another *estancia*, over there. Falcón came to get me. We've been friends for years. "This is what Roddy wants to pay you," he said. It suited me fine, so I came back. I've got a family in Mercedes, boy and a girl. Daughter about the same age as this girl here. She's gone to school, learned how to type. She can work in town, now. The boy's still studying. I want him to learn something so he can get a good job, so he doesn't have to work in the fields. I like it, done it all my life, but he can get better money in town. If he wants to. We'll see. My arm's still stiff, look: can't lasso so good any more. When we were young, Falcón and I used to ride out on our days off to practise roping cows, just for the hell of it. We were good. The best. Can't do it any more. Falcón got knocked off too, once. Happened right here, in a ditch over there behind the house. Damn horse fell on top of him. Knocked the wind out of him. Put him out for a few minutes. He says he's okay now. He's pretty tough. I used to go to the *Prado*, when I was younger. Boy, they sure have some mean horses *there*! The meanest. It's for the show, you see. Pony doesn't buck, they send it home again. It's what the audience likes, lots of bucking and jumping. You can get to ride the rough ones there. Throw you all over the place. More fun for the people who come to watch, see. I used to get prizes. Everybody knew me there. I used to come up to the other gauchos, they'd be standing around drinking *mate*, waiting for their turn. You know who I am? I'd say. Yeah, we know who you are, they always said. Paid good money, the *Prado*, if you could stay on. And there were dances, and that. Women, too. But I tell you something: after that horse over there threw me, I came this close to never riding again. Jeremías, you're getting too old for this, I said. You don't want to do this nonsense any more. . . . Thought maybe I should stay on the ground, go out in the fields instead and plant stuff. To tell you the truth, I was scared to get back in the saddle. But I had to. Couldn't just give up, just like that. I tell you, I got hold of that very same sumbitch that threw me, too. He'll never do *that* again. Taught him a lesson he won't forget in a hurry. Meek as a lamb, now. The ladies ride him.'

He murmured on in his quiet, unassuming voice, skipping from one memory to another as we rode across the billowing range, his eyes never leaving the distant horizon. Beneath his gruff manner he was something of a dandy. His dark blue *bombachas*, now dusty and worn, were delicately stitched and pleated. His black boots, too, although scuffed and abraded, were decorated with ornate welts and patterned perforations. His thick, sun-bleached workshirt, checked in shades of blue and criss-crossed with a thin red line, was smart and well chosen, and he wore his tattered blue beret at just the right rakish angle. The hilt of the knife which he carried thrust through a broad leather belt at the small of his back was filigreed in silver and gold.

Grazing in the valley ahead of us, beyond the creek, we found the herd. So that we could come on it from the right direction, we circled wide through a whispering wood and across a *bañado* where a spring filtered to the surface to form a shallow, muddy marsh. Jeremías nodded eloquently at Jorge and, nudging their horses, they cantered off to the left. My mare, having understood more than I had of the exchange, peeled off to the right. Thinking it might be best if we sat this one out, I reined her in and stopped to watch. Whistling and calling, the two men started the cattle moving. Moving straight towards me, in fact. Without consulting me, the mare broke into a canter and nimbly tucked a couple of stragglers back into the restless mass. I was impressed, but still wanted no part of this adventure. Giving her a congratulatory pat on the neck, I tried to get the mare to retreat to a discreet distance, but something must have been lost in the translation because she spun abruptly on her hind legs to race after a cow and her calf that had split away from the herd and were making for the woods. We galloped across the *bañado* to cut them off. It sounds good, that: 'we galloped'. To tell the truth, I was nothing more than a passenger as the mare flew across the sodden ground, her hooves lifting musical fountains of water with every powerful stroke. Fingers entwined in the sheepskin saddle, I hung on as best I could. I was getting a bit worried: if an expert like Jeremías can get thrown, well, so can I, I thought. I jammed on the brakes and only just saved myself from being catapulted off between the horse's ears.

'Sshhh, easy now, that's enough, no more, okay?' I whispered. Bang-bangbang went my heart. But however much I tried to restrain her, the mare was determined to reinstate herself as a working horse and be finished for good with this business of pulling carts. She stamped and bridled, eager to be up and at the cattle. Foolishly I loosened the reins. She was off like a shot. Only after alternately embarrassing and terrifying me several times in rapid succession did she stop again, somewhere in the middle of a distant field, a million miles away from the action. I held her there, nailed to the ground, until the herd had passed. On our slow, leisurely return to the stables, Jeremías was too kind to mention my disastrous performance.

'Riding a bicycle all the way round the country, eh?' he said. 'I couldn't do that.'

My heart went out to him.

Patricia was in a fractious, stormy mood. She was tired, she said, as we walked across the meadow, kicking up the camomile. She didn't want to walk. It was too hot, there were too many bugs, the weeds scratched at her legs, she'd just had a shower. . . . On the principle that it might bring her round, I tried some hearty, encouraging advice on the lines of *cheer up, old girl* and *pull yourself together*. Wrong approach. In no time at all we were tangled up in a very silly argument, which started mildly and degenerated quickly into full-blown war. Patricia had the last word:

'Go away! Leave me alone!' she snarled as she stamped off on her own, her anger billowing behind her like a flag.

Women! I thought. Bah! Ptui! I let her go, over a ridge and out of sight. We'd wandered quite a distance from the farmhouse. It was nowhere to be seen. In fact, I no longer even knew in which direction I should look. The sun was very hot, so I took my shirt off.

I was still rehearsing the conversation in my mind, feeling angry and unsettled and wondering why my wife was so unreasonable, when a movement in the grass caught my eye. Looking more closely, at first there didn't seem to be anything there. I turned away, then looked again. On a couple of blades of grass at my feet little beads of fresh, wet blood sparkled in the sunlight. Not fully believing my eyes, I crouched and looked more closely. There on the ground before me lay a short length of tiny intestine, neatly clipped off at both ends and, very near it, another minute piece of unidentifiable gut. They looked so moist and fresh I could almost see them quiver. A pace or two away something did quiver, and rustle. I strained to see what it was. Then it moved again, and this time I saw it although, once again, I had trouble adjusting. Twisting sinuously through the grass I saw a large brown snake with wings: two broad, outstretched, grey-feathered wings. I knew it was impossible, but there it was in front of me. The serpent turned to face me, and then I understood. Its jaw obscenely unhinged, it was halfway through swallowing a *tero*. The bird was lodged in the snake's throat, only its wings still protruding, one to either side, giving the impression they belonged there. At first I was relieved that I hadn't chanced upon some previously unrecorded freak of nature, but then my thoughts returned with a bang to something else: what if that damfool wife of mine, stomping angrily about the countryside, were to meet a snake, get bitten and die? I charged off the way I'd come, looking for her. Of course, I couldn't find her. Oh you stupid, lovely girl, *please* don't tread on a snake, I muttered, bogged down up to my ankles in the marsh I'd galloped across so easily the day before. When at last I found her she was squatting by the creek, looking at something. She hadn't seen me, so I kept my distance. She's alright, I thought, relieved. She's thinking, I can tell. Better leave her to it. After all, she told me to go away. She won't get bitten, I said to myself as I hiked back to the farmhouse.

Once there I had an uncomfortable hour or two while I waited for her to return, which was probably just as well as it gave *me* time to think, too. Lying cradled in each other's arms, we promised to try harder.

'I got lost,' she said.

'Hm.'

'I saw some *nutrias*, in the creek.'

'I saw a snake with wings.'

'I'm sorry. You were right.'

'No no: I'm sorry. You were right.'

'I'll try to behave a little better.'

'So will I.'

CHAPTER SIX

ACROSS THE RÍO NEGRO

Outside the gates of La Sirena we turned left. We were going to cross the Río Negro at the Palmar dam and continue north along the Ruta 3. Although the road was still by no means good, it was good enough to cycle on, provided we were careful. We were happy to be on the move again. It was a beautifully clear day, and we were bursting with energy. The track twisted and turned, dipping into wooded hollows in the never-ending plain. Yellow fields of wheat alternated with open pastures where enormous herds grazed. We stopped at a stone bridge and watched the stream glide by beneath our feet. Downstream, the water tumbled and foamed over the remnants of another bridge, long since fallen between the willows.

In a delicate glade by the side of the road we found a little whitewashed cottage, surrounded by fruit trees and flowerbeds. A large, incongruous ANTEL sign protruded from the thatch. We decided to stop and phone 'base camp'. Chickens scattered as we walked up the flagstone path. A young woman stepped out through the curtain in the open doorway and ushered us into the house, waving us towards a row of severe, straight-backed chairs along the wall. Ferns like feather dusters spilled from pots along the windowsills, and a veritable jungle grew in a collection of buckets and tins against the pale, terracotta-coloured walls. At one end of the room, like an upright piano sawn in half, stood the telephone exchange, bristling with wires, its varnished wooden case polished until it shone. Partly hidden in the flora on the floor were rows of interconnected truck batteries.

The operator sat down at the switchboard, put on her headphones, and gave the lever a hefty crank. She yelled down the cone-shaped mouthpiece at a succession of other operators until, at last, the connection was made. She beckoned me towards the telephone that hung on the wall.

'Not a very good connection, I'm afraid,' she murmured.

'Hello?' my mother's voice came down the wire, faint but clear.

'Hello, mum. How are you?'

'Hello?'

'Hello, mum, it's me! How are you?'

'Me who?'

'Me your *son*. Your *only* son, remember?'

'Oh. I can hardly hear you. Who did you say it was?'

'YOUR SON!' I bellowed, swallowing a string of curses, 'the line's not very good. Can you hear me now?'

'No. Not a word.'

'I said it's a very – bad – line!'

'Dreadful. Can't hear a word you're saying. Can't you speak up? You've always been such a mutterer.'

'I **AM** SPEAKING UP!' Stifling a laugh, Patricia put her fingers in her ears.

'Well, it's a very bad line, then.'

'Yes, I know, that's what I've been saying. Hang up and I'll try again.'

'I think you'd better. I can't hear you at all.'

The operator went through the chain of connections again. A couple of chickens wandered in from the yard and walked around the room, pecking and scratching at the stone floor.

'Okay, it's me again. Is this better? Can you hear me now?'

'No. It's still too faint.'

'Well I'll just have to call from somewhere else, then.'

'Yes, this is an awful line. That's what I've been trying to tell you.'

With the sun directly overhead in a cloudless sky, the fields around us shimmered in a heat haze. Little *apereás* darted in and out of the undergrowth along the margins of the road, and *teros* rose screaming from the grass, raising the alarm. Parrots hurled their insults at us from their perches high in the eucalyptus trees, occasionally bursting across our path like squadrons of turquoise missiles. We saw a weasel and a snake and a very large eagle, and for several kilometres the baking air was heavy with the smell of skunk.

At last the rough earth track emerged from the wood onto a straight, flat tarmac road that dwindled into nothing in the distant reaches of a broad, featureless plain. The stark, geometric perfection of electricity pylons marched towards us from the far horizon, graceful parabolas of thick high-tension cable draped from one to the next. We were getting close to the dam. Across the grey black ribbon, on the brow of a low ridge, we saw an *almacén*. We were hot and thirsty and our mouths were full of dust, so we pedalled up the rise to buy ourselves a drink.

On a bench in the shade beneath the eaves, three men interrupted their conversation to study our approach through the gate, across the paddock, around the grazing horse and up to the porch. As we rested our bikes against the wall, one of the men stood up. He looked the perfect Indian chief, as though he'd been hacked out of a mountain with an axe. Square jaw, high hard cheekbones and a broad flat forehead sloping back to a glorious head of long, lustrous blue-black hair, now greying at the temples, combed back onto his shoulders. Nose like a razor blade; lips full and finely drawn; eyes like bullets; broad shoulders; arms like tree trunks and a broad, muscular chest. He wasn't tall, but he radiated power.

The other two were a mess. Not only because of their unkempt, careless appearance: they were also drunk as lords. Sitting Bull greeted us with a slow nod and a soft 'good day', leading us into the dim, cool bar. His appearance fascinated us. There are no full-blooded Indians left in Uruguay: the Spaniards and the settlers killed most of them off and chased the rest into Paraguay and Brazil. In early colonial days there was some intermarrying – or at least some interbreeding – and traces of it are still plain, especially in the interior of the country, but we'd never seen them quite as plain as this. I was dying to ask about his ancestors, but didn't know how to begin. Not that he was in any way intimidating, quite the contrary. In fact he probably would have been quite happy to talk about himself, but I couldn't very well just say: 'Two Cokes please and what sort of Indian are you?'

We made inconsequential conversation, talking of the heat and the distance to the dam, while I tried to find a diplomatic way to approach the subject. By the time I'd steeled myself to ask, the two drunks outside had discovered our bikes and come indoors, both of them talking at once in slurred, slippery tones, holding each other up.

'Marblush m'sheensh . . . hic? . . . ' said one, waving his glass around under my nose.

I had the feeling that our Indian was embarrassed by his friend, and it occurred to me that while I'd been getting ready to ask him about himself, he'd been doing the same with us but, with the drunks tugging amiably at our sleeves, the moment of ripeness passed. They hovered around like friendly flies, breathing beer all over us, asking complicated questions and embarking on anecdotes they forgot halfway through. With regret, Patricia and I retreated to the road, our curiosity unsatisfied.

To the east of the flat black ribbon the land fell away into distant valleys, some of them flooded by the lake behind the dam. From a height we looked down on a herd of cattle grazing along a treeless bank, wallowing in the shallows. We stopped to take a photograph. A wire fence that ran parallel to the road interrupted the view. I didn't want it in the frame, so I wandered about in the bracken looking for a path. Thick, low bushes and bulky tufts of fibrous grass blocked my way. There was only one thing for it: just wade in.

'Be careful,' warned Patricia, 'you never know what might be lurking about in there.'

Nonsense, I thought, if I make enough noise I'll frighten everything away.

Halfway to the fence I had one of the biggest surprises of my life. It felt as though someone had driven a hot spike into my leg with a mallet. There was no transition from normality to pain. One moment life was fine, the very next I thought I was going nuts. With one leap I crossed the intervening gap and sat down hard on the tarmac, squirming and cursing my head off. Oh no, I hope it's not a snake, please don't let it be a snake. I couldn't sit still so I jumped to my feet, only to fall down again with a thump. Afraid of what I might find, I had a look. At the bottom of my calf, just above the Achilles tendon, was a tiny crimson bead the size of a pinhead. It was hard to believe that something so small could be so irritating. Gingerly I looked for another: oh shit, I hope there's only one. I didn't want to find the mark of another fang.

'How many holes can you see, Patita, how many holes?'

'Only one,' she said.

'Oh praise the Lord! Ow ow ow . . . '

'But it could have been a snake with just one tooth.'

I could vaguely remember seeing some large, black, slender-waisted wasps hovering in the grass, and hoped I'd been attacked by one of them. As I watched, the skin around the puncture first went red, then turned to white and then began to swell. Luckily the first shock wore off quite fast, although it still looked and felt as though I had half a walnut buried under my skin. It was hot to the touch.

'I might as well at least take the picture before we go, now that it's cost me so much. It may be the last one I take.'

Patricia neither laughed nor said I told you so, but it was in her eyes so I said it for her.

'Just be more careful next time,' she answered mildly.

'If there *is* a next time,' said the voice of gloom.

We coasted down a long hill into a small, prefabricated and whitewashed village, originally built for the construction team working on the dam, and now occupied by the electricity board's staff. The identical, boxlike houses reminded us of army barracks. Thirst again our number one priority, we stopped at a guardhouse by the dam, where the man on duty directed us to the Parador by the lake. The inn was on the other side of the village, in the 'posh' neighbourhood. Erected for the dam-building élite, it had the air of a small country club which, in a way, it once had been. Now the provincial government ran it as a hotel.

As we sat at the bar, gorging ourselves on ice-cream, I noticed a poster extolling the virtues of *dorado* fishing in the Río Negro. Like salmon, *dorado* swim upriver to spawn. Presented with the dam's formidable barrier, they gather in vast numbers at its foot. The waitress told us that 15-kilo fish were fairly commonplace. Patricia and I didn't need to discuss it: we left our luggage at the inn and raced down to the river.

In our haste we'd overlooked a minor detail: bait. We eventually managed to catch some minnows, using a white cotton scarf as a net. It wasn't easy. Holding onto its four corners we spread it out and sank it in the shallows, squatting nose to nose, keeping very still.

'I think I'm going to sneeze.'

'No, don't, you'll frighten them away.'

'Frighten who away?'

'Oh shush, you're making too much noise. The fish, of course, they'll be here any minute.'

'Who's making too much noise? Stay still, why don't you?'

'I can't. Something's nibbling at my bottom.'

Silhouetted against the white background we could see the fat minnows swimming back and forth between us.

'Now!'

'No no, wait a minute, I'm not ready yet. You have to give me more warning. Now?'

'There's nothing there now. You frightened them all off.'

'Oh for heaven's sake! Now!'

We stood up in a rush. There in the bottom of the sagging, sodden square were three or four tiny minnows. Flushed with our success, we repeated the trick a couple of times. A modest beginning, but it was a solemn occasion none the less. We were no longer mere hopefuls: we'd caught our first fish. They were also our last. We stayed an hour or two, baiting and rebaiting our line, casting here and casting there, but not even a nibble did we get. What made it most infuriating of all was that we knew the fish were there.

We'd underestimated the strength of the sun. From one moment to the next my face began to burn and I started to feel very sick and queasy. Perhaps the wasp sting had something to do with it. We had to walk our bikes up the bank: the sun's heat had turned the tarmac ramp into toffee. We'd originally planned to set up our tent on the lakeshore, but by the time we reached the inn I wasn't feeling at all well, so Patricia took command and checked us into a room. It wasn't very large, but it was spotlessly clean and had a wonderful view across the water. I stood with my face under the cold shower for about half an hour, trying to bring my temperature down.

'A good idea, checking into the hotel,' I said afterwards, feeling a great deal better.

'You see? You're wife's not such a thickie after all,' murmured Patricia as she plastered me with cream.

We'd been told that the 14-kilometre stretch of road leading north from the dam to Ruta 3 was very bad, so we asked around to see what the locals thought. As every story we heard was worse than the one before, we spent the rest of the morning trying to find a truck or van that might be going our way. The electricity company had a pickup truck, but it had already gone and wouldn't be back until late. It might be going again tomorrow, if we were prepared to wait. The watchman in the guardhouse suggested the police.

We found the *comisaría* on a backstreet near the lake. The corporal on duty was on the telephone, so we looked around the small station house while we waited. On the wall in a rustic wooden frame, decorated with a small posy of plastic flowers, hung a blurred photograph of a young policeman in uniform. The inscription honoured the man, fallen in the line of duty. At a rough guess, it had happened while the dam was being built.

The corporal came off the phone and said hello. He already knew all about us. News travels fast in small towns. From an inside office he fetched the *comisario*, dressed in bathing suit and sandals. He was a slight, grey-haired, rather nervous man. Yes, he said, the police had a van, and of course he'd be happy to give us a lift to the Ruta 3. There were, however, a couple of problems. The van had broken down, and wouldn't be ready before nightfall. And secondly, his budget for petrol was shot: could we afford to pay for the fuel? It looked as though we had no choice but to stay another night, so we agreed to meet at eight o'clock next morning, and wandered back to the inn.

Out in the lake we could see the naked tops of trees sticking out of the lake. Uruguay is mostly open savannah, and whatever natural forest it has – estimated by the only statistic I've seen at 3 per cent of the total surface area – is concentrated along the rivers and streams. Eucalyptus and pine, which possibly grow more abundantly, are both planted by man. The forests of the Río Negro, with the complex eco-system they supported, used to be thick and dense. With three large hydroelectric dams built across it, which in turn have created three massive lakes, the river's habitats have been radically changed. When the dams were built, the responsible government agencies devoted a considerable amount of time and effort to discussing re-forestation and promising comprehensive programmes to restore the riverside environments along the shores of the new lakes. Sadly, we saw no evidence that any of those promises were being kept. In a country such as this, hydroelectric power is a natural, obvious solution to the nation's energy requirements, and, for a number of reasons, infinitely preferable to the various alternatives. Provided that the natural habitats can be restored and protected, there is no reason why the dams should have a lasting negative effect on the environment. Uruguay's greatest wealth is its clean, open countryside, a resource which many countries in the world have already lost forever. It should be treated with the care and respect it deserves. Without that, whatever benefits the dams provide can't be considered complete.

Another tremendous storm woke us up in the middle of the night. We leaned on the window-sill, watching it billow and crash out over the lake until the wind changed and started blowing it straight into our bedroom, forcing us to close the wooden shutters. By next morning the rain had stopped, but the sky was black and pregnant, threatening more. No sooner had we packed and set off for the *comisaría*, than it started all over again. We were soon soaked to the skin.

The *comisario* apologized: the van had not been fixed yet. We raced across to the engineering depot at the electricity company. The foreman apologized: he wasn't going across until late afternoon. The clerks in the office apologized: they had no other van. The sky didn't apologize at all, it just kept right on chucking down water. We huddled in the guardhouse, our eyes on the highway, hoping a truck might come by. At about eleven o'clock, when the rain had dwindled to a fine, driving drizzle, one appeared over the hill and pulled up at the *almacén* across the road. We caught up with the driver as he came out of the shop. Yes, of course he could give us a lift: plenty of room in the back. A boy and two other men were travelling with him, and they helped us to hoist our bikes up. The truck had come from delivering some horses, and the wooden bed was padded with a thick layer of sand, wet and sodden from the rain. One of the men climbed into the back with us, the gate clanged shut, and we were on our way.

Beyond the dam we understood at once why everyone had spoken so disparagingly of the road. The truck slowed to a crawl. It took us over an hour to lurch and grind our way over those meagre 14 kilometres. The rain had turned the monstrous pot-holes into lakes of mud. Some of the holes had been hastily filled in with stones, which only made them worse. Several times the driver had to stop and get out, to hawk about on foot for the best in a selection of awful ways to pass. More than once I thought we might all have to get out and push.

The sun broke through the cloud, lifting filigrees of steam up from the ground. The heat became dense and oppressive. I tried to take some photographs, but the lorry was bucking so much that not only could I not focus the camera, but I also needed both hands to keep myself from falling over. After one of those bumps I caught a sheepish grin from our travelling companion, who'd been keeping to himself until then. He looked away startled as I returned his smile. There was something unusual about him. It wasn't just his carrot-coloured hair or even his clothes which, admittedly, were remarkable. In principle he wore the standard gaucho get-up of *bombachas*, *alpargatas* and a shirt. But the *bombachas* and *alpargatas* were white, and the shirt a shrill and brilliant yellow. But that wasn't it. There was something about his manner. . . . As I puzzled, he gave me a shy, slantendicular look and another smile, and somehow I understood. Patricia had suddenly spotted it too: her eyes opened wide. He was, as they say, a *maricón*. A gay gaucho! With the recognition I felt a deep, heavy sorrow. In this rough, aggressively masculine society, where the *campesino*'s most important boast is his manhood, this poor boy's life must have been hell. Although, at the same time, he must have been pretty damned tough to have the courage to parade about dressed up like that. And then, as though he knew we knew, he shrugged and grinned again, but this time really wide, to show that several of his front teeth were gone. I can live wth it, he seemed to say.

The truck driver dropped us off when the track rejoined the highway. On this side of the river the land was quite hilly, and we had to labour with a headwind, but we made fair progress and quite enjoyed ourselves. At least it wasn't hot. Stopped by the side of the road we saw an old man whose bicycle was even more heavily laden than ours. Untidy parcels tied up with string bulged out in every direction. A blackened Primus stove was perched on top of one of his bundles, and a saucepan hung from the handlebars. Thinking he might have had a puncture or something, we stopped to offer our help, but he'd only paused to roll a cigarette. He spoke in a thick, impenetrable patois, littered with broken Portuguese and something else I couldn't recognize. He told us he'd been moving around the country like that for years, stopping here and there when it suited him.

A little later we passed the Colonia El Ombú, a farming community centred around some of the last immigrants to reach the country as a group: Menonites fleeing the Danzig Corridor at the outbreak of World War 2. About 100 kilometres almost directly west, on the banks of the Río Uruguay, lay Fray Bentos, the provincial capital, where the celebrated Liebig's Extract of Meat Company was first set up in 1860. The town's name also became famous in Europe from the labels on tins of corned beef and other meat products. We were headed northwest for an *estancia* which has quite a reputation for breeding fine cattle. It took us another hour or so to reach the gates, through a landscape which was amongst the loveliest we'd seen so far. From the very beginning the *estancia* felt special. We pedalled up the broad, straight avenue towards the house, which we could just see at the end of it. On one side of us a grandstand, used for cattle auctions, faced some corrals, and on the other stood long, low, stone sheds, whitewashed and very old. The old stone house at the top of the drive was surrounded by carefully manicured lawns, tidy flowerbeds and ornamental bushes. A wrought-iron gallery, embraced by a vine laden with grapes like green chandeliers and a wisteria whose trunk was as thick as the spread of my arms, shaded the gravel path to the door.

The arches along the veranda, such an integral part of these old country homes, had been glassed in generations ago. The glass doors, made to match the windows, bore the additional embellishment of an ornate 'RS' engraved upon the central panes. A large brass bell hung on a wooden post. Patricia grabbed its rope and rang it hard. For a while nothing happened. Then a man's voice called out from behind us: it was the foreman, peering over the hedge. The *Señor* and the *Señora* weren't here, he said with regret. They were in Montevideo. But Mr Zabaleta was at the other house: why didn't we try there?

We crossed the cobbled courtyard and followed the rutted driveway through a dip and up a knoll. At the top of it we found another, more modern house. In answer to our calls, a slight, strawberry-blonde woman appeared from the garden behind it carrying an armful of honeysuckle and a pair of secateurs. She listened quietly as we introduced ourselves.

'Well, you'd better sit down,' she said, leading us to some chairs at the table on the porch, 'I'll get you something to drink.'

She returned a moment later with a jug of iced water and some glasses on a tray.

'Call me Maureen,' she said, joining us at the table and listening intently to our story, growing steadily more excited and amused.

'I wish my sister were here,' she said, clapping her hands, 'she'd love all this. I'll have to get hold of her. You don't mind, do you?' Her blue eyes opened wide in anticipation. 'What a pity mummy and daddy aren't here.'

The screen door opened with a squeak and a slim, fair-haired girl of fourteen came onto the flagstone porch, rubbing the siesta from her eyes with the back of one hand.

'I'm Luisa,' she said, unaffectedly kissing us hello before sitting down next to her mother.

A few moments later the scene was repeated when her sister Veronica, a year older, also came out of the house.

'Well,' said Maureen, getting up, 'where shall we put your tent? You can put it in the garden, if you like, but that's not really very adventurous, is it?' She wrinkled her nose, 'Or there's a lovely spot by the *Tala* over there in the meadow.'

Chatting about this and that as though we'd known each other for years, Maureen and her daughters guided us down to the elderly tree. Perhaps struck by lightning or torn by the wind, two heavy branches had peeled away from the trunk, one to either side. There they had lain, spread out like arms, and somehow continued to grow. In the cup of this leafy embrace the ground was cushioned with a perfect carpet of clover and grass. This was the spot: no question at all.

We returned to the house for our things. Maureen disappeared indoors, saying she had things to do.

'The girls will take care of you,' she said.

Wheeling our bikes through the tall, yellowing grass, the four of us went back to the tree. The girls had a delicate, enchanting manner: completely natural and unaffected, full of laughter and questions and talk. Out

here in these wide open spaces, there was no hurry at all to pretend to be
grown up.

'Gosh, these are really good bicycles.'

'Yeah . . . where did you get them?'

'In England? Wow!'

'How did you manage to bring them on the aeroplane?'

'My dad used to race when he was at university.'

'Yes, we still have his bike.'

'It's up at the house.'

'We can show you, later.'

'It's pretty old now. It's big, like yours . . . '

'But I can ride it.'

'So can I, but it's not very comfortable.'

'No, the brakes don't work, either.'

'Yeah, and the saddle's all funny.'

'Well, it's old.'

'Yes, it's the same one that dad used to race with.'

'And he's old.'

'Yeah. Well . . . not *that* old . . . '

'Well, he's older than *they* are. How old are you?'

'Yes, he's older than they are.'

'Crumbs: is that the tent? In that little packet?'

'What a lovely colour!'

'Shall I help? What do you want me to do?'

'Look: it's round!'

'Oooh . . . '

'And you're Peruvian, are you?'

'I've never been to Peru.'

'We've been to Buenos Aires.'

'Yes, but that's not the same.'

'No, but it's good there. Mummy got us those really pretty dresses,
remember?'

'Yeah, there are lots of shops.'

'My cousin goes to school there. Did you go to school in Peru or in
England?'

'We go in Young. It's not far.'

'Gosh, it's big in here! Look how big it is in here!'

'Yeah . . . what a good tent! It must be lots of fun. Is it lots of fun?'

'Crumbs . . . do you ever get wet?'

'Do you get frightened? I think I'd get frightened. Sometimes.'

'I wouldn't. It depends where you stay. They're not going to get
frightened *here*.'

'No, not here.'

'And they're together, anyway. And he's big.'

'Yes, you're big. I bet you're bigger than my dad.'

'But not *much*.'

'Well, a little bit. Daddy's belly is bigger.'

We wandered down towards the stream, knee deep in the meadow, Patricia and the girls picking a posy of tiny flowers, pale blue and lilac and white, as we went. On the brow of a small ridge alongside us, half a dozen horses interrupted their placid grazing to watch us go by. At the foot of the field we came to a thick, gloomy wood, the trees gripped precariously onto the steep, muddy slope. Below us, through the branches, we could see the sunlight sparkling on the water.

'You have to be careful here.'

'Yes, step on the stones or you'll get your shoes all dirty.'

'Hey, Luisa, it's better over here . . . '

We slipped and slithered down, grabbing the overhanging branches for support, to emerge again into the sunlight on the bank of a fast-moving stream. Patricia was at first a little wary, in case there were insects about. We told the girls about how we'd been attacked on the beach at Agraciada.

'I don't like bugs either,' said Luisa, brushing away a large, bottle-green mantis, 'they bite.'

Stepping gingerly from stone to stone, Veronica had made it to a flat rock in the shallows. She squatted awkwardly on it, poking at the mud with a stick. Something rustled and splashed in the rushes nearby.

'Probably a *nutria*.'

'Or a *lobito de río*. There are lots of them here.'

'My brother comes here fishing sometimes.'

'Well, not right here: a little further up.'

'Yes, from the old pier.'

'We used to go out in a boat sometimes, when we were little.'

Sunbeams filtered through the thick canopy, catching luminous motes of dust and little things with wings. Dragonflies flicked and hummed back and forth, skimming the water. The stream gurgled and sucked as it passed. Every now and then a frog called out: a plaintive, solitary cry. The air rang with the voices of birds. The peace seemed impregnable. We felt transported to another world, a land in the middle of Lewis Carroll's golden afternoon. We threw pebbles into the water, just to hear them plop.

Close to our new home we found a broken well, its wheel and tackle long since gone, lichens and weeds poking through cracks in the stone. We leaned over the edge and listened to the echo of our voices. It was near the tumbled ruins of a cottage. A donkey shied away as we approached.

'The foreman used to live here.'

'A long time ago.'

The foundations were still clearly visible, even though overgrown with grass. It seemed very small. We paced out the rooms, wondering which was what, using a gap in the wall, where we guessed the door had been, as a clue.

'This was the bathroom,' said Luisa flatly, pointing at a hole in the ground.

Amongst the broken tiles a few shards of white porcelain still clung to its rim. I picked up a piece of flooring tile and wiped off the dirt with my finger. It was red and black. We tried to work out what the pattern might have been.

'There are three different sorts,' said Veronica, rooting about for some samples. 'That one; a yellow one; and a black and white one.'

The lowering sun had begun to brush a different colour onto the world. We sat in a row on one of the *Tala*'s outstretched arms.

'Look: there's mummy and Monica!'

We looked. Coming across the meadow towards us we saw Maureen, her sister and three teenage girls – Monica's daughters. From time to time, her head barely clearing the tall grass, we caught glimpses of a little girl in pink.

'That's Virginia. My little sister.'

It was like meeting part of our own family. No sooner had we said hello, than they were fussing over us, teasing and poking friendly fun. Of course, everyone had to get into the tent and check out the gear and ask whether we were eating properly and bathing regularly and wrapping up warmly at night. In our honour, Maureen had changed into a smart new outfit, done her hair and put on some make-up.

'We've come to take you to tea,' she said.

Luisa and Veronica had been visibly dying to try out our bikes, but hadn't dared to ask. They didn't need a second invitation.

The table was groaning under the weight of the display. As well as dressing up and getting hold of her sister, Maureen had found the time to bake a couple of cakes and prepare a selection of goodies. The ten of us gathered around like wolves, making a tremendous racket of teacups and clanking of plates with everyone talking at once.

The ranch known as Rincón de Francia has belonged to the Stirling family since the early nineteenth century, and is famed in Uruguay as a *Cabaña*, a breeder of fine cattle and sheep. Even as a boy I knew of it. I used to go to the *Prado* fair at Easter and wander about the cattle-pens gawping at the animals. Rincón was always there, exhibiting bulls the size of houses and seven-pullover rams. For some reason I had always assumed that the musical name – which I interpreted as 'A Corner of France' – was a nostalgic reference to the *estancia*'s physical similarity to that country. The first Mr Stirling, a cabinet-maker, sailed from England to Buenos Aires with his friend Mr Young in the 1820s, commissioned to carve the doors for the new cathedral. The job completed, the two of them wandered into

Uruguay, brought some land and settled down. Mr Young's fame is assured by the town which now carries his name. Stirling bought an *estancia* nearby, nesting in a bend of the Arroyo Don Esteban. That 'corner' of land belonged, at the time, to an old man called Francia, hence the name by which it was commonly known: 'Francia's Corner'.

CHAPTER SEVEN

SHEEP THIEVES, INJUNS AND A RUNAWAY BULL

We dismantled the tent slowly, sorry to be breaking camp. In the distance, impatiently walking back and forth in front of the house, we could see Veronica and Luisa waiting for us to get up. They came out to meet us halfway across the dew-drenched meadow. Luisa greeted Patricia with a kiss and a small spray of the jasmine she loves so much.

Fortified with hot cups of tea and wedges of bread and butter, Maureen took us on a tour of the *Casa Grande*. Built by the first Mr Stirling, subsequent generations have all added bits here and altered bits there to make it a house of considerable character. Indoors, too, every item told a story. We climbed the spiral staircase to the roof and looked out across the orderly gardens and the tumbling meadows beyond. Near the house was a small orchard and vegetable garden growing produce, as on so many *estancias*, for the family and staff. Here, however, it was run more efficiently than any other we'd seen, to the extent that the deep, cool basement was stacked to the ceiling with large jars of pickles and conserves. When I later commented to Oscar that we were impressed by how well organized everything seemed to be, he laughed and jokingly complained that a full third of the staff of nearly forty was engaged in what he described as 'non-productive' work, i.e. running the place. We had caught up with him in one of the long, cobbled sheds where he'd been artificially inseminating some of his prize ewes. He was standing up to his chest in a square pit in the floor, surrounded by instruments and containers. The last of a long queue of sheep was being brought past him. They all had numbers painted on their backs, which were carefully noted in a logbook as each of them was served with the contents of bottle A, B or C.

The weather was perfect for cycling. The sky was patchy and overcast, making the day pleasantly cool, and we had a strong wind behind us. We stopped briefly in Young for supplies, and were surprised by the bustle and activity. The focus of a highly productive agricultural region, it's very much a small cattle town, but an extremely busy one. Along the short main street, banks crowd shoulder to shoulder with all manner of shops selling everything from tractors to toothpaste. After the pastoral tranquillity of the last few days it was quite bracing, but we were glad to get out again and back on the open road. Although we had a couple of fairly steep hills to contend with, we cycled 67 kilometres in record time. Oscar had given us the name of an old friend of his who, he was sure, would be happy to let us camp on his land. By two o'clock we were standing in front of the gates. The track to the house, lined on either side with tall, whispering eucalyptus trees, seemed almost as long as the trip from *Rincón*. When at last we reached the hub we found that everyone except for the elderly cook was indoors having a siesta. Even the two dogs – a large collie shaved down to stubble by the sheep shearers and a small, nondescript mutt with terrible scars on his face bearing witness to some battle in his youth – lay asleep on the tiled veranda.

With time on our hands and quite an appetite after the long haul, we unpacked our shopping and stretched out on a soft, shaded patch of lawn. Here beneath the bough, with a loaf of bread, a flask of wine, a lump of cheese and a length of spiced sausage, we had our lunch. The 100-year-old farmhouse consisted of three long, low buildings set at right angles to each other along the sides of a broad central square. The walls were white, the woodwork dark blue. The ubiquitous sloping roof shading the veranda was made of large sheets of corrugated iron, painted red. The manufacturer's name and Liverpool address, printed on the underside of the sheets, was still clearly legible. In the centre of the gravel quadrangle was a small garden of bushes and shrubs and, at the centre of that, a white, elaborate cast-iron gazebo with defiantly uncomfortable hinged seats suspended between its pillars.

Alberto was the first to emerge from his siesta. He shuffled sleepily out of his bedroom and sat down on a bench on the veranda to pull on his beautifully polished boots. Still blinking and rubbing his face, he came over to us, obviously puzzled to find us there. He was tall and robust, balding on top, with penetrating, surprisingly pale blue eyes. He stood quiet and expressionless while we introduced ourselves and explained what we were doing. The directness of his gaze was almost unnerving.

'You eat water-melon?' he asked gruffly, when I'd finished.

'Well, er . . . yes, sometimes,' I said lamely.

'C'mon then,' he turned on his heel and led the way into the kitchen. 'Best time for *sandía*, after a siesta,' he said, taking one out of a large refrigerator and banging in onto the wooden table.

'Knife . . . ' he muttered, rummaging in a drawer. Producing a two-foot sabre he cut through the fruit as though it weren't even there. You could have shaved in cold water with the damned thing.

'I've got some work to do,' he said after a while. 'You been on an *estancia* before?'

There was a light, mocking challenge in his manner, but the humour and wit that played constantly across his face drained it of all malice.

We climbed into the station wagon and set off. At first he was guarded and cautious, measuring us up. Later, looking back, I realized that I'd missed a vital clue: his surname. Whilst I was still in my early teens his father, a wily old fox if ever there was one, had been President of Uruguay. But once Alberto realized that we weren't digging for political dirt and that, having no particular axe to grind, our presence on his estate was coincidental, he relaxed.

After stopping to check the work on some new drinking troughs for the cattle, we went to the dairy. The veterinary clinic in a room off the barn was tidy and well stocked. Spotlessly clean, the medicines and implements were laid out neatly on shelves around the walls. In one corner stood storage vats of liquid nitrogen in which he kept the sperm collected from prize bulls. He had a card file listing every cow on the *estancia*, its pedigree, offspring, medical history and milk production. From there we went to the 'hospital', a corral in a distant field, to tend to a cow with a throat inflammation of some sort. The animal was put into the same sort of clamp we'd seen at La Sirena and, thus immobilized, was given an intravenous injection in its neck, down a rubber tube from a sterilized wine bottle.

Like so many of the landed gentry of Uruguay, Alberto had taken a degree in agronomy. His studies completed, he went off to Europe on a trip which obliquely reminded me of the pilgrimage to Paris indulged in by so many of America's literary lions between the wars. For Alberto, the trip culminated in a sojourn on a Danish dairy farm. He was so impressed by the methods he discovered there, that he returned to the family estate determined to put into practice all the things he had learned. Today he manages a dairy farm widely regarded as one of the best in the land, but that enviable position was not achieved overnight, nor without some difficulty. He found himself having to wrestle every step of the way with the entrenched inefficiency of the pastoral tradition which, ironically, had arisen thanks to the benevolent climate and inordinate generosity of the land, with its flawless natural pastures and immediate reward of the slightest of efforts. His eventual solution – simple, but far from easy – to those pervasive bad habits surrounding him was to dispense with them altogether. He decided not to employ anyone with previous experience of dairy farming or who, however romantic the traditional image of the gaucho, was too old or set in his ways to learn a new trick. It was a calculated risk but it paid off in the end, although not without some serious soul-searching. Nowadays, with a few counted exceptions, all the men who work for Alberto are young, and most have learned their trade from him. He cited the foreman of the dairy as a case in point. He arrived at the *estancia* as a virtually unemployable teenager, and has blossomed to become indispensable. He carried the entire record book in his head, recognized all the animals on sight and made it a point to be present at every calving. Since he'd been on the job not a single animal had been lost, in itself something of a record. Even today in some parts of the country it's not unknown, when a cow goes into difficult labour, for the calf to be dragged into the world by a tractor, with all the frightful consequences that usually ensue.

The milking shed was clean, modern and well equipped. What is perhaps commonplace in Holland and Denmark is not necessarily the rule in Uruguay. The cows were comforted and their udders carefully rinsed with warm water before they were connected to the milking machines. Care for the livestock extended to the way the animals were treated when, as we saw the next morning, they were put through the medicinal dip. The cows were not beaten or goaded as we saw being done on one or two other *estancias*. They were kept moving by noise alone: whooping war-cries and the clatter of sticks on wooden fences.

We were coming back along the wooded drive towards the house, after giving the cow her injection, when Alberto trod on the brakes and cursed. A fresh sheepskin was draped over the top strand of a nearby wire fence.

'At least he left me the skin!' he muttered.

'I'll pick it up later,' called one of the chaps travelling in the back.

Sheep farmers in Uruguay accept as 'normal' a certain rate of loss to poachers, and take it into account when doing their arithmetic. From time to time the local poor or unemployed will take a sheep from one of their more fortunate neighbours to feed their families. It is almost a tradition, part of the contribution the farmers make to the region, and an unwritten code of behaviour seems to go with it. The animal is slaughtered and skinned on the estate, albeit secretly, and the hide is left carefully on a fence where it will not spoil and is sure to be found, so that the landowner doesn't suffer a complete loss. Sheepskins are not only useful on the *estancia*, they also have a fair commercial value. Very often the *estancieros* even know who the poacher is but, unless things get out of hand, they seldom prosecute. There are, of course, exceptions, notably those who steal for subsequent sale, but their behaviour is usually different. To begin with, they're never content to take just one animal, as the risk versus profit equation makes little sense in that context. Since leaving half a dozen sheepskins draped like laundry on the wire might attract unwelcome attention and disposing of them, unless you sell them regularly, isn't as easy as it might seem, the poachers usually hide or bury them along with the offal. The animals are very rarely stolen alive. When they are, on the other hand, it's usually the whole flock!

Alberto told us about a neighbour of his who, not long ago, had been surveying a remote corner of his estate, plotting irrigation ditches when, much to his surprise, through his theodolite he saw three men gutting some of his sheep and loading the carcasses into a van. He watched them long enough to see which way they were headed, overtook them on the road, and alerted the police, who sat down to wait on the verge. A few moments later, the van clattered over the hill. They stopped it, found half a dozen fresh carcasses in the back, and promptly arrested the men. So far as the *estanciero* was concerned, that was that. That evening, however, he had an unexpected visit from the local *comisario*, who'd come to plead on the poachers' behalf. Could he please drop the charges, he'd be generously compensated for his loss, it would never happen again. Alberto's friend was understandably reluctant to agree. After all, one of the thieves was a well-known butcher in the town! The sheriff readily conceded that excusing him might not only set a dangerous precedent but also earn the *estanciero* the contempt and derision of his neighbours as soon as the word got about. The second poacher was from out of town, a friend of the butcher's, and no, the *comisario* didn't much like the idea of strangers coming into his parish and creating havoc, either. So what was the problem, then? The third man was the problem, the special case. You see: that coming weekend he was due to marry the *comisario*'s daughter.

We were up early next morning, as we were going to see the herd put through the dip. It was bitterly cold and very windy. Or colder than usual, anyway: 17° centigrade. We were glad of our jackets. The job done, we loaded our bikes onto Alberto's station wagon and he drove us into the town of Paysandú. We entered it along a broad *arroyo*. For some distance along the bank, we drove by a row of rough, hastily built shacks. In many of the riverside yards we could see the flames of large bonfires and smouldering, pyramid-like mounds. People and horses and trucks moved feverishly amongst them, everyone intent on a different part of the job at hand: they were making bricks.

All the work was done manually. The rich loam taken from the bed of the stream was mixed in large troughs with various sorts of vegetable fibre, as much for binding as to aid the baking. Some used sawdust and some used straw but the best, we were told, was horse dung. The thick mix was pressed into wooden moulds and the resultant damp, black cakes were then stacked in towers around carefully heaped firewood, leaving appropriate gaps for ventilation. When the tower, or oven, as they called it, reached the required height, it was shielded and the fire was lit. It had to be fed and carefully tended day and night, until all the bricks were properly baked. Like peat, the mud actually ignites, glowing red-hot, although it's not allowed to burst into flame. The heat was tremendous.

Giving us the address of some friends of his further along our intended route, Alberto dropped us off in downtown Paysandú. Perhaps not so affluent as it has been in the past, it's a busy, fair-sized town with a well-established middle class. The trip from there was uneventful. We cycled against the wind most of the time, although fortunately the terrain was fairly flat. It was also decidedly uninspiring, without a hill or a tree to lift a man's eyes and heart from the relentless anonymity of the plain. Our lunch lay heavy in our bellies, making us feel jaded and drowsy.

In the late afternoon we reached the *estancia* Alberto had suggested. Beyond a dense thicket of bamboo we came to a broad gravel yard, shaded by large *timbó, paraíso* and jacaranda. On the top step of the wooden veranda sat a man with his shirt off, being fussed over by two women. His bare skin was covered in large, red lumps and he seemed to be in considerable discomfort. He was the *estanciero*'s brother, on a visit from his own piece of the inheritance which lay a couple of kilometres further along the road. He'd been doing something in the garden when he'd accidentally upset a hive. The bees had set upon him *en masse*, and had stung him very badly. To make matters worse, he was allergic to their bite, and was in some fear of being hospitalized, which had happened once before. With some difficulty, as we understandably didn't have his full attention, we introduced ourselves. He suggested we talk to his brother, who was out in the fields at the time but was sure to have no objections to our camping there for the night. He even offered his own *estancia*, where we could pitch our tent by a stream if we liked, but we weren't really in the mood for any more cycling that day. A third woman had joined the little group, hovering on the edges until the others got into their car and drove away. Peering disdainfully down her nose at us, she said, 'I supposed you'd better go over there somewhere, outside the garden,' before disappearing into the house.

The stream the man had spoken of fed into the Río Queguay, which we'd crossed an hour before. It was the scene of a shameful episode in the nation's history. The skirmishes between settlers and Indians were a perennial part of life in the north, but it wasn't until General Fructuoso Rivera became the first President that the *Charrúas* were finally ousted from their homeland. The *hacendados*, unencumbered by any preoccupation about who had been there *first*, were heartily fed up with the Indians. They banded together and, offering a substantial sum of money 'to help finance the operation', were able to prevail upon the General. Having served under Artigas, whom the Indians trusted and respected and with whom they'd fought Spanish and Portuguese alike, Rivera had inherited some of that esteem which, with the perversity that typified the man, he put to good use.

In the autumn of 1832, while Charles Darwin was pottering about in Argentina, Rivera sent envoys to visit the *Charrúa tolderías* along the banks of the Río Cuareim and Río Arapey, inviting the Indians to join him in a war against Brazil. The tribes would be rewarded for their help with a vast reservation, several thousand head of cattle, a share of the booty and promises to be left alone. Although they had good reason to feel resentful towards the Brazilians, at first the Indians were wary and had to be visited again and again before they finally agreed. Led by their chiefs Venado and Polidoro, they left the forests and marched south to the meeting place at Boca del Tigre, near the Río Queguay. For the last few leagues Colonel Bernabé Rivera, the General's brother, whom they trusted for the same reasons, guided them into the carefully chosen encampment.

Familiar with their suspicious nature, Rivera concealed the bulk of his army and awaited the *Charrúas*, accompanied only by an unarmed detachment under the command of Major Luna. None the less, the Indians faltered. Seeing their hesitation, General Rivera rode up to his old comrade Venado and engaged him in friendly conversation, coming the rest of the way into the valley alongside him. Polidoro, reassured, followed close behind. Reaching the appointed spot, the braves dismounted, planted their spears in the ground, and made ready to camp. At that point the treacherous Rivera asked to borrow Venado's knife, to cut some tobacco from a plug he carried so that they might have a smoke together. Trustingly, the Indian handed over the blade. By way of thanks Rivera drew his pistol and fired point-blank at the unarmed *Charrúa*. It was the signal the soldiers were waiting for.

Miraculously, the bullet missed. At a run, Venado remounted and galloped towards his tribesmen in a frenzy, raising the alarm. In the tumult that ensued, the Indians raced to mount up and escape but, as planned, Major Luna's squadron gained control of the *Charrúa* lances before the braves could reach them. With a blare of trumpets and a crash of steel, Colonel Bernabé Rivera galloped in at the head of his cavalry, spread in a giant, encircling horseshoe. The slaughter was terrible. Indians cut down by sabres, spears and bullets fell to the bloodsoaked ground one after another. Venado, pierced by many lances, went down at the heart of the fray, resisting until the end. Polidoro suffered the same fate. Pirú, another brave and indomitable chief, mortally wounded, picked himself up and ran through the ring of steel to where the imperious Fructuoso Rivera, who was reputed not to have a taste for bloodshed, stood watching the massacre.

'Look, Frutos!' the Indian screamed into his betrayer's face, using the name by which he knew his old comrade in arms, 'See your soldiers killing friends!'

The valiant Chief Sepe gathered the last braves around him and, in a final desperate assault, escaped with eighty of them through a breach in the line. They made it to the forests of the Río Cuareim, hotly pursued by Colonel Bernabé Rivera and men of the second cavalry regiment. But Sepe, of whom the Jesuits had never made an altar boy, felt deeply that it was up to him to avenge Rivera's treachery. Drawing the soldiers to the Cerro de Las Tres Cruces, he fell in furious ambush upon their flank. Only one sergeant, who was thrown wounded from his horse and amidst the savage battle was able to hide beneath a bush, survived the Indians' anger. The perfidious Colonel was taken alive and, for two days and nights, tortured by the remnants of the tribe for his deception.

According to Brigadier General Antonio Díaz, who later spent some time collecting accounts from *Charrúa* survivors of the action, Sepe had his men bind up the heads of their lances so that only half an inch of steel was exposed, and with those cruel tips they inflicted cut after cut on the body of the unfortunate Rivera. He pleaded for his life, begging them 'By God to torture him no longer' to which Sepe, implacable, replied: 'For you, you want God, and yet for our fathers and brothers you had none.' The Colonel promised to return the captured *Charrúa* women and children to Sepe if only he would stop, a mere letter from him would see them released . . . 'And who will bring back Venado, and Polidoro, and the rest of our brothers killed at Queguay by your treachery?' Like the Apache further north, the fierce *Charrúa* were fiendish masters at keeping their victims alive whilst visiting hell upon their flesh.

Later the same year, several people who met him reported that Sepe had bound Rivera's sinews on the head of his spear, which he proudly displayed as a trophy of his revenge. As a footnote to the tale, the last three surviving *Charrúas* in Uruguay were later taken to Europe as curiosities, to be exhibited at the Paris fair of 1889 – commemorating the French revolution and the declaration of the rights of man – where they died in squalor and ignominy.

Alberto had said he would telephone ahead, to let his friend – the newly married daughter of yet another brother – know that we were on our way. Patricia and I had retreated disconcerted to the shade, where we were wondering what to do next, when two young women in fashionably faded jeans and designer T-shirts, little trinkets sparkling on their fingers and wrists, appeared from the general direction of the stables leading horses along by the reins. One of them gave us a friendly smile.

'You must be the backpackers Alberto called me about,' said the other, a petulant, hard-nosed little blonde who wasn't too painful to look at but promised to be hell to get along with. She had 'spoiled brat' written all over her in luminous letters.

We passed the time of day for a minute or two and then, without adding to our wisdom or comfort, they mounted up and cantered off.

'They can't *all* be hospitable, I suppose,' Patricia said as we looked for a spot to put up the tent.

Near the house we could see a woman in an apron playing with a small boy. As Patricia wanted to use the bathroom, we walked up and asked.

'Yes of course,' she said, 'it's down the hall on the right. And the *Señora* said to give you anything you needed.'

The maid was short and squat and by no means beautiful, but she had a gentle, friendly manner and a delightful smile which lit up her face in a most engaging way. As I waited in the courtyard for Patricia, I realized that I needed to use the bathroom too. I'd been having some trouble with my bowels, probably due to a combination of cycling, a steady diet of meat and my continuing lack of expertise at 'going' in the middle of a field. Once inside the bathroom, however, I performed with such astounding success that the antediluvian plumbing was unable to cope with my contribution. I had a deeply embarrassing few minutes while I waited for the ancient cistern to fill and refill. I was sure that my delay and frequent flushing was not going to endear us to our hostess, who hadn't exactly welcomed us with open arms in the first place.

Having pitched our tent by a large, spreading pine, I sat at one of the garden tables by the *parrilla*, once again to fight my losing battle to bring my notes up to date. The slim, grey-haired *estanciero*, wearing black rubber boots and a peaked cap, came over the fence and walked resolutely towards the house, seemingly unaware that we were in his path. I stood up and introduced myself. He was courteous but brief, and seemed very nervous. He lifted his cap to Patricia and, telling us to carry on, marched into the house. About an hour later, bathed and changed into clean clothes and followed by his wife, he came back. Hesitantly, with laboured formality, he asked whether we might like to join them for dinner that night. The wife said nothing. Her posture made it clear that this was not *her* idea. The set of her face would have curdled milk at ten paces.

'I'm afraid we shan't be able to dress properly,' I said, not without mischief, 'we're travelling light, you see.'

'Quite all right,' he said, 'quite all right. It will just be the two of us.'

Patricia stifled a giggle, and we agreed.

'Very well then. I'll come and collect you here at nine.' With a stiff, solemn nod, they were gone.

The night came down quite cold again, and the ground was beginning to dampen when our host came out to fetch us at half-past nine. We followed him straight into the dining room, where his wife was waiting amongst the heavy, solid wooden furniture. The floors in the handsome old house had settled over the years, and in the dining room the boards sagged so deeply towards the middle that some of the cabinets ranged around the walls had wedges driven in beneath their legs to hold them upright. Patricia and I had been rudely making bets about the quality of the meal awaiting us. We were very pleasantly disappointed. The main course was a boneless joint of roasted lamb from which every ounce of fat had been meticulously trimmed. Lest you find that unexceptional, I should explain that it was the only time in our nine weeks of travel that meat was presented in this way. Unless we prepared it ourselves, we usually had to work our way through slabs of grease and gristle to get at the meat. There was a fresh salad to go with it, and a bottle of very acceptable wine. Our host was indeed a nervous man – he even apologized for it – but he calmed noticeably and became engaging and agreeable company once he'd downed a glass, which is more than I can say for his pretentious wife. I suspect that she was probably at the root of much of her husband's nervous disposition. Once she realized that we were neither tramps nor cannibals, she thawed a little, and even deigned to talk to us. So much so, in fact, that I found myself wishing she wouldn't deign quite so much.

'Oh! You live London?' she shrieked, 'such a wonderful city. The most wonderful city in the world. I absolutely love it. The people there are all so elegant.'

She became rather cross and argumentative when I suggested that well, yes, but perhaps not *all* of them nowadays, but it didn't distract her for long.

'I love *all* of Europe. I know it well, you see.' (According to hubby, who let it slip later, they'd been on a whistle-stop tour of the major capitals twenty years ago.) 'It's so much more refined than all this,' she gushed on, 'of course, we have masses of land but you know what it's like . . . ' she said, dismissing the entire estate and, for all I knew, perhaps the entire country as well with a contemptuous wave of her hand. 'Now Rome . . . I absolutely *adore* Rome. And Paris . . . Paris is a lovely city too, don't you think? I think that Paris must the loveliest city in the world. So cultured. So sophisticated. People say that Buenos Aires is like Paris but it's not a patch, my dear, not a patch.'

She droned on and on, threatening to warble her way through the entire Michelin guide, until hubby stepped in to ask whether or not Patricia had ever tried *mate*.

'I love it myself, but I can't drink it. My nerves, you see. Too stimulating. Turns me into a rocket.'

'Ugh! *Mate* . . . ' his wife curled her lip, 'Do you know: I've never tasted it,' she said, as though this conferred upon her some exalted state of grace, 'Never let it cross my lips.'

I commented that Alberto had told us about sheep thieves, and asked whether it was common around here, too.

'Oh, yes,' he said, 'it happens. But the little people, you know, there's not much you can do. I don't have any more trouble with larger theft any more. I buy the *comisario* a couple of tanks of petrol a month now, and he keeps an eye open. Had a couple of chaps a year or two ago: they came in and slaughtered four lambs. We caught them on the highway, the meat in bags, waiting for the bus!'

After dinner he was all for retiring to the study and snorting a brandy or two, but his *Señora* quickly put a stop to that, on the grounds that we all had to get up early next morning. As he walked us back to the tent, lighting our way with a torch, the *estanciero* invited us to join him for breakfast.

Having gone to bed later than usual, we were late getting up. It was almost eight o'clock when I crawled out of the tent, just in time to see the farmer walking by.

'I waited for you for breakfast,' he said, 'but I couldn't wait any longer.

I've left some things on the table for you, and the maid will get you some hot *café con leche*.'

I was very sorry to have disappointed him. He seemed such a kind man, and had probably been looking forward to some company. The maid was expecting us. She was very chirpy and bouncy as she brought in the toast and the coffee. The *Señora* was still asleep: in fact, she was still in bed when we eventually left after ten o'clock. So much for *her* idea of early rising. Her husband, however, came back from the fields in time to see us off and wish us well and, much to our surprise, the maid gave Patricia and I a warm, strong hug and a big kiss, getting quite emotional about it.

As usual, there was hardly any traffic. Cycling in the wake of one of the few cars to overtake us, we found a furry little *apereá* lying by the side of the road, probably killed by that very car. Its mate, looking agitated and disconcerted, nose twitching, was sniffing nervously at the still warm body. Patricia promptly burst into tears.

The flat had become rolling once again, as we travelled through fields of grain, sugar beet and potato and the ubiquitous herds and flocks of grazing livestock. We pedalled over countless limpid streams, speculating about the quality of the fishing, and through dense, dark forests of eucalyptus and pine. We had just emerged from one of these, into a broad valley, to be greeted by an unexpected sight: the meadow was filled with rank upon rank of tall, nodding palms. Sheep grazed in the grassy spaces amongst the slender trunks. A thin haze veiled the sun, blunting its edge and softening the texture of the light, giving the palm fronds a dark, hand-painted sheen. More than the Uruguay we'd come to know, it looked like a scene stolen from *The Arabian Nights*. To add to the surrealism of the picture, a long, straight line of electricity pylons marched with mathematical precision from horizon to horizon. Straight down the middle stretched the black tarmac ribbon. The *palmar* continued around us for several kilometres, never dense but sometimes more and sometimes less sparse, sometimes scattered into isolated clumps like small oases or reduced to a thin, solitary row like a fence along the skyline. In amongst all this was a tapestry of vegetable fields and a vast emerald carpet of corn.

We stopped at the Guaviyú thermal springs for a bathe. Expecting a natural pool, instead we found something more like an amusement park. Neither of us had ever been in a hot spring before, and it was at first disconcerting to be in what looked like a perfectly normal blue swimming pool, where the water was 38° centigrade. We were amused by a large green hoarding by the pools which listed all the 'do's and don'ts'. Amongst them was the stern admonishment: 'It is expressly forbidden to drink *mate* in the swimming baths'. Being Sunday, the cushioned lawns were absolutely packed, children swarming through the picnicking crowds with the jerky, unpredictable synchronization of shoals of fish.

An hour later, deliciously refreshed and changed into clean clothes, we continued on our way. To our horror, only a few minutes later, we came upon a great upheaval of tractors, trucks, bulldozers, cranes and teams of burly men beavering away, tearing and terraplaning kilometre after kilometre, kicking up choking clouds and making an abominable racket. In seconds all our cleanliness was gone beneath a layer of grime. One of the greatest joys we'd discovered about cycling was the constant feeling of communion with the land, the direct contact with everything it bore and everything that happened in it, the romantic, soul-stirring sensation of being an integral part of everything around us. On this occasion we quickly came to rue that closeness.

We'd been hoping to camp on the Meseta de Artigas, a bluff overlooking the Río Uruguay, where Artigas had the encampment he named Purificación. Our hearts sank when we saw the state of the track leading to it. It was rutted and broken and, for us, impassable except on foot.

If any man can be said to dominate Uruguayan history, José Artigas is that man. The grandson of one of the six patriarchs who founded Montevideo in 1726, he rose to become the father of the nation. Born into what were then the privileged classes, he had as good an education as could be had in those rough, colonial days. When he came of age, his brothers had already taken charge of the family holdings, so he had to rely on his own initiative to make his way in life. Immediately he rode into the interior, where for years he lived amongst the gauchos and became one of their most trusted and beloved chiefs, sharing with them a lifestyle on the fringes of the Spanish law. Years later, taking advantage of an amnesty for outlaws – which in the eyes of the law he was – he joined the newly formed regiment of Blandengues, whose remit was to patrol the countryside, pacify the Indians and put an end to the cattle thieving from the northeast and the west, now Brazil and Argentina. The experience he'd gained in his years in the wilderness combined with his military career to temper a character already devoted, by family tradition, to public service. He fought against the British when they invaded in 1807, and when the nation later revolted against Spain he was chosen by popular acclaim Chief of the *Orientales*, the natives of the Eastern Province – as Uruguay was then known – and dedicated himself to the cause of independence. His aim was a federation of the provinces on either side of the Río Uruguay, the Federal League. Despite its encouraging beginnings, the League faltered and never reached maturity (its enemies were too great in strength and number) but Uruguay exists because of him. He was ultimately defeated by the Portuguese, who invaded Uruguay from Brazil with the connivance of the perfidious Buenos Aires. (An excellent account of these years is to be found in John Street's *Artigas & The Emancipation of Uruguay*.)

Just ahead, on the opposite side of the highway, we could see the village of Chapicuy nesting in a hollow.

'Let's go there for a beer, and talk about it.'

The tiny hamlet was deserted. The *almacén* by the solitary petrol station was shut.

'Everything's shut,' said a despondent young man in a dusty red shirt, waiting at the bus-stop. He looked tired and fed up, as though he'd been waiting for years. He brought down the tiny transistor radio he'd been holding to his ear, drilling the silence with the frenzied, metallic commentary of a far-off football match, 'except the *comisaría*.'

'And where's that?' I asked.

He pointed along the highway to the opposite edge of the village.

We knocked at the grey metal door. Two panes of glass were missing, and we could see into the murky station. There didn't appear to be anyone here, either. Looking around, we saw a corpulent man detach himself from a family group in the yard of a house on the corner and saunter loose-limbed towards us. His black hair was curly and thick, touch of grey at the temples, several days' dark stubble on his square chin. A hairy belly struggled to escape between the buttons of his straining shirt, forcing down the waistband of his baggy trousers.

'*Sub-comisario Duque a las órdenes*,' he said mildly, lips pursed, thumbs hooked in his pockets, feet apart, an enormous joke rippling just behind his eyes. I explained.

'I can give you a water-melon,' he said, scratching the back of his head, grabbing a handful of curls, 'You like water-melon?' Here we go again . . .

'We were hoping to find some bread,' I said, 'something to drink. Some tomatoes, maybe.'

He thought about it.

'All shut,' he said. 'But you might find someone at the shop round the corner. It's shut too, but they live there. Bang on the door, tell 'em I sent you. Hard work that cycling, eh?' he grinned.

There was a rustle and clatter from the highway behind us, which passed as if on a dyke a bit above our heads. Over the top of it, pouring down towards us, came a herd of cows. A small, filthy gaucho cantered past them and dismounted in front of us. He doffed his battered hat and shook hands all round, nodding his grubby head up and down. His face was the colour of an old suitcase, and his calloused handshake felt like a lump of wood. He stretched his lips into a toothless smile.

'*La tropa*, officer, with your permission. We'd like to move it along the road a piece here, if we could.'

He produced a scruffy wad of greying, dog-eared paper from the recesses of what looked as though it had once been a green velvet jacket, and held it out to the policeman.

'Call back in on your way out,' said Duque to us, leading the little man into the station house, 'and I'll give you that melon.'

On a sidestreet, just as the *comisario* had said, we found the shop. The only thing that differentiated the house from all the others was the spray of soft-drink stickers in the window. By the hedge a little girl with long, brown plaits played with pebbles in the dusty road.

'Hello,' I said, 'do you live here?'

'Yup,' she said, without interrupting her game.

'Are your parents here?'

'Yup.'

'Could you call one of them, please?'

She looked up at me, and thought about it for a while. Her game was obviously at a crucial stage.

'Okay!' she sang out at last, and scampered off through the yard to the back of the house.

A moment later she returned, peering at us from behind the skirt of a young, neatly dressed woman. Dark haired and cinnamon skinned, with traces of Indian in her fine, delicate features, she was very lovely.

'We're sorry to bother you on a Sunday,' I said, 'but the *comisario* told us you might not mind. We're cycling around the country, you see, and we'd like to buy a few things.'

She smiled gently.

'Yes, of course,' she said in a soft, liquid voice, 'come on in.'

She unlocked the door and opened it wide. We followed her through. Two or three tables and a few chairs stood on the bare concrete floor. There was a counter at the end of the room and, behind it, wooden shelves tidily arranged with a modest display of basic goods: rice, dried noodles, biscuits, tinned goods and packets of *mate*, whose distinctive perfume embellished the cool air. She chattered happily as she collected the few items we needed, asking where we'd been and what we'd seen and, recognizing Patricia's Spanish as non-Uruguayan, what she thought of it all. We stood slumped against the counter, sipping cold water.

When we returned to the station, *Sub-comisario-Duque-a-las-órdenes* came out to meet us. He'd taken his shirt off and draped a towel over his shoulders. Half his face was covered in shaving cream, and he was waving a razor about.

'Any luck?' he asked, standing on the doorstep with us, continuing to shave by his reflection in the grimy window. 'Melons are on the floor in the back room,' he said, 'help yourselves.'

Inside the dingy *comisaría* a young policeman, clad only in his underpants, yelped and jumped for cover behind a rusty filing cabinet when Patricia came in.

'Don't worry,' she said, 'I've seen it all before.'

'Next room!' he said, agitatedly, 'In the next room!'

In the damp, grimy kitchen all but a small patch of floor was covered in shiny *sandías*.

'Neighbour gives them to us,' said Duque, wandering in behind us, 'Most of them are still green. No, no, not that one. Here: here's a good one, try this one.'

He pointed with his foot. Patricia, who'd squatted to look through them, picked it up. Duque prodded it with his thumb.

'Yeah, this one'll do. Very nice. Pity you don't have a fridge,' he added, stretching his neck to shave under his chin, 'they're better cold. But still, you can't carry a fridge on a bicycle, I suppose!' He laughed sonorously at his own joke.

Weighing it in my hand, I wondered how we were going to manage the blasted melon, never mind the fridge.

'Yeah, the meseta's nice,' he went on, approvingly, as we steered the conversation towards campsites, 'but the road's *una porquería*. You missed a good spot a few kilometres back. Very pretty stream. But I guess you don't want to retreat. Lovely one up ahead, though, at the Chapicuy Chico. About ten kilometres. Great spot there, *precioso*, on the left, just past the bridge. Clean. Safe. Can swim, if you want. You'll like it. I'd go *there*, if I were you.'

By the time we reached it, we were truly exhausted. The sky had cleared and the late afternoon sun was pouring its fiery heart out, making up for lost time. On the way we passed the travelling herd, lowing softly, hooves padding and clicking and picking up the dust. The little gaucho and three others, welded onto their horses, interrupted their whistling, singing encouragements to wave as we pedalled by.

The bridge hung high above a deep, green gully, the glassy stream gliding silently along its leafy bed. We crossed it to the promised glade on our left. Mottled with the bottle-green sunlight that filtered through the canopy of pine and *paraíso*, we found our enchanted, secret spot. We slid down the embankment and pushed through a lacy thicket and across the soft, tall grass to a clearing. Old *Sub-comisario-Duque-a-las-órdenes* sure knew what was what. Underneath the pines at the far end, on a patch of clear earth, a few blackened stones around a small mound of ash bore witness to past campfires. Delicate flutterings and the intimate cooing of invisible doves decorated the whispering breeze. The smell of pine sap hung in the air. For a few minutes we slumped against the bole of a tree and soaked up the silence. We saw the vanguard of the shuffling herd, a dozen or so horses under the watchful eye of a portly, grey-haired gaucho, amble across the bridge and into the woods on the opposite side of the road. The rider stretched, pulled himself stiffly from the saddle, and disappeared into the undergrowth.

We did a bit of stretching ourselves, and set about looking for firewood. There was plenty on the ground. We collected it gingerly, piece by piece: heaps of old sticks are favourite hiding places for spiders and snakes. From the bank of the stream we could see, deeper into the woods to our right, a blackened iron railway bridge spanning the gully high above our heads, at the same height as the road bridge on our left. A couple of days later we were to meet a railway worker in Salto who, in the course of a meandering conversation, told us he'd worked on the repairs of that very bridge, damaged by a flood a few years before. Looking at it then, so high up, it never even occurred to us that this limpid, innocent water could rise that high.

While I got the fire started, Patricia poured out a hefty snort of the *nacional* whisky we'd bought in Chapicuy. It was no-nonsense stuff, the kind that makes you wince and gasp and flap your wings. We thought it was marvellous. This was roughing it in style!

The muffled rustle of hooves and the lowing sound of bony, wet-nosed voices drew our attention to the bridge, where the herd was pouring across in a brown and white tide. The cows were being guided into the clearing across the road, where we could see smoke rising from a campfire. They came and they came and they came across, grunting and murmuring until, bringing up the rear, a bull the size of a motorcar refused to go over the bridge. The last two gauchos patiently tried to persuade it to cross, but the majestic animal didn't want to know. He stumbled down the embankment, broke into a cumbersome canter, and ploughed straight into the undergrowth. The gauchos conferred on the verge for a moment and followed it in, deeper and deeper into the brush until they were a stone's throw away from us on the opposite side of the stream. Seeing us watching, one of them waved, just before nudging his horse into an ambush ahead of the recalcitrant steer. They waded back and forth amongst the weeds for several minutes before they got Ferdinand back on the road. Flanking it on either side, they tried again. I told you I didn't want to cross this thing, the bull seemed to say, as with a clumsy lunge it shouldered one of the horses aside and vanished down the embankment again, this time off the other verge. '*Aijuna!*' The men laughed and cursed amiably before following the animal down. The bull soon appeared on the beach beneath the spans of the bridge, cornered at the water's edge. It circled once or twice, looking for a way to escape. Out of our sight, the gauchos were closing. One of them appeared on foot, cracking his whip in the air, saying nasty, improbable things about the bull's mum. Or mums, as it happens, since the bull was being credited with the laudable achievement of being the son of a thousand whores. Obviously not one to tolerate that sort of language, he bellowed a war-cry in reply, feinted, threatened to charge, thought better of it, and, wheeling with surprising agility for one so large, plunged into the stream. Pursued by catcalls and shouting and laughter he swam across, lumbered with dignity up the opposite bank, and marched proudly into the concealing bushes.

Our fire was going great guns by now, so we scooped off some embers and piled them between the stones across which we'd suspended the grille. Patricia laid out the *chorizos* and succulent *colita de cuadril*. The first wisp of the perfume of cooking reduced us to ravening savages. We had another swig on our backs in the grass while our impatience mounted in aboriginal crescendo. To help pass the time we put up the tent. Even though by now we were real experts at it, we'd never done it so fast. Beyond the bridge the gauchos stripped and went for a swim.

Our meal was plain: we accompanied the *asado* with *galletas de campaña* and water-melon. It went straight into our top ten, competing for the top slot with the Asado San José. We had masses of meat left over, of course, but we'd planned it that way. There was no question at all in our minds that this was simply the best beef in the world. Lusciously bloated, we rested against a tree, watching the sky turn purple and gold, painting the stream. We went down for a wash in the mirror-like water, and set the two pink-hearted melon halves floating away like Moses. The herd, we saw, had already moved on: we hadn't heard them go.

The sun set almost without warning, and the dark silence ignited with the scraping of the creatures of the night. Beyond the branches the stars lit up in the infinite black of the overhead vault, every one a sun, how many holding worlds within their sway? Is there anybody there, looking up at me looking up at you? Selene, the luminous moon, harnessed the team and sent them racing. We retreated gratefully to our travelling home and in the blue, whispering darkness, like Endymion we slept protected.

CHAPTER EIGHT

THE LAST TRAIN TO SALTO GRANDE

Beams of sunlight were penetrating the glade when we woke. The tent was so comfortable, and the view through the net so enchanting, that we didn't want to get up. It was ten o'clock before we started pedalling again. I don't know whether it was because we stayed in bed so late or because we were getting the opposite of our second wind: a sort of 'second worn-out', but we found the going tough, with far too much uphill. The terrain wasn't, of course, really very different from anything else we'd cycled across.

Despite our excellent progress of the last few days, all we wanted was a comfortable place where we might stop and eat lotus all day. We'd picked the wrong place for that sort of wishing: Ruta 3 climbed gradually but steadily onto a broad *meseta*, wild and windswept and completely deserted, with nothing at all in the way of 'comfortable places'. Luckily, it didn't last for long. An hour or so later we came off the plateau down a slope as welcome as a long-lost friend, and crossed the river Daymán into the province of Salto.

Not far beyond the bridge, a fork led off to the left. A signpost pointed down it to the Daymán hot springs. As we put our backs into the curve, a swarm of schoolchildren cheered and whistled us past as though we were leading the pack in the *Vuelta Ciclista*. We couldn't have felt less like champions. Only the thought of a swim at the end of it kept us on the road.

At the gates to the springs, for reasons I still can't fully understand, we were quickly embroiled in a bitter and totally unnecessary argument with the attendants about where we could or could not leave our bikes while we bathed. The springs are owned and maintained by the Salto municipality and, in a Kafka-esque parody of civil servants, the men at the gate were rude, pedantic and absurd. I was just getting ready for homicide when we were rescued by the proprietor of the Parador, a restaurant straddling the perimeter fence: he invited us to leave our things in his storeroom.

As at Guaviyú the water had been channelled into swimming pools, but there the resemblance ended. The grounds were far larger and more imaginatively landscaped, and there were perhaps twice as many pools, beautifully cleaned and maintained. We decided then and there that the city of Salto could wait another day: we were going to stay here and rest, soak our bodies in the medicinal waters, and lie like lizards in the sun. Which is exactly what we did. The water was hotter here, 42° centigrade. It did wonders for our aching limbs.

In the course of our lazy afternoon we learned that it was Daymán's policy to be 'accessible to the general public'. In a rare demonstration of fiscal enlightenment, the entrance fee was risibly low. One could even buy a bus ticket in downtown Salto, including entrance to the park and pools, for 105 pesos, equivalent to 20 English pence. Perhaps, because it was Monday, there were few people there; although in the evening, as people finished work, the place began to fill up.

That night we camped in a nearby paddock, also belonging to the owner of the Parador. There were two or three other tents there already and our neighbours visited back and forth all night, playing their radios loud, but we were far too tired to really notice, or to care.

Dawn had barely caressed the eastern sky when our alarm clock buzzed. We wanted to get an early start. The grass was soaked with dew and the air was sharp and crisp. Through the railings we saw the gardeners draw the tarpaulin covers off the hot pools. The roiling, climbing clouds of vapour were caught like sluggish ghosts in the first rays of the rising sun.

On the road we met another construction team, putting the final touch to their work with Brobdingnagian, wood-fired steamrollers. I remembered them with affection from my childhood in Montevideo. Their twins had laboured noisily for weeks half a block from my home, in the company of wreckers and bulldozers and Lord knows what else, in a memorable summer when the Ministry of Public Works decided to yank up all the tramrails and remake the roads, and I prayed constantly that they would also plough down my school at the top of the hill, only another block away. But even these majestic machines paled into insignificance beside the great favourites of my youth: the barrenderas, the street-sweeping machines. They were enormous, the size of a house, bristling with brushes and rollers, squirting jets of water in every direction as they lumbered along making their wonderful dinosaur noise. My boyhood ambition for years was to drive one as soon as I grew up: I wanted to be a barrendero.

We entered the city along a backstreet, through a poor neighbourhood.

An archaeologist could deduce the entire chronology of the availability of building materials, just from studying that backstreet. The residents had built their homes of whatever they could get their hands on: bricks; wood; tins and oil drums cut open, hammered flat, and nailed to a wooden frame; mud . . . But despite the evident poverty, people had held onto their dignity: most of the houses were freshly painted, the tiny patches of garden were carefully tended and the entire quarter was clean and tidy.

At the ONDA bus station we collected our parcel from base camp and sent another one back. We were getting through film at a ridiculous rate. The bus depot was on the main square, and we sat at a pavement table at the café next door to watch the world go by. The nation's second city, there is a certain stately sobriety about Salto, with its solid official buildings and cobbled, tree-lined streets. It has an air of establishment about it, a flavour of age and experience, as befits a city founded in the mid-eighteenth century. Although it has suffered from the country's general decline since the 1950s, the shops are well stocked and seem to thrive, and the pavements are alive with colourful activity. Outside the busy heart of town all is calm and quiet: tidy suburbs, careful gardens, peaceful streets.

In pre-colonial days the region was crawling with Indians, coming in great migrant waves from Brazil. The first to sweep across were the *Yaros* and *Ibirayás*: primitive, nomadic tribes. They were dislodged by the *Chaná-timbúes*, drawn by the abundance of fish around the falls of Salto Grande. The most recent were the piratical *Bohanes*, part of the great *Guaraní* nation, who travelled the waterways raiding along the banks, and the fierce *Charrúas* who went all the way down to the coast, where the first Europeans to arrive reported seeing 'one behind every tree'.

Being north of the Río Negro, the first Europeans were predominantly Portuguese, and many took Indian women as mates although never *Charrúas*. They were too damned rough, and fought tooth and claw rather than be touched by a white man. The poor suitors usually ended up with their guts all over the floor before they'd even got their trousers down. Not that the girls would have been particularly attractive anyhow, mind you, thanks to the *Charrúan* custom of rubbing their skins with animal grease, which quickly went rancid in the sun. Apparently you could smell them coming long before you saw them. It is said that the only times *Charrúa* blood mixed with European it happened in a white woman's belly, and seldom with the lady's consent. As in the rest of the country, Salto was then visited by the usual tide of Spanish, French and Italians, with a smattering of African slaves. The industrious Basques came later, as did the British. The first settlements were precarious and unstable, under constant siege from the war-loving *Charrúas*. There was one greatly feared chieftain, known as Black Cat, who regularly came down from his hideout in the eastern hills for an entertaining slap at the isolated *estancias* on the fertile plains of Arerunguá.

In time the Indians learned to trade (beads, mirrors, tobacco, rum, and knives in exchange for hides, *ñandú* feathers and horses), but they never developed the white man's concept of property, and continued to take from the land whatever they needed, to the extent that the *hacendados* were frequently offered hides taken from their own cattle. Nor did the 'redskins' fully appreciate the idea of trade as a permanent arrangement and often, returning to a spot in the course of their constant wandering, they would reclaim goods they had bartered away. A local *estanciero*, surveying his herds, once came across a group of braves cantering away on the horses he had bought from them only months before. He tried to explain to the Indians that one didn't do that sort of thing, ending with what for him was the irrefutable argument that the horses now bore his mark branded onto their rumps.

'Yes,' agreed the leader of the braves without demur, 'Mark yours. Horses mine.'

We wanted to visit the Salto Grande dam, built jointly by Uruguay and Argentina across the Río Uruguay, which supplies electricity to a vast area in both countries. As we headed out of town we passed the railway station, sidings and shunting yards spanning the road. In contrast with the city around it, it was a scene of utter desolation. Crumbling, ancient railstock stood discarded and forgotten on rusted, weed-covered sidings. AFE, the nationalized railway system, has been in trouble for as long as I can remember, and longer. Through negligence, mismanagement, corruption and constant labour disputes, it has fallen far since its glory days as a British company, the Uruguayan Midland Railway. It started dying around the time of the First World War, when president Batlle, (about whom more later) in an attempt to break the foreign monopoly on transport, built highways next to the most important routes. My great-grandfather, who ran the railway at the time, is probably still turning in his grave. But he saw it coming: he packed his bags and ran off to Brazil with his mistress, to run the Leopoldina railway instead. Which is a different story.

We had hoped to travel at least a short stretch by train, if only to be able to say later that we'd done it, but by recent government decree the few trains still running no longer carried passengers and closure of the entire network was imminent. The already sadly shortened list of freight customers, tired of having their produce rot in shunting yards for any of a million reasons, was growing shorter every day. The company was on the verge of collapse, lumbered with dilapidated stock, kilometres of unusable track and labour troubles that would make even The Iron Lady tremble. The government wanted to close down and forget the entire enterprise. The modernization demanded by the syndicates and a body of public opinion required sums of money which, unsurprisingly, simply did not exist in the national coffers. Rumours about potential foreign investors abounded, although none of them showed any substance, which is hardly remarkable as only a certified lunatic or the most misguided philanthropist – preferably both – would even consider the venture. So severe is the neglect and so entrenched by now the concept of disuse that, although I forget the place, we passed a row of cottages adjacent to the tracks whose back gardens had been allowed, nay, *encouraged* onto and beyond the rails.

At one end of the yard, beyond some derelict sheds, we saw smoke rising from the blackened funnel of an ancient locomotive. We hurried over to the enormous, obscenely dirty hulk. At some stage in its history the furnaces had been converted to diesel, but otherwise it was still a steam train and the boilers were well fired up. A single freight car was hitched to the front of the engine. As we walked around it, in silence, the engineer dropped down from the cab and started talking to us. Patricia wanted to go for a ride, and asked whether the train was going anywhere. Yes it was: to the dam. Well, so were we! Could he give us a lift? she asked. The engineer, whose name was Juan, told us to wait while he went to *consultar*.

A few minutes later we were in the freight car and, whistle blowing, we were clattering across the countryside towards Salto Grande. The 15-kilometre trip was noisy, dirty, smelly and tremendous fun. At the end of the line we pulled up at a surprisingly handsome brick and stone station. Juan, who had attached himself to us, explained that it had been built by the same company that built the dam. We were the first, and probably the only members of the public ever to alight there. By the time the route was inaugurated, it was already obsolete: AFE no longer carried passengers.

We walked with Juan to the head of the dam. On the way we passed an imposing customs building, in the same general style as the station, and just as hauntingly vacant. Once built, the joint Uruguayan–Argentine commission had decided that there was no need to have an *aduana* on each side of the bridge: one could do the job of two. All customs inspections were now conducted in a building presumably just like this one on the opposite bank. It wasn't completely abandoned: there were a few soldiers on duty, although besides keeping away squatters they had nothing to do.

Intrigued by a signpost pointing the way towards the Public Relations Department, we followed the road to yet another handsome building rising in splendid isolation from the plain. A sign outside it advertised guided tours of the dam, so we went indoors. The entrance hall was spacious and airy, carpeted in soft, spongy black rubber, with large picture windows looking out over the open countryside. Along the walls in the cavernous lobby, glass cabinets crammed with exhibits told the story of the dam's construction through core samples, tools, sections of cable, models of the turbines, maps, aerial photographs and reams of statistics. A door led into a small auditorium, complete with a screen and cinema seating, an elevated podium and a soundproof projection room. Upstairs there was a canteen, and suites of offices led off the halls. It was a modern office building just as one might find in the heart of a city, but the place was deserted. So far as we could see, there were perhaps half a dozen employees there, including the minibus driver and the cleaners, and it was difficult to make out what they all did, besides guided tours, to keep busy. Even the tours couldn't have kept them greatly entertained: on that midsummer Tuesday we were the only customers.

We bundled into a minibus with the driver and a young, bespectacled girl wearing a smart beige uniform and a smart line of chat. No doubt she had fascinating data to impart, but she lost us as soon as we were up on the dam. From high on the rampart we could see that the river was boiling with fish, especially around the 'fish gate'. It was a walled enclosure, a flooded concrete pen, jutting outward from the dam. It was joined to the river below the water line and, up a sluice, supposedly provided a route through the dam for the *Dorado* (*Salminus maxillosus*) to continue upstream to their spawning grounds. We had tantalizing glimpses of their black and golden backs as they thrashed about in the pen, queuing up to get through. Far out in midstream two men in a boat, rod bent practically double, struggled to bring a gigantic specimen aboard. We stood at the parapet and watched them bring in another before reluctantly going in for a look at the massive Russian turbines, promising ourselves all the way that one day we'd be back to 'ketch one o' dem fish!'. I don't know why we were suddenly so keen. Before coming on this trip I was ready at the drop of a hat to denounce angling as the second most stupid and boring sport known to man, surpassed only by golf.

Our guide was motoring seamlessly on about tonnage and megawatts and litres per hour, when I heard her mention wildlife. As at Palmar – which, compared to this, was a toy – despite all the high-blown rhetoric, there was no sign at all of any attempt at re-forestation. Oh but the funds were there, oh yes of course, or, rather, had been there, but she couldn't say how or where they had been spent; nor by whom. For the next couple of days we cycled around the perimeter of the lake behind the dam, and I can't tell you where or how either. With the sort of pressing problems that countries like Uruguay have to face, this may seem a trivial complaint, but I don't believe it is. It's not that I'm 'against' the dam: I just consider and will continue to consider the job incomplete until the forests are replanted with native species of trees and the vanished habitats of all those animals and birds are re-created.

As the girl talked about the tonnes of wood that had been used in the course of construction, I asked idly whether any of it had come from all the forests that were felled to make way for the lake. No, she said, it had not. All specially imported for the job. From other forests, somewhere else. I asked what had happened to all that wood.

'They burned it,' she said, although she flinched as she said it, 'enormous bonfires. Cheaper than storing or recycling, you see. Until a neighbourhood committee, after months and months of trying, finally managed to persuade the contractors to donate it so that the poor could use it to build homes.'

We cycled through orange groves, one of the main sources of revenue for the province. Beyond the orchards the countryside grew increasingly bare until there was practically no cover at all on the rolling plain. At first glance we thought the pastures to our right were strewn with grey, feathery shrubs until one of them moved, and then another. Ostriches. There were about 30 of them, grazing in a group across the field. Besides the occasional *tero* which rose screaming from the grass as we rode past, or the partridges, whose whirring, whistling escape startled us as much as we had startled them, the only sound was the humming of our tyres. We were almost out of water when at last, after hours of empty prairie, we saw the blades of a windmill turning slowly above some trees on the horizon. As we approached the house another flock of ostriches fanned out in front of us. One ran alongside, as though offering a race, but he was gone long before we had any hope even of rising to the challenge.

From the house came a slight, scruffy man, who eyed us suspiciously through thick, heavy glasses. A revolver hung from his belt. I was intrigued: I'd never seen a gaucho wearing a gun, and thought people only did that in Hollywood Westerns. Behind the stubble on his chin I could see the long, thin line of an old scar. Hands on his hips, tan leather jacket drawn back from the holster, he studied me from under his eyebrows. I stuck out my hand and introduced myself. Only after shaking hands with Patricia too and hearing us out did he loosen up a bit, but it took him another few minutes to relax completely. I wondered to myself whether he had something to hide, or was just naturally glum. He cheered up when we were joined by his pretty, dark-skinned daughter Alfonsina.

Fernando took us into the house. It was small and, except for a table and chairs, completely bare. He didn't live there: his home was on another piece of land a league or two away. This property wasn't his, it was leased from a solicitor in Salto, a family friend. As time passed he became friendlier, even extroverted, and offered us *mate* and food. Having worked our way into his confidence we felt sorry to turn him down, but we had all we needed and all we wanted now was access to the well and a place to pitch our tent. I said no thank you, and had the fleeting impression that, having offered us his hospitality, he was offended by our refusal. He went into a momentary sulk, and for a heartbeat or two we reverted to one of those awkward, cross-wired conversations while we both tried to recover our poise.

We had to hang the outer skin of the tent on a branch to dry: it was still soaking wet from the morning's dew. We cleared a spot and left the inner frame assembled, to ventilate in the breeze and the last fading rays of the sun. The ground beneath the trees was a thick, peaty *milhoja* of eucalyptus leaves and dried pellets of sheep dung. For a second, until I forced the thought out of my mind, the spectre of disease raised its ugly head. There were only a couple of things that worried me as we travelled: poisonous snakes or spiders and disease, primarily *quiste hidático* which, despite all efforts, is still quite common in some parts of the country. We cooked ourselves another 'top-tenner', and as we ate it in the gathering gloom Fernando appeared – he'd stopped on his way home to check that we were all right. In the short space of time since our arrival, he'd come to take an almost proprietorial interest in our welfare, touching when compared to his reserve on our arrival.

The sun set scarlet and the moon rose white. The next thing we knew the gauchos were galloping cattle right past our tent and the sun was high in the sky once again. We were refilling our canteens at the windmill when father and daughter rattled up the driveway to the house.

'Slept okay?' he asked.

'Here: this is for you,' said Alfonsina, 'I made it.' She held out two large wedges of cake, carefully wrapped in a clean, white napkin.

There wasn't a tree anywhere. We could see the occasional stand of eucalyptus in the distance, but nothing close to the road. The sun was hot and dry, beating down from a cloudless sky. The roll of the land had become wider, broader, the slopes far longer. The prairie was studded with enormous rocks, washed smooth and round by centuries of wind and water. We saw no sign of cultivation, only natural pasture from horizon to horizon, covered in grazing sheep and cattle. There was no traffic at all, not even trucks or long-distance buses. We'd been pedalling along for an hour or two, with nothing but nature for company, when we came to a broad, shallow marsh. A few cows and horses, up to their fetlocks in water, grazed on the emerald grass. One of the mares was suckling a foal. Spoonbills and herons strutted amongst them. The sight of all that water made us desperately keen to go for a swim, so we promised ourselves a bathe in the Río Arapey which we knew lay not far ahead.

In the days before the dam, the Arapey was a strong, moderately sized river, winding and looping through dense forests, long ago one of the main Indian homelands. Now it was a naked, featureless expanse of still water, spanned by a road bridge almost a kilometre long. The land dipped towards it. The wire boundary fences of the roadside *estancias* continued down the slopes and out into the lagoon where, following the contours of the land, they disappeared beneath the surface. We scrambled down the embankment, to the shade beneath the bridge where a twisted, broken remnant of the old road jutted out into the sluggish river like a pier. We hadn't bathed since the Daymán springs; that was only a couple of days ago, although it seemed much longer. Our clothes, on the other hand, we hadn't been able to wash for almost a week and they were so stiff with grime that they probably could have cycled home alone. Stripped to the buff we did our laundry first and spread it over the bikes to dry in the sun while we had our bathe. Although open and exposed it was a peaceful, private spot, invisible from the road – not that there was anything travelling along it – and set in deserted countryside. We lounged in the sunlight with nothing on and breathed deep the deliciously cool breeze that whispered across the water.

Still trailing wet laundry, we crossed the bridge. At the opposite end a portly policeman came out of a wooden shack by the roadside and stood in our way, clipboard and pencil at the ready.

'*Buenos días, muchachos,*' he sang out as we slowed to a halt, 'enjoy your swim?' Two or three men were huddled in the gloomy hut, puffing away at evil-smelling cigarettes. For a moment I wondered whether they'd all been having a jolly good ogle at my wife, but they'd probably seen us get off the road and back on again. It didn't really matter, anyway.

'Oof!' we said in unison, 'and how!'

'Hope you didn't drink any of the water,' the policeman went on, 'It's not safe. Won't be for another ten years, on account of all the forests breaking up. Mind if I have a look at your documents?'

As he made a note of our names and numbers I asked whether he was looking for anyone in particular but no, he said, just routine. In a slow, roundabout way he teased from us all he needed to know. All we wanted to know was where we could get a nice, cold Coke.

'Hm,' he grunted. 'Not around here. Closest shop is in Colonia Palma, 30 kilometres ahead.'

We hadn't been planning to cycle that far. In fact, we'd almost done our daily quota of 50 kilometres, but in the end our taste buds won out. Colonia Palma it was.

All alone in the world, we worked our way across the open savannah. By the bank of a small stream, a few metres back from the road, we saw a small stone monument set within a weed-choked, fenced-off square. An inscription commemorated some soldiers who'd died there doing their duty some years before. Intriguingly, it said no more. For a moment we considered filling our canteens in the stream but, remembering what the policeman had said, decided against it. In any case, we could see the silhouette of a windmill in the distance.

The gate was crooked and rusty. The track to the house was surfaced with brightly-coloured pebbles, polished and round as though taken from a riverbed. It was our first contact with the quartzes so abundant in the north, but if we were hoping to find a fortune in amethysts lying at our feet, we were doomed to be disappointed. However pleasing to see, these polished pebbles are as common and valueless as unpolished pebbles.

From the yard in front of the stable an unsavoury group of men watched us approach. Something felt distinctly wrong. Under their lugubrious, threatening stares we regretted our decision to stop, but when you've come that far onto a man's land you can't just turn tail and walk off again without even saying hello. Anyway, if they were half as mean as they

Wheat turning gold along the Kiyú road.

Milking time at the Galarzas'. Note the single sheepskin used in place of a saddle.

Barefoot girl with ducks. María-Ethel Galarza guiding her charges back to the house.

Left: 'In the dark, aromatic shed the boys walked barefoot through the luminous sludge from one animal to the next.'

Advertising comes to Carmelo. Publicidad Laser doing the rounds.

The farm house at La Sirena.

The campsite at the Arroyo Chapicuy Chico. Patricia feeding the fire.

Patricia preparing the water-melon, donated by the wonderful
Sub-comisario-Duque-a-las-órdenes.

We stopped at a butcher's shop in Salto for provisions and were immediately swamped by hordes
of chattering, inquisitive children. The tallest chap in the back row is the butcher.

Sugar-cane at Bella Unión.

Left: Juan, the engineer, aboard his locomotive at the Salto Grande dam.

Edenes Picón. Sipping his afternoon *mate*, a Thermos of hot water gripped under his arm, he seemed shy and unexceptional – until he started to talk.

A fruit and vegetable stall at Bella Unión.

Looking into Brazil. Or is it Uruguay? The customs shed and contested border marker at Masoller.

The infamous Heartbreak Hill, *La Bajada de las Penas*, coming out of the Cuchilla de Haedo.

The view from the top of Bald Mountain. The buildings of Estancia El Boquerón can just be seen amongst the trees on the right.

The industrious Alvarez takes a break to talk about his life.

The sandmen mining a temporary bank in the Río Tacuarembó.

'Stuck on the back of a galloping gale that rattles your teeth and tears at your bones, a minute is stretched into years'.

Tomás, the foreman at
El Arazá.

'. . . we passed a *tropilla* on
  the move . . .'

Sunset over Cerro Largo.

Right: 'We sat there in the half-light of the old *almacén*, watching the locals come and go . . . '

'Ricardi rolled another cigarette, and stuck it in the corner of his mouth'.

The view from our dune at Punta del Diablo. The white, beehive-shaped mound by the house in the foreground is a traditional wood-burning oven. We baked bread in it one evening and it was magnificent.

looked I wasn't too keen to offend them by turning my back. We'd just have to bluff our way through and hope for the best. They fanned out in silence around us as we drew up.

'Good afternoon,' I said.

Nobody answered. Maybe none of them thought it was really that good.

'We're just passing through,' I went on, 'we ran out of water. We saw the *molino* from the road, and thought you wouldn't mind if we filled up our canteens.'

One of them detached himself from the stable wall and spat on the ground. He put a hand in his pocket and drew the other one out from behind his back, lazily balancing the weight of a long, shining knife. Time stopped. He was an ugly little chap. Holes for eyes, thin weasel mouth, face like a hatchet.

'Water, eh?' he drawled. His left hand came back out of his pocket, and he started to trim wafer-thin slices from a tarry plug of black tobacco.

'Sure,' he said truculently, 'over there,' pointing the way with the razor-sharp *facón*.

'Travelling far?' The question was full of ambiguous menace.

'Maybe they don't want us to stay, huh?' I murmured to Patricia as we filled the canteens and had a long drink.

'Neither do I,' she answered.

The men had moved over to where their horses stood tethered in the shade of some trees, but no one was yet in the saddle. I only had eyes for the knives thrust through their belts. Like intruders, we'd walked uninvited onto people's land day after day for weeks, to be met in all sorts of ways as we eavesdropped on their lives, but our reception here was in a brand-new category all by itself. These men weren't just shy or reserved, nor were they merely suspicious like Fernando yesterday. And as for the foreman, who'd now sheathed his blade and was rolling the tobacco into a corn husk, well, Fernando had relaxed, in the end. This son of a bitch would never calm down. His eyes never left me, flicking constantly from my face to my hands. Even when he looked away he was watching me. I tried to make conversation, asking about the stone memorial by the stream. He chuckled: it was a short, grating sound.

'They died,' he said simply, with another vicious cough. 'Truck turned over.'

As we passed them on our way back out, one of the men, a burly, stone-faced giant far too large for his horse, was pouring some liquid from a tin onto its hooves. Curiosity got the better of me.

'What's that?' I asked.

'Kerosene,' he bit the word but then, as though regretting his brevity; 'lot of stones. It stops the hooves from splitting.'

It was obvious that they weren't going to invite us for dinner, so we thanked them for the water and walked back down the track. Halfway to the gate they cantered past, riding in a tight pack like the bad guys in films. Doctor Kerosene was the only one to wave.

Within view of Colonia Palma, we passed our first sugar-cane plantation. We'd see many more over the next few days. Once in the small, dusty settlement straddling the road, we found the only bar and dragged ourselves indoors.

'You made it,' said the bartender, grinning. 'I wondered where you were going. I saw you in Salto the other day. On the Post Office steps.'

The two *quinteros* who'd interrupted their game of billiards to watch us come in resumed the match with slit-eyed intensity, muttering dire threats to each other about how now, my friend, you will die, it will cost you a week's worth of beer. A young gaucho, covered in dust, his beer on the table in front of him, had fallen sound asleep balanced precariously on the edge of his stool. His hat had slipped off his head and lay on the floor at his feet. A long, thin thread of spit hung from his lower lip.

The bartender dug deep into the fridge and brought out the coldest drinks he could find. Patricia was so keen to get to hers that she gulped down the first glassful in one go. She immediately curled up with cramp, and fell onto the bench trying to catch her breath, nursing her stomach with one hand and rubbing the aching bones in her face with the other.

'Oooh, I'm going to die,' she whimpered. 'I think I'm going to die.'

Placing bets on whether she would or she wouldn't, the bartender explained that this was his summer job. He was helping out his parents, who owned the place. For the rest of the year he was a law student, in Montevideo.

STOP: POLICE CHECKPOINT said a large crooked sign in the middle of the road outside the *comisaría*. A tall, lanky policeman, a hand-rolled cigarette poking out from beneath a bushy brown moustache, was lounging against the fence leafing through a dog-eared girlie magazine. He had to tilt his head right back to peer at us from under the brim of his kepi.

'Yes . . . ?' he said dreamily.

'The sign. It says stop.'

'No, not *you*!' he exclaimed with mock impatience. 'You're not a truck! It's only for trucks. And cars.'

He spoke *Portuñol*, border Spanish, thickly laced with Portuguese and heavily accented. Although it changes slightly from region to region – sometimes, I suspect, even from speaker to speaker – it's the lingua franca all along the frontier with Brazil. Having lived in Río for some years, I speak Portuguese as well as Spanish so, unless the accent was particularly obscure, I could usually deduce what people were trying to say. It reminded me of the mishmash of Spanish and English we used to speak at school to confuse and annoy our teachers. We became so successful at it that in desperation the headmaster issued a stern edict in assembly one morning forbidding the use of *Spanglish* whilst in school uniform. Didn't work, of course.

The village fell far behind and out of sight as we mounted the long, gradual slope to a ridge. Over the years the bare red earth on both sides of the road had been torn and deeply scored by the rush of rivers of rainwater. To our left stood a dark, dense forest of coppiced eucalyptus and, to our right, plantations of sugar-cane, soybean and corn. In 1976 I travelled from Montevideo to Rotterdam on a freighter, its holds filled with what the bill of lading described as soybean expeller: crumbling, greasy pellets the shape and size of sticks of blackboard chalk. They were the solid by-product of oil extraction, destined for the poor cows of Europe who didn't have pasture to eat. The cold room, stocked with frozen fish and orange concentrate, was above the vast central hold in which that noisome stuff was carried loose. Something had gone wrong with the refrigeration plant, and condensation from its sides was dripping very slowly onto the dunes of fibre which, when wet, fermented rapidly, generating enormous heat. These damp patches could, if left untended, burst spontaneously into flame. I used to join the crew on filthy mountain-eering expeditions over the sticky dust, to collect the fermenting expeller in metal buckets. On more than one occasion we collected glowing embers.

Just beyond the ridge we came to a small, frivolous stream, tap dancing over the stones at the foot of a steep, twisted gully. Like a gash in the ground, its banks ruptured and disfigured as though attacked by a giant, angry hand. It was eloquent testimony to the ferocity of the flash floods that occur in the north with monotonous regularity. Entire swathes of the province of Artigas are frequently isolated by them. A local journalist, writing in the 1970s, complained that 'while the Yanks go to the moon, we get cut off from the world by a little bit of rain.'

We'd just about had it when we met a man with a wheelbarrow by a white wooden gate. He was hoeing away at the ocean of weeds that sprouted on the driveway, a thankless, never-ending task if ever there was one. Amongst the trees on the bluff in the middle distance we could see the shadows and shapes of farm buildings. We stopped to talk. The man was glad to be interrupted. He greeted us with a clear, open smile and we gave him a condensed version of what we had come to call The Famous Writer Routine: we're cycling round the country, collecting material for a book, may we pitch our tent on your *estancia*, and could we have some water please?

'Go on up to the house,' he said. The *capataz* would let us stay, no sweat, probably even give us something to eat.

As we trudged up the coarse track, pushing bicycles that seemed to grow heavier with every step, the man nipped past us, tools clattering in the metal barrow.

'Had enough of that,' he muttered, 'done enough for one day. Go on, go on, up up up!'

Three remarkably tame ostriches watched us until we were almost upon them and them moved disdainfully out of our way. To our left, in the deep shadow of a tangled grove, stood a large, two-storeyed L-shaped house. Its walls were flaking and scarred with damp, and the windows were dark and forbidding, but there was a certain imposing, stately elegance about the stark, uncompromising severity of the building's lines. Wooden scaffolding leaned precariously against one of its faces, where some restoration had begun. Mock spearheads tipped the tall iron railing that enclosed the gravel courtyard in the house's elbow. Around it a large paddock, once perhaps a garden, was full of bleating, jostling sheep.

In front of us across our path stood a row of massive, gnarled ombú and beyond them, one of the most enchanting buildings I've ever seen. It had no walls. A low, thick thatch with a long, shallow rake was supported on pillars, the unadorned trunks of sturdy ibirapitá. Except for the joins, which were beautifully cut and expertly fitted, the spars and trusses and rafters and beams were all made of equally natural, unadorned wood. The earth floor, eroded and beaten into a hard, shallow bowl by generations of hooves, was slightly lower than the surrounding ground. Bridles and harnesses hung from hooks on the posts and, on poles slung between them, sheepskins and saddles. Open to the elements and having no stalls, it wasn't a stable in the conventional sense of the word: it was only used for saddling and grooming the horses, which were all loose in the fields when they weren't working. So harmonious were the building's proportions, and so soothing and joyful the rough, uncut lines – everything in warm, palpable browns – that it was more like a primitive temple than a stable. The only enclosure within it was a small storeroom at one end, its walls made of compacted mud, standing under the eaves like a sacristy. I've been in very few places which combine weight and light so effectively. One is the Norman chapel in the Tower of London; another a hall in William of Orange's house in Delft.

Facing the stable across a bare yard was a long whitewashed lodge, like a barracks, where the farmhands lived. Back from a long day in the fields, they were gathering on the porch for the ritual evening mate before dinner. They rode in, singly and in pairs, unsaddled in the stable and rinsed the horses off at the pump, before retiring indoors. Showered and changed into clean clothes, they drifted back outdoors, bringing wooden stools, many just lumps of light wood cut from the trunk of a ceibo, and Thermoses of hot water from the fogón, to settle in a ring, to rest and talk and listen, sipping at the gourds of mate. The fogón (literally large fire) was in a square room at one end of the lodge. On a raised brick hearth in the centre of the floor a fire, fed with cumbersome pieces of tree trunk and branch, was kept constantly burning. Close to the embers a cluster of blackened kettles stood purring and steaming. Over the coals hung a grille, where the men could roast their breakfast of *asado*. Suspended from chains, now drawn away from the heat, a black witch's cauldron straight from Macbeth. In the winter, when the days are cold and sitting outdoors is no fun, this is where the men gather. The blackened walls seemed to reverberate with stories overheard through the years. A single large window faced east towards the gate and the prairie beyond.

As we approached, the young houseboy, a towel draped over his bare shoulders, hair still wet and yet to be combed, came out of the building to greet us. The foreman was still out *en el campo*, but of course we could stay, we could camp over there, under the *ombú*. He brought us a couple of stools and set them on the ground. No offence was intended, and certainly none was taken, but we were amused to see that he'd seated us outside the gathering circle. Looking us over with care, nodding a taciturn greeting, they went back to their meandering conversation, studiously ignoring us, although for our benefit they talked amongst themselves a little louder.

A rheumy-eyed old farmhand who was also sitting outside the ring, asked whether we would like any *mate*.

'We have our own things,' I said, 'but we'd appreciate some hot water.'

We mentioned we'd visited the dam.

'Used to be a waterfall there before. And caves in the banks. Spooky they were. All gone now, covered in water. Used to be clear when I was a boy. You could drink it. All muddy and brown now.'

Which it is, thanks to the brutal de-forestation that spreads like a ravening cancer upstream, in Brazil, where the world is rapidly changing. History is certain to condemn today's Brazilians as vandals. Not, on the other hand, that history is likely to be any kinder to the rest of us.

One of the lads threw a pebble at an ostrich, which was digging into a dustbin for something to eat. Unhurriedly, the bird stalked away in disgust. The old man told us of the *ñanduceros*, the ostrich hunters, who in his youth used to lasso the birds and pluck out their tail and wing feathers for use in dusters and fans.

'But nowadays it doesn't pay, so they don't do it any more,' he said, 'which is just as well, really. They didn't kill them, but it still couldn't have been much fun for the *ñandú*.'

Carpincho and *mulita* are still hunted mercilessly for their flesh, a fate which the ostrich seems to have escaped. I wondered whether their meat was too tough to be edible.

'Oh no, not at all,' came the reply, 'I've eaten *ñandú*. Very fat, roasts very well. Tasty. But what's the point? No need to kill them for that, *son bichos preciosos*, part of the country, part of our lives. We've got plenty of food.' With an eloquent wave of his arm he included all the livestock in the fields, 'we can leave the old ostrich alone.'

As new arrivals joined the group they came up to us and shook us courteously by the hand before sitting down, but even then it took us the best part of an hour to work our way gently into the ring. It's not that we were being rejected, quite the contrary. The men were just shy and reserved and wary of strangers, especially such strange ones as us. But slowly they warmed to our presence, and began to include us in the conversation. They talked of wages and women and the dance soon to be held in the town, and the time that Pedrito fell off his horse into the stream. They poked fun at each other and tore at the flesh of the government. Two of them, the houseboy and his brother, both in their early twenties, controlled the transistor radio and quarrelled amicably about which cassette to play next.

The blue shadows were long and getting longer as the sun sank in the west. Dinner was ready: would we like to join them for a bowl of stew? The table was almost as large as the small dining room. Benches were ranged against the walls around it, and we clambered over each other to get to our places, a noisy, raucous procedure. On the table was a basket of bread, two enormous jugs of cold milk and a steaming cauldron of mutton stew. In with the meat had gone lentils, noodles, onions, potatoes, carrots, garlic and corn. It would have kept Napoleon's army going all winter in the wasteland outside Moscow: good, belly-distending, temperature-raising stuff. Here, in the heat of the summer night, attacked by this ravenous crew, it didn't last for long. The houseboy served up mountains, egged on by everyone in chorus.

CHAPTER NINE

NEST OF SEDITION

The muffled sound of hooves and men's voices pulled me from a deep sleep. I stuck my head out of the tent to find myself eyeball to supercilious eyeball with an ostrich, so close that I could count its eyelashes. Another two, not far away, fed on fruit and leftovers laid out for them on a wooden shelf nailed to the trunk of one of the *ombúes*.

'Quick! The camera!' I said to Patricia, not daring to move.

'Nngh?'

'The camera! An ostrich . . . '

'Fnf, nf, nf . . . cmmacktobed.'

'Oh, never mind; it's gone now . . . '

Yelping and whistling, gauchos on horseback were chasing sheep out of the paddock by the house and into 'our' field. Pursued by men and barking dogs, the bleating, agitated animals boiled around the tent in a woolly white tide.

'*Buenos días!*' called one of the lads as he galloped past, a metre away from my nose.

'What's going on?' asked Patricia, her mouth full of sleep, 'What time is it?'

'Time to get up, I think. C'mon, let's go!'

The sheep had been herded into a pen, and were now filtering back out again down a wooden alley through a footbath filled with a bright blue medicinal liquid.

Seeing us wander up to the lodge, the *capataz* came away and offered hot water for *mate*. We filled a Thermos from one of the kettles on the hearth, looking covetously at the remains of mutton *asado* hissing quietly on the *fogón*. Bringing a pair of stools out of the dark, smoky room we breakfasted on a forgotten tin of peaches Patricia had found in one of her panniers. In the stable, the *casero* was scooping up horsedung and hosing the hard earth floor to settle the dust before sweeping it with a broom made of *mio-mio* branches.

Mio-mio is a tough, fibrous weed that grows uninvited in much of the country. It is caustic and poisonous, comparable to strychnine, and extremely harmful to cattle. Not only does it cause nasty mouth sores, ulcers, and even death, but it can also injure their hooves. Cows reared on *estancias* were *mio-mio* grows wild have learned to stay well away from it. The problem only arises when animals unfamiliar with the plant are moved into a region where it is common: they invariably try to eat it, and as a result many of them die. Hence the salutary codicil often displayed at cattle auctions: '*conoce mio-mio*' – familiar with *mio-mio* – which can add a few pesos per kilo to the price.

The *capataz* was in a talkative mood. I commented that we'd found the old farm buildings very lovely, and that the men seemed well cared for.

'Oh!' he exclaimed, '*Luxury* compared to the quarters I was given when *I* started out! My first job was in Paso de los Toros. We didn't have beds then, didn't even have bedrooms. Slept in the barn, like animals, a few old hides for cover . . . hell, when it rained. If the skins got wet they wouldn't dry out for days. Lost count of the times I lay down to sleep in a soggy bed. No wonder the lads were in such a damned hurry to get into the towns. You'd think that now, with labour so scarce, a working man would be able to find better conditions, but they're not all like this, you know: on some *estancias* things are still exactly as they were when I was a boy. Except that now there's not much in the way of jobs to go into town for, and some people take advantage of that. Government says they don't, but they do.'

We had a strong following wind, and fairly flew towards Bella Unión, the republic's northernmost city, hotbed of revolution and modern economic miracle. Considerable fuss had been made of the *co-operativas* in the region, and we wanted to see them for ourselves. At about noon we reached the junction with Ruta 30, which would bring us to our first port of call. Twenty metres into it the tarmac ended abruptly and once again we had to get off our bikes and push, searching all the time for the path of least resistance over the rubble. By the time we reached CALVINOR we were covered in muck. A hoarding by the gate announced that the co-operative vineyards had been set up with help from the Interamerican Development Bank. The gatekeeper – who lived in the gatehouse with his wife and children – directed us down the track. We noticed as we went that there was no fruit on the vines. In Carmelo we'd been too early for the harvest: here, about 400 kilometres further north, we were too late. At a warehouse on the shore of a large reservoir, the last boxes of newly picked grapes, bees swarming noisily all over them, were stacked in the loading bay. The air was full of their rich, sweet scent.

In the days when the tracks were being laid down, Bella Unión was the end of the line, and much of the workforce elected to take plots of land here in part payment for their labour. Amongst those settlers was a sizeable contingent of Italian peasants, who found the stony soil remarkably similar to that of the Old Country. They proceeded to work it in much the same way, planting vegetables and vineyards. Those first vineyards have long since disappeared, as have most of the original families, but some of the old cellars survived and with them the knowledge that grapes could be grown in the region. When the members of CALNU, the sugar-cane growers' co-operative, were looking to spread their investment, wine-making seemed a natural choice. It was their good fortune that the military rulers of the day, spotting a heaven-sent propaganda opportunity, were keen to underwrite the venture. The value to the government, quite apart from the obvious benefit of encouraging a new industry, was in being able to put to rest once and for all the spectre of revolution. The 'Tupamaro' National Liberation Movement was widely held to have begun in Bella Unión, amongst the disgruntled sugar-cane workers.

Sadly, the wine press wasn't on the property, but housed in one of the old Italian cellars closer to town. We would have to visit it later. A young manager we'd dug out of his office installed us in a Volkswagen Beetle in such ruinously bad condition it was a miracle the thing was still on the road. The drooping body was barely visible through the dirt and the dents, and there was nothing left of the seats but the springs, covered with a moth-eaten horse blanket.

'Cars don't last very long around here,' he said, 'and we use this one as though it were a jeep!'

Gears grinding and engine complaining, we raced off over the dyke across the reservoir, our guide occasionally looking forward to see where we were going, from time to time interrupting his hand-assisted speech to touch the steering wheel. He made a comment (later echoed by the Chairman of the cane-planters' co-operative) that although the members of the association all enjoyed the benefits of sharing equipment, expertise and all the marketing machinery, the enterprise was run on commercial lines as severe and uncompromising as those of a private company.

In my ignorance I had formed quite the wrong idea of these *co-operativas*: I had assumed they were vaguely socialistic, owned by the workers who ran their neo-Utopian enterprise with fraternal concern. Wrong. The co-operators were the investors. The workers, well, they were the workers. As usual they got the short end of the stick, certainly in the early days when there wasn't much of anything to share and CALVINOR enjoyed the dubious distinction of paying the worst salaries in a region known for decent wages. Naturally enough, that made it impossible for them to recruit good personnel or hold on for very long to whatever staff they *could* get. To make matters worse, conditions for the workforce were so bad they would have embarrassed the slave traders of the South Sea Company. Together it all added up to the wrong environment for making a reliable product in sufficient quantities to make the money to pay the wages to draw the staff they needed to make a reliable product . . . a bit like the house that Jack built. Our host was refreshingly frank about it. But things had, he said, now changed for the better. He showed us the new housing being built for the farmhands as proof of the new enlightenment. Although the lodges were unfinished, they were already in use, and a dramatic improvement over the old housing: tin sheds where up to 15 men in three-tiered bunks had shared each tiny room. In those days, during the summer months, one of the men would be put in charge of 'cooling'. His job was to hose the building down with cold water at regular intervals around the clock, to prevent the temperature indoors from soaring high enough to bake the men alive. Even then, there had been more than one medical emergency. One of the old corrugated iron sheds, although vacant now, was still standing. The ramshackle, lop-sided building was quite frightening. In desperation, trying to get some air into the place, previous tenants had hacked holes in the metal walls.

When we eventually arrived at the CALNU refinery, in the middle of miles of sugar-cane, the factory bell was about to go. We went into the management office block and introduced ourselves at the desk. To our great surprise, moments later we were ushered into an office with one of the Directors. Mr Carnelli, a dark, tousle-haired man with a management waistline, wearing the first white shirt we'd seen for weeks, seemed completely unaffected by our dusty, dishevelled appearance, and talked quite freely about the company and its history, which in many ways is the history of modern Bella Unión. We'd been listening for some minutes when a solemn man in a powder-blue, open-necked shirt came into the room. It was Dr Sosa, the Chairman.

'I heard you were here,' he said earnestly. 'I'd very much like to have a chat with you, but I'm afraid I'm a little tied up at the moment. Perhaps we can meet tomorrow. Will you be here tomorrow? Good. Could you see to it please, Carnelli? Excellent. Must be off. Delighted to have met you.'

With that he shook our hands again and left the office as suddenly as he'd entered. Carnelli picked up where he'd left off.

'But you must need somewhere to stay,' he said, after a while.

'Well, yes. We were hoping you might be able to recommend a place where we could pitch our tent.'

'Tent? Well . . . er . . . yes, I suppose so. But wouldn't you rather stay in our hotel? We have a hotel, you know, which belongs to CALNU. You can be our guests. Nice rooms. Hot shower . . . '

'We'll take it!' Patricia leapt in. He laughed.

'Fine. I'll let them know you're on your way. We can talk again in the morning. I'll arrange for you to take a tour of the factory before you meet the Chairman.'

We returned to the factory the following morning to find that Mr Carnelli's secretary, María Elena, had been 'put in charge' of us. She led us across the yard to the factory, where she handed us over to Rodolfo Cardoso, one of the managers, who was to take us on the grand tour. He was a cheerful, good-natured man, dressed in blue overalls and a yellow safety helmet. The plant wasn't working at the moment, it not being harvest time. The personnel were doing their annual maintenance of the massive machinery, most of which had been dismantled and lay in enormous chunks all over the place. We started our tour at the gates, going past the weighing scales, beneath the huge cranes, through the presses and the filters, all the way to the packing plant. By modern European standards, said Rodolfo, it was a modest, rather old-fashioned refinery but, never having seen another, Patricia and I were impressed by the sheer size of the sleeping leviathan. The presses, where the cane was broken down and crushed to extract the sweet sap, looked particularly fiendish. I commented idly that they must be very noisy when operating.

'Terrible!' said Rodolfo promptly. 'Years ago I used to work here, in the receiving end. My hearing is permanently damaged. There's a constant buzz in my head. When I'm here it sort of blends into the background noise, and I don't notice it all that much, but when I wake up in the mornings, or on the weekends when I'm at home, it can drive me nuts!'

One of the packing plants was working, churning out an endless train of kilo bags. The clanking machinery that filled them also filled the air with fine, white dust: accidental icing sugar. It settled in snowy drifts against the walls, on the window-sills, on any flat surface. The men packing the bags into boxes for shipment were covered in the fine powder. In the midday heat, with the sun beating onto the distant tin roof, it was inevitable that the men should perspire. Their body moisture mingled with the sugar and ran down their skins in sticky, syrupy streams. They looked up and laughed as we entered the hall, reading, in the looks on our faces, the thoughts that ran through our minds. At least they'd kept their sense of humour.

In a shed behind the factory the *bagazo*, the cellulose waste, was piled up in cliffs. The cane had been shredded and tormented until it had given up its last drop of sweet moisture, and the leftover fibre would go into the furnace as fuel. Rodolfo told us of a project, currently under review, to sell some of that waste to the paper mills, as was done by the rice mills in the southeast.

The conversation strayed to the days in the early 1960s when the sugar industry was plagued with labour problems, and the workers formed the union that was credited with spawning the 'Tupamaros'. Whilst it is true that Raul Sendic (a lawyer, founder of the National Liberation Movement) cut his teeth helping to organize the cane workers' union in Bella Unión, he was not alone in that task. Sendic also differed from the union leadership in that he wanted a political dimension to their activity, having taken the Cuban experience as a model for popular revolution. The phlegmatic sugar-cane workers, however militant and anomalous as trade unionists, were not seeking to revolt, but only to obtain better working conditions. As a result, the activists shifted their focus from rural areas to the towns, notably Montevideo, to form a clandestine urban guerrilla movement (the MLN, also known as 'Tupamaros') which drew its support, at least in its early days, from an intellectual élite; a fact which determined its potential as well as its limitations.

Montevideo was ripe for political renewal. There was rampant inflation, injustice, the autonomy of the beloved University was under threat, civil liberties were being abused and the traditional political parties were showing themselves to be far too occupied with internecine bickering to act constructively. Corruption in high places was also the order of the day. The Tupamaros made their 'official' public début in 1968, launching a campaign of Robin-Hoodesque banditry which demonstrated a shrewd, pragmatic understanding of the national mood and, in its idealism, initially captured the popular imagination. They exposed crooked financiers by 'borrowing' their account books and delivering them to the Press; they stole warehouses of purportedly unavailable food which they unloaded in poor neighbourhoods and, by making plain their incompetence, subjected corrupt politicians to ridicule.

They scored some formidable propaganda successes but failed to galvanize the public into active support. With the kidnapping of several eminent figures on the political and diplomatic scene, amongst them the British Ambassador (who was later released) and an American 'counter-revolution and torture expert' (who was killed), and the simultaneous capture and imprisonment of its original leadership in 1970, the MLN lost its clarity of vision and certainty of touch. An important consequence of the new militarism was the sudden and complete loss of what little popular support the Tupamaros *had* managed to foment. The nation, having no taste for bloodshed, was not ready for violent revolt, even though the armed forces were able to exploit the threat of it to take power and set in motion the dreadful machinery of repression.

But if the people were not ready for insurrection, they were also not ready for the horrors that followed at the hands of a military government. However anarchic, Uruguayans are fond of debate and enamoured with the principles of democracy. It was this which led a record turnout of voters to reject the dictatorship's clumsy attempt to achieve constitutional legitimacy in the national plebiscite of 1980, which led ineluctably to the general elections of 1984, the first in thirteen years.

The Chairman received us in his office, apologizing for not having been able to talk to us the day before. He was an eloquent and entertaining speaker and retraced the history of CALNU back to the first plantations of cane and the origins of the sugar industry. In the days of the labour troubles it did not yet exist, the cane growers having joined forces only in 1965. Without a refinery to absorb their crop, their chances of survival were bleak. They therefore decided to build one, but in order to obtain the necessary loan, they had to post a guarantee: even together, they couldn't raise the funds. They were, after all, small farmers – one or two had plantations of 200 *hectáreas*, but most of them only had 20 or 30 in cane production. Then something miraculous happened: all the shop-keepers and tradesmen in Bella Unión, from the butchers to the bakers to the newsagents and the corner grocers, realizing the opportunities that a large factory in the area would create, spontaneously signed as guarantors for the loan. If the enterprise failed, they all stood to lose everything they had. CALNU had its refinery.

By later founding CALVINOR, the members of the co-operative made another contribution to the region's growth. The next project, and perhaps the most ambitious of all (in which CALNU also has an interest), is to be CALAGUA. Like the other two, it will be a co-operative of small farmers, this time in the crescent of land around the town. When the irrigation system is completed, it will be a vegetable growers' co-operative that, by virtue of the sheer number of its members, is sure to change completely the face of northern Artigas. Dr Sosa made no bones of the fact that the support all these projects had received from the military government was politically motivated but, he said, provided it helped Bella Unión to prosper, he was happy to have it.

Before we knew it, the factory whistle had gone. We'd arranged to meet María Elena in town after she'd finished work. Dr Sosa (before becoming a sugar manufacturer he'd been a dentist: 'I went from fixing teeth to ruining them.') put us into a company van. Like practically everyone we met in Bella Unión, the young driver was bursting with energy and optimism. There seemed to be some sort of electricity in the town, the anticipation of great things just about to happen. He could hardly sit still while he told us of his hopes for CALAGUA, the horticul-tural project. His girlfriend, who worked in the hotel, had some land in the irrigation area. They were hoping to marry, and as soon as the project became a reality, they could begin to work for themselves in earnest and secure a more promising future.

We found María Elena trying to get her car started. Not that there was anything wrong with it: it was brand new, she'd only just bought it. She simply wasn't a very experienced driver.

'Not to worry,' she said, 'we're going to pick up my friend Mercedes, who's much better at cars than I am.'

The wine press was in an old, terracotta-coloured house. Three enor-mous stainless steel vats stood in the yard in front of it. Although they were in the full glare of the sun, they were cold to the touch. A grizzled old man in a rocking chair watched us from the porch as we arrived. Breathing deep the smell of fermenting wine, we walked into a long shed on one side of the house. Rows of vats ran all the way down to the opposite end, where some men were unloading grapes box by box from a truck into a sort of centrifuge. The juice and the crushed grapes – and, by the look of things, a fair number of crushed bees too – were channelled in one direction, whilst the rejected stems came whizzing out in another. A pump carried the fruit down a hose to the press. We were rather disappointed to learn that there was no wine on the premises for us to taste. It was too soon after the harvest, and all the fresh pulp was still busy fermenting. Last year's model had long since left the cellar.

'In a couple of years we'll have moved the presses and the warehouse out to the vineyard, where they should be,' said the young oenologist, 'come and visit us then! I can let you have some juice, though.'

It was made from an Argentine white variety which, intriguingly, was called Moscatel de Alejandría. It was absolutely magnificent.

A mere 12 years old, CALVINOR are still too new at wine-making to have settled into deliberately producing the sort of vintages that require ageing. For the time being 'Cash-Flow Rules, O.K.' has to be their motto, and all the vintner's attention is concentrated on producing what he described as 'young' wines, experimenting with grape varieties and different blends. Over the next few weeks we were able to try a few and, although quality was irregular, some were excellent. Their most serious problem was the corks, which seemed perpetually to conspire against them.

For much of its life, Bella Unión has been little more than another dusty border town, lying in that northern corner of Uruguay where the country meets Argentina and Brazil. It is still far from glamorous. The homes are small and modest, many of them poor. The few paved roads are ravaged by a smallpox of pot-holes and the rest are just the naked red earth and bones of the land. But it has something about it, some mysterious vitality that made me think at once of the gold-rush towns of the North American West. Smuggling has always been a major industry in Uruguay, nowhere more so than along its borders with Brazil. Manufactured products come in and raw materials – primarily cattle – go out. It's not only limited to bulk shipments: everybody does it, all the way down to the housewives who compare notes on prices in each of the three countries, but so entrenched is the habit, that people often automatically shop across the border even when things are cheaper in their own town.

Ironically, the land across the Río Cuareim was part of Uruguay until 1851, when it was negotiated away as the price for Brazilian support against the blood-thirsty Argentine dictator Rosas. He had been quick to take advantage of the feud between the Uruguayan political factions and was avidly nourishing the civil war which would become, in ever-changing forms, the dominant feature of the country's political life until early this century. During that bitter nine-year conflict, *La Guerra Grande*, which left the country in ruins, Uruguay once again had help from Britain (about to get drawn into the Crimean calamity) to resist Argentine attempts at annexation. France also contributed, although perhaps she acquitted herself rather less than honourably. Neither European power, of course, was *entirely* disinterested.

We found the address we were looking for in one of the poorer neighbour-hoods, in the shadow of an army barracks. We had come to talk to Edenes Picón, the leader of UTAA, the sugar-cane workers' union with which Raul Sendic had been involved. Sheila, his wife, invited us to sit down in the little patch of garden in front of their modest brick house. Her husband had just come back from work: he'd be out in a minute.

He came through the curtain, *mate* and Thermos clutched in his hands. He was a short, slight, olive-skinned man, wearing thick, heavy-framed lop-sided glasses; white shirt buttoned all the way up to the neck; baggy, threadbare trousers and rubber flip-flops. His black hair was wet, and combed back from his forehead. He seemed shy and insignificant: it was difficult to imagine this little man ever involved in such momentous affairs. His wife fussed over him, placing his chair to face us, and making sure he was comfortably settled. He lifted his eyes and smiled sheepishly. His teeth were crooked and stained. And then he started to talk, and at once he was transformed. This man could move mountains. In a casual, anecdotal style, peppered with humour and insight and a deep concern for his fellows, he talked with enormous natural dignity about his life and how he had arrived in Bella Unión as a young *campesino* looking for work, and how things had developed from there. He even managed to make light of his involvement in starting the union.

'But it's hard to talk objectively about important events in which one has taken part,' he said. 'At the time we were caught up in our own little world. We didn't know we were making history, we just happened to be there.'

I wanted to know, having heard plenty of second-hand stories, what working conditions were like in those days. Were things really that bad?

'No, of course they weren't,' he answered at once. 'When I first went to work for CAINSA (the sugar refinery which existed before CALNU) I was on top of the world. I'd never seen so much money! I bought myself a little motorbike. I used to zip about on it after the girls. I even bought an electric razor. God knows why, because I was too young to shave! If you had a job with CAINSA you were okay, they paid the best wages for miles. . . . But it wasn't all perfect, some things weren't right, there was a lot of injustice, and you know how it is – people always want to make things better. So we had to organize. And we did. I was reading a lot at the time, and my head was full of ideas. When I was a kid, living in a *ranchito* out in the country, my mother and father were always going on at me to read. I can't thank them enough for that. I didn't want to lead the union, though, but the other chaps insisted that I had to be their representative, that I should be the leader, and they voted me into the job. What could I do? I had to do it properly, then,' he said, with disarming simplicity, without making it seem like a boast. I could well understand why they had chosen him.

He spoke very clearly and lucidly, showing he had a firm grasp not only of political principles but also of the social environment, the aspirations and characteristics of the people he'd worked for and with. He talked about how the situation had developed, the troubles they'd had and the solutions they'd sought, how his initial infatuation with Marxism had gradually diminished, his relationship with Sendic and how he was imprisoned for seven long years for his beliefs. That chapter of his life was obviously no fun to remember, and I was hesitant to ask him about it. Mercedes had no such reservations.

'But they didn't beat you, did they?' she said, half statement, half question, referring to the vicious tortures that the military indulged in so systematically.

'Beat me?' he said, 'Beat me? They beat me until I had bruises on my bruises! I used to ask them why. Carlos, I used to say – because they all call themselves Carlos, you know, – Carlos, I said, why are you doing this? I tried to explain that it wouldn't do any good, not for their bosses and not for themselves in years to come, when they wouldn't be able to forget it and when at last they would come to understand that they'd just been used to do someone else's pointless dirty work, but they didn't want to know: they just kept on going, day after day.'

I just couldn't imagine that anyone would indulge in such bestial behaviour for no reason at all, however misguided, so I presumed that they'd been trying in their savage fashion to get Edenes to talk about something they considered important to know. I said so, and asked what it was that they had wanted Edenes to tell them.

'Tell them? Tell them what? I didn't know anything that they didn't know already. I would have answered if they'd asked, but they never asked me anything. They just hit me. And as for a reason, I don't believe they had one, apart from wanting to spread fear, so that their nefarious regime would work more efficiently. It was just an expression of their impotence. In the end they failed, anyhow.'

They may have beaten his body to rags, but they hadn't broken his spirit. But this isn't really the place to try to capture that extraordinary man: Edenes deserves a story all to himself. Night had fallen without our even noticing it, so enraptured had we sat and listened.

In mid-afternoon the following day Mercedes and María Elena drove out to pick us up and take us to visit Don Juan, one of the founder members of CALNU. As a Company Director in the days of CAINSA, he'd had a great deal to do with the unions. He was a wily old patriarch, and entertained us with his version of events.

'Sendic? Weeeell . . . ' he mused; 'he was just roaming the country trying to find a revolution he could join. A troublemaker, really. Pain in the arse. Oh, he was intelligent all right, very sharp, very shrewd, very political. But he wasn't from around here, wasn't in the industry, had nothing to do with sugar-cane. I doubt if he even knew what it was before he turned up on our doorstep. He wasn't really in the union, anyway. He was their so-called legal adviser. I've never understood why anyone ever followed him. He had no personal charisma, no charm, no spark. . . . Edenes Picón? Now *there's* a man for you. His appeal I can understand. A man of the people, a natural leader.'

As I listened to Don Juan, I detected what I thought was too fine a thread of irony to be true. Everything he said as he talked about the co-operativist ideology and promoting business in Bella Unión seemed to arrive, over a different route, at the same conclusions which Edenes had struggled so hard to achieve: the equitable distribution of wealth. And yet these two men had stood on opposite sides of a line that yawned like a gulf between them. Sendic had complained of the geography upon which his revolution had foundered. Edenes, with a different perspective, had attributed the ultimate failure of the union to excessive involvement in politics. And here was this man, espousing the principles which once, when enshrined in a cause, he'd opposed.

CHAPTER TEN

INTO THE HILLS

For some reason we didn't want to leave without a last look at Bella Unión. We told ourselves that it was because, in all the excitement of the last few days, we hadn't taken any photographs of the town; but as we pedalled around, clicking the shutter, we found ourselves drawn inexorably towards Edenes Picón's house. We didn't want to arrive empty-handed, so we stopped at a fruit stall before knocking on his door (or, to be more precise, calling 'Anybody home?' through the curtain).

They were in the kitchen finishing their lunch. Sheila insisted that we join them, refusing to accept 'no' for an answer. While we ate our ravioli, she bubbled over with stories and questions. She thought she might like to have a baby, and quizzed us implacably as to whether or not, in case it were a boy, there was a masculine form of 'Sheila'.

'Are you sure there's no English version of it?' she asked, 'I'm certain there is. How about Sheilof? Isn't there a name Sheilof in English? Are you absolutely sure?'

Her husband, by contrast, was quiet and subdued, watching his exuberant wife with evident affection.

Their home was very modest. It was built of rough bricks, with no proper pointing or finish as such, and the floor was bare cement. The furniture was rudimentary and worn. There was no bathroom in the house, for the simple reason that there was no plumbing, and that was because the mains hadn't yet reached this far along the road. They only had water at all thanks to a neighbour a few doors away, whose house *was* connected to the mains, and who had let them hook up a hosepipe across the back gardens. Their back yard, although fairly large, was a tangled and overgrown jungle of weeds, through which a few chickens squabbled and scratched.

'I'll have to do something about this one day,' said Edenes; 'tidy it up, maybe put down some vegetables. You know, after you left the other night, with you saying you wanted to write a book, I started to think about all the things we were discussing and I realized that nobody's ever written properly about those times, the growth of the unions here and all the things that happened. Maybe *I* should. I'd like to. But I've tried to write before, and I've never been happy with it. I'm more of a talker than a writer, really, my thoughts flow better that way. Maybe I should get hold of a cassette recorder and just talk, and then I can write it all down afterwards.'

I made him promise to try.

He laughed, 'It's funny, you know, how people you meet quite by accident can have such unexpected effects on your life.'

We had almost reached the intersection with the road to Tomás Gomensoro, where we would pick up the road to Artigas, when the two girls came racing up in the car.

'We were looking for you,' they said, 'we were afraid you might already have gone. We brought a picnic.'

María Elena indicated a basket in the back seat, covered with a red and white checkered cloth.

'We just have to pop into town for a minute, but we'll come back and meet you.'

We turned into the road east, cycled to where the tarmac ended, and settled in the shade of a large eucalyptus to wait. The road ahead was truly appalling. Patricia was bursting for a pee, and relieved herself right where we were, and only just in time, because a moment later Mercedes and María Elena were with us again. They unpacked the picnic: fresh rolls, salad, cold meats and some cheese. As we were helping ourselves, María Elena sat down on the grass and leaned back, resting her weight on her hands. For a moment she looked puzzled, and then deeply suspicious, and then she promptly stood up once again. The poor girl had placed her hand right in the wet spot Patricia had made. Although maybe she guessed, she said nothing, and we certainly didn't have the heart to confess. She was such a sweet, gentle girl, that the realization probably would have been quite a shock.

It was quite a while before a station wagon appeared. Crowded into the small cab were a man and his wife, their son, daughter-in-law and a small baby. They weren't going far: only to the Fiesta Criolla in Tomás Gomensoro. We spent a few minutes moving the picnic equipment which was tumbled any-old-how into the back – deck chairs, folding table, baskets and polystyrene boxes – to make space for ourselves and our bikes.

They dropped us off at the turning into the little town. For a moment we wondered whether or not we should break our journey here and go to the Fiesta too, but in the end decided against it. We had no idea what sort of terrain lay ahead of us, nor how long it would take us to cross it.

All we knew was that the road was fulfilling all the worst predictions we'd heard. We trudged off across the open farmland, yellow fields rippling in the breeze, praying that the stones wouldn't puncture our tyres. From the distance to our left the wind occasionally carried the cheers of the crowd at the rodeo. Five kilometres later we joined up with the Ruta 30. If anything, it was worse than the Gomensoro road. We could well understand why even the truck drivers avoided it. We settled down to wait in the shade. There was no traffic at all.

A couple of hours later, heartily fed up with hanging about in this deserted middle of nowhere, we saw a pillar of dust approaching slowly from the western horizon. It was being lifted by a cattle truck, a large articulated lorry with a steel cage at the back. Stopping in reply to our waves, the driver dropped down from the high cab and walked around to open the iron gate. Fortunately, he carried no cargo. The cage was set up for transporting sheep: mud-caked wooden planks had been laid across it halfway up to form a second floor. I climbed in and moved a few of them out of the way to make space for us. Dry dung was gathered in loose drifts everywhere, and the air was laden with the pungent smell of urine. Patricia joined me, the driver slammed the gate shut, and we started off along the road.

The rattle and clang was deafening as the truck bounced violently over the endless succession of pot-holes and rocks. We moved at quite a speed; the draught picked up the dust and the loose flakes of dung and sent them spinning around us in gritty mini-tornadoes that scratched at our eyes and stuck in our ears and our mouths. Patricia was leaning with her back to the gate, hanging onto the bars for dear life with one hand and holding her bike with the other. I stood facing her, legs wide apart, the wooden boards pressing into the small of my back.

'Oh, my tits!' she yelled.

'What?' I yelled back. I could have sworn she'd said something about tits.

'My tits!' she shouted again.

'Yes, very nice!' I said approvingly. In the heat she had long ago dispensed with her bra.

'No, you dingaling! I mean they hurt! All this bouncing!'

As we shook and jolted along, being thrown about by every bump as though we were feather-light, I felt myself being pushed steadily forwards. Looking around, I saw that the entire second floor was beginning to slide, and the gap we were standing in was getting steadily narrower. There was no chance of our being able to get the driver to stop while we adjusted the boards. The cab was a million miles away and out of sight; Patricia and I, a mere arm's length apart, had to yell at each other to make ourselves heard. Scrambling and cursing, struggling to keep my balance, I shifted the planks one by one before they cut us in half, while Patricia held on to the bikes.

The road twisted and dipped through countryside ever more desolate and wild, fording innumerable streams in deep, rocky beds. Some had washed up onto the road. Through the bars we could make out the scars of continual flooding. At last, after what seemed an eternity, the shuddering stopped. We had reached the fork in the road where we and the truck would part to go our separate ways. Although it meant that once again we were left on our own, we were glad of release from that clattering monster. For several minutes afterwards our ears were still ringing.

It was late afternoon. A few kilometres to the north was the spot where old chief Sepe had entertained himself for a couple of days doing macramé with Bernabé Rivera's hamstrings. About a kilometre and a half ahead of us, on the crest of a ridge, was a small wood. If we were going to have to camp somewhere until morning, that seemed a better place than here, in the middle of this wretched wasteland. Picking sheepshit and sand from our hair, we made our way to the top.

The western sky was turning to gold, and still we'd seen no signs of life. We sat disconsolate under the trees, wishing we'd gone to the Fiesta instead of trying to get to Artigas.

'I suppose we'd better choose a place for the tent, before it gets too dark.'

We wandered into the wood, kicking about in the carpet of leaves. Patricia picked a small posy of wild flowers. It looked as though we'd have to spend the night here. Then, looking up, we saw a column of dust moving along the road.

'Charrúas!' I said, pointing.

'Or maybe the cavalry!' said my wife. We raced back to the roadside, afraid that whoever it was might drive past without stopping, but we had to wait for several minutes before the car came into view. We realized then how deceptive the distances were.

The station wagon slowed to a halt in front of us. Crammed into the cab were half a dozen leering, shirtless, pot-bellied drunks. In the back were more drunks, a couple of large dogs and a mountain of furniture. They all laughed and cracked good-natured jokes, but there was no way on earth that we'd fit in there with them.

'Don't worry, don't worry,' slurred one of the chaps in the back, 'some friends of ours are coming along in another pickup like this one a couple of kilometres behind. They're pulling a trailer, they can fit you in there no sweat, bikes an' all. You jus' stay there, don't go away. Bye bye!' he waved, as the driver stepped on the gas.

Sure enough, a while later we saw headlights in the distance. The shadows were deep, darkness beginning to close. It was a pickup truck all right, just like the other, and just like the other it was stuffed full of drunks. The trailer behind it was filled – yes, you guessed it – with furniture, dogs and more drunks. Someone was obviously moving home but, considering the state they were all in, it was anybody's guess whether or not they would ever get there.

Night had fallen for good, and the stars had started to blink. We were about to surrender and put up the tent when another pair of headlights swept over the horizon and onto the plain. We watched them come slowly towards us. It was another pickup truck. A young gaucho with a large blond moustache slid out of the driver's seat. Luck was on our side: he was going all the way to Artigas.

'Now let's see, let's make you some room here . . . '

As I followed him round to the back of the truck, another man stepped out of the passenger seat. He was an older version of the driver, almost his twin but for the twenty-year difference in their ages.

'My father,' said the driver. A young boy peered at us through the windscreen: 'My son.'

Huddled against the cab in the back were two young men, surrounded by luggage, a large bottle of butane gas, nine bags of cement, a box of freshly caught fish, a sheep's carcass in a blood-sodden sack and masses of boxes and bags. We made space for the bikes and myself, and Patricia climbed into the cab with three generations of Arvizas.

For all of its 60 remaining kilometres, the road was an utter abomination, but our driver treated it as though it were smooth as new silk. He plunged through the darkness, oblivious to the stones, the holes and the rubbish thrown up by his wheels. In the back, the two young chaps and I were soon covered in dust and flying cement that had leaked from the bags. They were *zafreros*, itinerant labourers, moving from one job to look for another. One had already been travelling for years, chasing the crops and the seasons, and he was teaching his sidekick the ropes. He was full of advice about places to stop and those to avoid. Through the rear window I saw that the little boy had fallen asleep with his head on Patricia's shoulder. Now that the sun had gone, the air was chilly. In the open truck, buffeted by the wind, it was getting quite cold. I wondered what we would do when we eventually reached Artigas, and hoped that my wife was working out the details. I needn't have worried: when we stopped to drop off the *zafreros*, Mr Arviza came around to tell me that up in the cab the committee had decided we were going to a hotel, since at this time of night we'd never find anywhere to camp.

My teeth were chattering when we pulled up under a lantern in an Artigas backstreet. As soon as she saw me Patricia burst into peals of hysterical laughter.

'You're filthy!' she shrieked, 'you look like a panda!'

We had stopped in front of a run-down *pensión*, the Residencial Concordia. Mr Arviza said it was cheap and clean. I went in to check, and got a very odd look from the man at the desk. He showed me a room which looked good enough at a glance, so I came back outdoors with the news. Thanking our rescuers, we wheeled our bikes into a storeroom and mounted the stairs.

The footworn floor was chequered in black and white tiles. The lopsided furniture had been painted white *a la buena de Dios*, with all the edges picked out in virulent pink. The bedclothes were orange and the curtains were a mixed salad of bilious greens. On top of the bed, two drooping, threadbare, mismatched blue towels were folded in a failed attempt at decoration. The full effect was overwhelming.

'Aaargh!' said Patricia from the bathroom. SLAP! went her foot on the tiles. 'Cockroaches . . . '

I saw something peculiar looking at me from the mirror, and realized it was my reflection. My hair was matted and standing on end and, except for two paler patches around my eyes, all the rest of me was crusted and brown. Panda indeed . . .

'I need a drink,' I said, and we went off to find one before climbing into the shower. From a little shop around the corner we bought a bottle and a couple of packets of crisps. I managed to knock over my glass before even taking a sip, spilling grappa all over the floor.

'Never mind, it'll keep the mosquitoes away,' said Madame, as the smell of it rose in a dense cloud that made our eyes water for the tenth time that day.

I don't think I've ever been so dirty in my life: it seemed to take hours to wash it all off. The water poured off my body in a thick, muddy stream. Since so much of the dirt was cement dust, I wondered whether it might set in the pipes. It doesn't matter. Bed: just get me to bed.

The bikes, of course, were filthy too. The night man had said we'd be able to wash them in the morning, in a little patio beyond the back garden. The *pensión* was a rambling old house built around a tiled central courtyard choked with plants. On wooden benches along the veranda, half a dozen old duffers were drinking their *mate* and staring into space, fretting about the state of the nation, the state of the weather and the state of their livers. We wheeled our bikes through an archway, across an overgrown garden, and to a tiled square next to what must once have been stables. Against a wall stood a row of large, grey concrete washbasins. A couple of women were doing their laundry. I searched in vain for the promised hose. In the end I went back into the hotel to ask again. A woman with a face like a tin-opener scowled at me across the desk.

'Of course there's a hose,' she muttered, barely controlling her temper, and marched back outdoors with me.

It was in a small shed. She dropped it contemptuously at my feet, and stamped back indoors again. When I tried to connect the hose to a tap, I realized that there were no fittings on either end of it, and its diameter was smaller than the thickness of the taps. It didn't fit. Not by any stretch of the imagination.

'I know it doesn't fit,' scowled the concierge.

Back out she stormed, stopping on the way for a pan of boiling water. She dipped one end of the hose in it, to soften up the rubber so that it would stretch. Now it fitted on the tap. Without a word she left us again.

Artigas, capital of the province of Artigas, is a small, noisy city. We weren't in the mood for cities, we just wanted to get out. We were now heading south or, as Alberto had put it some days ago, downhill. But far from downhill, all of the slopes that we met travelled up. We were entering the foothills of the Cuchilla de Haedo, the first proper mountains we'd met in our trip, the first brown bits on a map which, so far, had remained persistently green. Of course, in Uruguay the term 'proper mountain' is relative: the highest in the land is a mere 501 metres, the sort of thing that doesn't even register on a map of Peru, but when you're on a bicycle your perspective is different. The landscape was craggy and broken, even the vegetation had changed, taking on a tropical look. The soil was as red as cayenne pepper. Coming out of town we flew down a long, steep slope, perhaps our last now for several days, and laboured up an identical one on the other side of the valley, racing two boys in a horse-drawn cart. We won, by the way.

Buzzards circled high on the upwind over the stony plateau. Dense forests loomed on either side of the road. Through occasional breaks in the wood we saw fields of tobacco and even, surprisingly, a rice paddy, its watery, emerald bed flashing bright in the sun.

Thirty kilometres later, at a bridge that spanned the dry, rocky bed of a stream, the tarmac petered out and disappeared. There was nothing to do but get off and walk. We reached a fork in the road, where a broken-down sign announced that the new highway was under construction. The branch to the left was no more than torn up, untidy ground. We identified the spot on our map and saw that the two ways joined up again about 20 kilometres further on, not that it made a great deal of difference to us now. Of far more interest, we saw that not too forbiddingly far into the woods up ahead was a stream.

'Perhaps we can go for a swim,' I suggested.

It was better than standing around hoping to hitchhike a lift in a car that didn't exist. We plodded on. The heat was so intense that my Japanese computerized speedometer gave up the struggle and died, its microchip guts in a mess. The stream, when we reached it, was perfect. We had just scrambled down the bank to have a closer look at the water when we heard the sound of an engine. Around a bend in the road a small lorry was coming towards us. Shouting and waving, we barely managed to catch the driver's attention in time. The lorry slid to a halt in the dust. To our joy there was plenty of space for us, even though we had to move a few pieces of timber before getting in. A small, corgi-type mongrel looked at us sleepily from under a bench. Robbed of our swim, at least we had managed a lift.

We sat back and relaxed, watching the country go by. Even the slip-stream was hot as the lorry charged through the broken, tumbledown hills. Enormous rocks jutted out of the grass all over the place. The ever-changing view was magnificent, but we were glad we weren't having to walk through it. We sped past the fork where the two branches of road joined up again, and soon after that reached the turning that led to our driver's estate. He stuck his bearded face out of the cab, and invited us up to the house. It wasn't far, he said, in soft *Portuñol*.

The driveway was steep and littered with pieces of quartz, but we weren't quite prepared for what we saw when we got to the house. To one side of it there was a large water-tank, like Jaime's at Los Macachines but, instead of cement, this one was built out of stones. A good third of the blocks were quartzes, broken open to reveal their glittering, crystal hearts. A barn and a cowdip were built the same way. I could never describe them as beautiful but here, where the ground was littered with mineral stars, they somehow seemed to fit. People spilled out of the house when they heard the sound of the lorry. Of course they wanted to know who we were, what we were doing and all that sort of thing. Surrounded by the family, we sat in the shade and drank our way through two large jugs of water. One of the children, disappearing indoors, came back to give Patricia a rough piece of amethyst the colour and size of a plum.

The road ran along through the scrub on the brow of a high, barren ridge. To either side of us the land fell away into deep distant valleys where the faraway groves of eucalyptus on the plain looked like small woolly caterpillars. Rising like walls in a haze, we could make out the purple-grey outlines of hills. In the late afternoon, the going was heavy. The wind had been against us for ages, but somehow that didn't explain it. We stopped to check whether something was wrong with our bikes. I squatted by my back wheel, fiddling with the chain, but everything looked in good order.

'Yuk!' said Patricia, a couple of metres away. 'So that's what it is.'

'So what's what it is?'

'That,' she said. 'Look . . . '

She lifted a foot. It made a sucking noise as it came away from the surface, leaving its imprint behind. We looked back the way we had come and there, sure enough, as plain as the nose on your face, were the tracks of our tyres in the tar. No wonder the going was tough: the road had turned to molasses.

A minuscule hamlet lay by the side of the road. We stopped at the police station on the corner, and sat on the edge of the porch with our feet dangling down, for a rest.

'I've had it,' groaned Patricia, 'I'm damned if I'm going any further.'

We walked our bicycles uphill to the end of the track, where the policeman had said we'd find a shop. A horse was tethered outside the small wooden shack. We went indoors and collapsed on a bench in the gloom. A dusty old gaucho, having a drink at the counter, squinted in our direction.

'Tired?' he asked.

'*Molidos,*' we both said at once.

The young shopkeeper looked us over, nodding his head up and down. 'Oof!' he said. 'Pah!' he said. '*Ahi 'tá!*' he added.

He was uncommonly tall. His nose was enormous and his ears stuck out like wings. The pendulous lobes wobbled as he nodded his head. He gave us a grin without any front teeth at the top.

'Yup!' he said, rubbing the bar with a rag.

'Could we have a large mineral water, please?' I asked.

'Oof!' he said. 'Pah!' he said, diving into the fridge as though trying to murder the alien he'd spotted inside. 'That's it!' he said loudly, banging the bottle onto the bar: 'Yup!'

We asked whether he could suggest a place for us to pitch our tent. He was very friendly and dreadfully keen to help, but he answered in so tangled and mixed-up a torrent of Spanish and rough Portuguese, that I doubt whether he could even understand it himself. Eventually we were able to work out that he meant the farm next door, but just in case we'd got it wrong, I asked once again.

'Yup!' he said proudly, 'That's it!' with a grin.

We walked round to the back of the house, where a radio in the kitchen was blaring the news. A young gaucho, dressed in his best, put his head through the door. His navy blue *bombachas* had a delicate pattern of flowers embroidered up the legs along the outer seam, and a white band around the crown of his hat proclaimed '*Defendiendo la Patria*' in bold red letters.

With the sun slowly sinking we put up the tent near the gate, and spread the tarpaulin on the ground. We dug out the food: tomatoes, pimentoes, cheese, a tin of sardines, a piece of sausage and some bread, and were just settling down for a little cocktail party when the *capataz*, looking tough and hard-bitten, came marching across the field toward us.

'You going to want to eat?' he asked without ceremony.

In any other situation such a gruff approach could easily have been misunderstood, but somehow we knew he was inviting us to dinner. We thanked him, but explained that we'd brought our own food and would hate to have it go off. Instead we invited him to join us, but he said he had things to do and stamped away again. A few minutes later, he came back.

'You *sure* you don't want to eat?' he asked. 'You should eat.'

We were sorely tempted to accept and we really didn't want to offend him, but neither could we afford to waste the food we'd already prepared.

'*La patrona* isn't going to like it . . . ' he threatened, meaning his wife.

'No, please . . . ' I said, 'we really appreciate your invitation, but we can't throw all this away. But thank you very much. Are you sure I can't interest you in a *grappita* at least?'

Somehow I knew that my urbane attempts at politeness weren't cutting any ice with this *paisano*.

'Hmph!' he snorted, casting a sceptical eye over our spread. It was clear from the look on his face that what he could see wasn't 'food'.

'*Hasta mañana*, then,' he said, and turned on his heel.

We lay there for a while, sipping our drinks and nibbling our feast, watching the sky changing colour. A woman and half a dozen children, astride two sleepy horses, ambled past on the other side of the gate. We waved.

'*Buenas noches!*' the children all called out in chorus.

When we awoke the next morning a thick, impervious mist lay in the hollows and valleys around us, cutting us off from the rest of the world. Invisible farmhands were gathering the flock in a neighbouring field. We could hear the drumming of hooves and the sound of their voices, and from time to time a man on a horse loomed like a phantom before disappearing again.

We managed to get an early start, for once. It was eerie to cycle through that dense opacity without being able to see beyond the bracken on the verge, but the sun soon gathered strength and slowly unveiled the blunt hilltops, for a while leaving them stranded like islands, before it finally stripped the last wisps from the land. We were still high on the Cuchilla. Lizards, basking on the road, darted under cover as we drew near. For some kilometres we travelled alongside drystone walls which might have reminded us of the north of England had not the heaths they enclosed been quite so vast. In the civil war of 1904, the *Colorado* government troops at last defeated the insurgent *Blancos*, led by Aparicio Saravia, amongst these hills. These very drystone walls were used very effectively as fortifications in the crude and bitter final battle which left Saravia mortally wounded and the field littered with dead. Many of the troops were untrained irregulars, and the machine gun had only recently appeared on the scene. The carnage was horrendous, with losses on both sides running at about 20 per cent, but it put an end at last to the long and destructive cycle of war on Uruguayan soil. Besides putting my great-grandfather out of business, Batlle, leader of the *Colorados* and president at the time, had a profound effect on the nation's development and system of government. He secularized the state, expanded even further the concept of public education and instituted far-reaching social reforms, including universal suffrage, women's rights (even an enlightened divorce law which rendered unnecessary the husband's consent), socialized medicine, a state pension plan and labour legislation which protected the worker and made compulsory a weekly day of rest.

We reached the village of Masoller in broad sunshine. On our left, at the side of the road, there was a large, rusty, corrugated-iron barn with a chipped enamel sign saying *Aduana* hanging on its wall. How quaint, we thought, checking our map, to have a customs shed so far from the border. Only with a second look did we notice the inscription 'border contested'. These bloody Brazilians are at it again, I complained, eating up Uruguay a mouthful at a time! I made the same observation when we stopped for a drink at the general store, which made the shopkeeper laugh.

'Not them,' she said, 'it's us!'

It turned out that Uruguay, and not Brazil, had taken to contesting the border, settled by treaty in the last century. The basis for the claim was that the intention of the agreement had been to lay the dividing line along the bed of the deepest stream. Not long ago a stream other than the one chosen was found to be deeper and, predictably, the underdog cried 'foul!'. In the interim, of course, a village complete with shops and schools and a sizeable population had sprung up on the Brazilian side, and the local inhabitants – never mind the government – understandably were none too keen suddenly to become Uruguayan.

We crossed the road and the no-man's-land of dry, well-trodden earth that marked the frontier, and went into a general store on the Brazilian side. There we bought some *goiabada*, a jam made from guavas which sets hard, like cheese. The storekeeper spoke the same impenetrable patois we'd grown familiar with on our own side of the border. He was quite happy to be paid in Uruguayan *pesos*.

Almost imperceptibly, the road had been climbing all morning, following the brow of the ridge. Small streams, sometimes no more than rain-water channels, ran down the sharp groins between the hills, nourishing ribbons of trees and lush vegetation. Gradually the landscape began to change, and soon that lushness was all around us: the slopes were woolly with trees, and the air echoed with the voices of birds. We passed a succession of signs that warned us of a sharp descent ahead, instructing us to keep our vehicles in gear and our eyes on the road, and not to exceed the speed limit. It was the infamous Heartbreak Hill, the *Bajada* or *Subida*, depending on how you approached it – *de las Penas*. We'd been looking forward to this for days, imagining the wonderful glide back down to the plains.

In the event, it was a severe disappointment. The land fell away far too sharply and the road twisted and turned much too tightly for us to let go of the brakes, so we had a hesitant, halting descent under the watchful eye of the *urubús* that hung on the wind. But one should be grateful for small mercies: at least we didn't have to go *up* it! To our dismay, *Penas* didn't mark the end of the hills. We found ourselves having to climb slopes far steeper than any before and, to add insult to injury, the road continually returned us to the plain only to make us climb upward again a little while later. Luckily, after a month on our bikes, we were fit and strong and, despite our curses and complaints, were able to manage quite adequately. Had we run into this at the start of our trip, it would probably have killed us. Or we'd have given up.

It was mid-afternoon, and unbelievably hot. Needing supplies, we took a fork into the town of Tranqueras, probably the dreariest and deadest of all the dead towns we'd seen. Physically it reminded us of Bella Unión, but whereas that town was vital and overflowing with energy, this one felt abandoned and unloved. We did our shopping as fast as we could, watched by a family as though we were monsters from Mars, and headed hastily southeast. Patricia was eager to get to Ruta 5, the main highway south to Tacuarembó.

At the junction, which we reached in late afternoon, highway repairs were in full, messy swing. We stopped to refill our water bottles at a *Policía Caminera* station. The patrolmen were playing cards. As we stood outside, leaning on the window-sill, chatting to them, one of them made a casual remark which caught our attention at once.

'What a coincidence,' he said, 'only a couple of days ago we had another chap here who was travelling around the country. A crazy Brazilian.'

Could it have been Florentino, the man we met in Colonia? We asked.

'Yeah, that sounds like the man. Carrying a flag and a whole lot of luggage. *Un loco*. He wanted us to drive him around all over the place. But we had orders from headquarters not to.'

'Luggage?' I asked. 'But wasn't there another man with him? When we saw him he only carried the flag. His companion was carrying the luggage. Didn't he have a companion with him?'

'No, he was on his own.'

'Well he did have,' said another, 'but not any more.'

'What happened? Did he give up or something?'

'No, not exactly . . . '

He seemed reluctant to say anything else, which intrigued me, so I insisted.

'Well, I suppose there's no harm in telling you. His companion's in prison for stealing.'

'Stealing? What did he steal? Poor chap: they were probably hungry.'

'No, no: stealing food when you've got nothing to eat carries no sentence. It's considered a crime with justifiable cause. It was theft, plain and simple, and they threw him in jail. And when he got caught it was found not to have been the first time, either.'

We thought of poor old Florentino, now having to plod his way to Brasilia alone. What a blemish on his mission for world peace!

The policemen suggested that the best place for us to pitch our tent was under the pines across the road. 'Nice spot there,' they agreed. We went for a look and found that they were right, despite the noisy roadworks yard not far away, so we decided to stay. The thick branches hung all the way down to the ground, hiding the clearing behind them. The neighbouring field was full of cattle, and in the failing light several curious cows wandered up to the fence behind our tent for a look at us. We hadn't heard them approach, and were startled when one started lowing. Soon after nightfall the generator in the yard stopped, casting the world into darkness and restoring the peace.

CHAPTER ELEVEN

A NIGHT ON BALD MOUNTAIN

The morning dawned misty again, and we set off in a fine drizzle. Miniature rivers of moisture seeped from cracks in the high stone embankments that stood like walls at our sides. Frogs croaked in the gutters, and a large brown snake wriggled across our path. As the mist cleared and the drizzle stopped, the air became less oppressive, although the sky remained impassively grey. The landscape opened up, and we began to see the table-top mountains so typical of the region. In some remote geological yesterday, all of this land had been a high plateau. Erosion over the ages had cut first grooves and then channels and then canyons, and these had spread out into plains. Along those plains we were now travelling, the road winding along in between the remains of that ancient *meseta*, now cut and reduced into massive, isolated hills, all the same height, all perfectly flat on the top, as though a giant scythe had come down from the sky and chopped off the peaks. Beneath the heavy, threatening sky, grey streaked with purple and black, bathed in a ghostly, glistening light, it was as though we were approaching the gates of Mordor. The illusion was heightened when, on the horizon, an electrical storm started flexing its dynamo muscles. Bolts of lightning raced like luminous whips across the charcoal grey. We could hear them rumble and hiss.

'Can you imagine what it would be like to watch the storm from the top of one of those mountains?'

The idea was enthralling. It obsessed us as we analysed each hill with a view to climbing it up to the top. They were all too far away from the road. We would have to hike across the heath for hours before even reaching their ponderous feet.

'Well, it still was a good idea,' I said. 'Maybe next trip.'

Unconvinced, Patricia looked at me out of the sides of her eyes.

By the road two men were guarding a pyramid of corncobs. Twenty-five pesos each, said a sign (5 pence, at the time). Being big spenders, we bought four.

On the horizon the storm was gathering strength. At any minute now it was sure to engulf us. The light was so unusual that we stopped to take pictures of some horses on a slope.

'We can climb up that one,' said the wife, 'it's close.' It was, too.

'But what do we do with the bikes? And we don't have any food, except for the corn.'

'Those *zafreros* the other day said that people would feed you if you asked them. And we passed a gate about half a kilometre back.'

At the end of the driveway we came to a barn, attached to a windowless wall with a single door in it. Enclosed by a fence overgrown with flowering ivy, we could see an orchard. Amongst the fruit trees were long trestle tables laden with halved peaches, laid out to dry in the sun. To the other side of the barn there was a low shed in the lee of a fig tree and, beneath it, two old men sat drinking *mate*. A very small dog came running towards us, yelling obscenities at the top of his voice.

'*Picho!*' called one of the men, but the dog paid no heed. Yap yap yap he yelled.

'*Venga p'acá, aijuna!*'

The watchdog relented. One of the men limped up to us. He was ancient. His face was covered in wrinkles that spoke of his years in the fields.

'Justo,' he said, 'pleased to meet you.'

I explained to him why we had stopped.

'Ah, you'll want to talk to the *patrón* then, just wait a minute.'

He walked through the door in the wall. The other man nodded and smiled. Over our heads, the sun was trying to break through the clouds.

Mr Jauregui was awfully close to Justo in age.

'Huh!' he grunted, which we knew was hysterical laughter, when we asked for permission to camp on the top of his hill.

'Food?' he asked.

'Well, actually, we don't have any, no, we usually stop and buy some before we make camp, but it's early for us today, you see, there weren't any shops on the way, we usually stop at a shop, you see, we were wondering whether you might be able to sell us a bit of meat or something . . . '

I needn't have bothered. He had long since gone back through the wall.

'This enough?' he said, holding up a shoulder of lamb with all of the ribs. The meat had been rinsed, but it still was covered in ants.

'Know how to start a fire?'

'Um . . . yes, well, yes, of course, but let me pay you for it, we don't want to abuse your hospitality.'

'We'll see about that,' he said gruffly. 'The hill's over there.'

Leaving our bikes in the barn, we chose what we needed and slung it on our shoulders. Justo and his buddy grinned as we passed.

From the road the hill had looked small. Standing at its roots, it loomed above us enormous. With a blunt, calloused finger Mr Jauregui had pointed out the best route of ascent. Over that hump, around the trees, along the brook, there, where the cows are, behind the rocks. It seemed to take us forever but then, at last, we were there.

We left our things on a stone, and set off to explore the *Cerro Chato*. Covered in yellowing bracken and grass it was almost completely flat, bulging slightly in the middle. Because of the high plateau's abrupt rim, one had the impression of being at the edge of the world. The *patrón* had mentioned a wood to the east. It was a precarious tangle of trees clutching on by the roots down a steep, sudden gully: a throat carved into the hillside, plummetting down to the plain. As we drew near, a flock of sheep ran bleating from the shade where they'd been sheltering from the sun.

I collected some branches and started a fire while Patricia settled down to trim the fat from the quarter of lamb. Once we had the embers glowing we spread the meat and a couple of corncobs on the grille, and lay down on our backs while it roasted, to watch the clouds chasing each other across the sky. Up there in the heights the wind must have been pretty strong. A fast, sudden movement in the grass at my side stole my attention. It was a lizard, a full metre long. Unaccustomed to people, it thought it had nothing to fear, and had stopped very near us. It stood like a statue and watched through patient, inscrutable eyes.

'Look,' said my wife, 'a *lagarto*! Let's give it something to eat.'

She picked up a piece of the fat she'd discarded, and threw it onto a stone.

'Here, López!'

For a while the lizard didn't move. Maybe it wasn't called López. Then it drew closer.

'He likes it,' she said, 'he can smell the meat.'

'Nonsense!' I said. 'It doesn't want meat. It wants the flies that are collecting around it.'

As though fired on the end of a spring, the reptile lunged forward and took up the offered morsel, fully as big as its head, swallowing it whole.

'You see?' gloated Patricia, 'I told you he wanted the meat.'

Chastized, I watched as she fed it some more, and some more, and then even some more, bringing him a little bit closer with every mouthful until, solidly stuffed and unable to move any further, López Lagarto collapsed in the sun an arm's length away. All told, he'd eaten at least 200 grammes of our leftovers. If he had children, and he talked to them, he would probably tell them for years of the day that fat fell out of the sky.

After lunch we went for a walk. The view from our mountain was truly spectacular. The road far below us looked like a piece of grey string, and a couple of articulated lorries moving slowly along it seemed no larger than Dinky toys. We could hear the faint sound of their straining engines carried on the wind. Around us we could see other table-top hills. From the ground they had seemed to stand alone, but from up here we could see how they all would have linked together to form that ancient plateau. Mr Jauregui had told us that there was a spring up here somewhere and, in case it was big enough, we'd brought our soap with us. We hadn't bathed for days, and were beginning to smell a bit ripe. We found the pool, but it was mostly mud and we couldn't even rescue enough water to drink.

Time had flown by, and the afternoon had turned hot. One thing we'd learned in all these weeks was how to get instantly neurotic when our water began to run out. I was elected to skate down the hill again to the house. A family of ducks floated peacefully on a pond. Some cows that had been grazing in the field ambled curiously up and followed me towards the gate, thinking it was time to be milked. A very large ox gave me a fright when it nudged the small of my back with its nose, pushing me forcibly forwards a couple of steps. A beautiful honey-coloured Jersey cow with large, liquid eyes designed by Walt Disney stood in my path, refusing to move. I stopped, and in no time at all was surrounded by cattle, huddling together, all watching and waiting to see what I would do. I could feel their hot breath on my skin. I knew they were harmless but they unsettled me, perhaps because they were so close and so keen to get closer. Behaving just like the crowds of people that gather when something unusual happens on the pavement, the ones at the back were pushing and shoving to get to the front: they wanted to see the card trick too.

'Come on,' I muttered, 'get out of my way, I have things to do.'

But perhaps, being Uruguayan cows, they didn't speak English, so I repeated my request in Spanish, inwardly kicking myself for such silly behaviour. High on the hilltop, silhouetted against the infinite blue, I could see my tiny wife waving and laughing her head off, slapping her hands on her knees. Positive, forceful behaviour is the only way out of this, I decided, and started walking forwards again. I had to push my way through, brushing against their bellies and rumps.

Having filled the bottles from a tap, I was on my way back when old Justo intercepted me for a chat. He used to be the foreman here, he said. He was retired now, seventy-two, but he'd been on this farm all his life and he was ready to die here.

'Yup,' he said with a grin, 'if I have to go, this is where I go from.'

This was his home, and the *patrón* and the *señora* wouldn't hear of him living anywhere else, which suited him just fine. He didn't want to live anywhere else. There were traces of Negro blood in his wrinkled, luminous face. One of his legs was stiff, perhaps the reminder of some old accident, which gave him a halting limp. I mentioned my encounter with the ox.

'Yeah, we use them for ploughing,' he said, 'stubborn, ornery bastards but a whole lot better than machines. Give you time to think and look around. Don't make any noise, either. You just walk along, gently gently behind them, and then, when you're ready, the field is done. Some folks use tractors. Can't understand what the damned hurry is. The field ain't gonna go away.'

He was on his way to have his bath in the duckpond, just as he'd done every day of his life, summer or winter. Yup.

I struggled back up the slope, to where Patricia had pitched the tent facing east, near the lip. We sat in front of it, soaking up the silence. The mackerel sky seemed to burst into flames as the clouds were caught by the sunset. By the time we made it to bed a haze was hiding the stars, but we woke up again around midnight and came out to watch the display. There was never a name more apt than Milky Way.

The morning broke misty again. Low-flying clouds were caught on the lips of the mountains around of us, drawn by the breeze into long, tattered strands. On our way to the path that would lead us downhill, Patricia said 'Look! Little snakes.' There in the grass at our feet were three or four, about the length and size of pencils, the criss-crossed diamond design on their backs giving way to a pale underbelly.

'I wonder what they are,' said Patricia.

'No idea. But let's avoid them, just in case.'

On the road outside the gate we saw another, squashed flat by a passing car. The weather was unsettled, alternating sunshine with cloud, and the air was hot and oppressive. We found the pedalling tough and unrewarding, and still weren't into the swing of it when, bathed in sticky perspiration, we reached the Rio Tacuarembó. By now we were smelling like foxes, so into the river we went, soap and shampoo and razor, the lot, let the cool clear water soak into our grumbling joints. For Patricia, accustomed to hot showers on demand, an impressive array of scented soaps and creams always within easy reach, the inability to bathe and groom herself properly every day was one of the most difficult aspects of the journey.

As we worked our way around the country we'd been very saddened to see the inevitable toll of animals and birds knocked down by the traffic. On this stuffy morning we kept finding large, mysterious stains on the road, like sticky splashes, although there was no trace of what might have caused them. More run-over animals, I guessed, despite the absence of carcasses. There were so many of them, though, that I grew more and more intrigued.

'Falling water-melons,' announced Patricia.

I looked cautiously up at the sky, feeling a profound kinship with Chicken Little.

'Do they fall very often?' I asked, not really wanting to know: 'From very high up?'

'From trucks, you clot. From trucks!'

Surrounded by wheat fields and enormous herds of cattle, we grew ever more tired, and I became ever more convinced that there are more hills in the world going up than hills coming down.

In Tacuarembó, while we sat on a bench eating an ice-cream, a gypsy came up to us and tried to sell us a set of enamelled cast-iron oven dishes. Heaven knows how she could carry them around. She wore a billowing, bright orange dress, cut low in the front to expose a magnificent bosom, and a bright green silk scarf tied over her hair, which was the colour of honey and twined into a long braid that hung down her back. Her eyes were a pale, transparent blue and stood out like lights in her cinnamon skin. In her youth she must have been very beautiful but, although only in her early thirties, she hadn't worn very well. Her face was lined and her hands were like garden tools. I'd been appalled to see her approach, as the gypsies in Uruguay just won't leave you alone until they've separated you from some of your money, but somehow Patricia charmed her to a standstill and, after chatting for a while, the woman wished us good luck and walked off in search of another target.

The tree-lined road climbed and dipped and climbed again. Patricia, her early difficulties completely forgotten, was steaming along like an Amazon but I was exhausted, and had to keep stopping. My knees just didn't want any more. Climbing that mountain twice in one day had worn me out. In a little hollow a man and a boy were trying to saddle a horse. We coasted down the slope and stopped alongside them. The man's car was parked by the fence. The name of a local firm of rural auctioneers was painted on its door. The man was dressed, although informally, in 'city' clothes. Could he recommend a place where we might stop for the night, preferably nearby?

'Yes, of couse,' he said, 'I've got a little place just up ahead. It's only a field, mind you, I just bought it a couple of months ago as pasture. I've got a man there now, he's mending the old shack. Go on ahead, I'll meet you there. It's up on the left.'

'On the left, how far ahead?'

'There, there, you can see it, at the top of the hill, first gate.'

It took all the willpower I could muster to pedal the last 500 metres, but we made it. The man overtook us as we followed the track to the shed. When we got there he was talking to another man who was banging and chopping away at some boards. As we drew up to them the auctioneer introduced himself as Páez, and this man as Alvarez.

'I was just telling Alvarez,' said Páez, 'that I was down at the *frigorífico* this afternoon, and bought some pretty good stuff. What do you say I come back tonight with my family, and we all have an *asado* together?'

How could we possibly refuse?

'So that's settled, then. I'll see you again in a couple of hours.'

'Come in,' said Alvarez gruffly, 'sit down.'

He waved us towards a rough wooden bench against the wall. I collapsed onto it gratefully.

The shack was very rough. A small, square, windowless room – containing a bed, a chair and some shelves – was set into the corner of a larger rectangle, the main body of the shed, where we now were. The bedroom walls were made of cut turves stacked on top of each other like bricks. Grass continued to grow from the joins, and hung down in fronds like living wallpaper.

'It's getting a bit whiskery,' said Alvarez, 'I'll have to give it a trim soon.'

The outer room was enclosed on three sides by walls of roughly cut eucalyptus planks, and open on the fourth. For much of their lengths these walls were only chest-high: the upper half was hinged along the top so that it could be swung open to let in air and light. The sloping roof was made of coarse thatch. ('Have to get that done next.') In the middle of the bare, beaten earth floor, the remains of a fire were still smoking.

'I can put some water on to boil if you'd like a *mate*,' said Alvarez.

Greying at the temples, he was lean and fibrous, his ropy muscles clearly defined. He seemed incapable of sitting still. Even while he talked he was hacking at bits of wood, sweeping the floor or tidying up his toolbox, a stained, disreputable hand-rolled cigarette permanently stuck in the corner of his mouth.

'I'll get you some water from the well. Dug it just the other day. C'mon, I'll show you.'

He led us outside the shed. Surrounded by heaps of drying clay, there was a perfectly round hole in the ground.

'Just have to line the inside, now. Do that next week, when Páez brings the bricks. He had the water tested. Pure as pure. Tastes good, too. Here, try some.'

He pulled up a bucket on the end of a rope. It was completely clear, ice-cold and utterly delicious, with a faint stony flavour. Back in the shed he filled up the battered black kettle, and balanced it on a wire frame over the embers.

'Ready in a minute,' he said. 'I suppose I'd better tidy up if Páez is bringing the family. Need firewood, too.'

I offered to help him but to my delight he turned me down. I was happy just to sit here at the table, leaning against the wall. As though infected by our host's nervous energy, Patricia rinsed some of the fruit we'd brought, prepared a *mate* for me and did all our laundry in a bucket with water drawn from the well. Then she rigged up a clothes-line and hung all the clothes out to dry. I just stayed put on my bench, and minded my own business.

'Right,' said Alvarez. 'That's that. Time for my bath now. If you want a bath,' he added, 'use the creek over there.' He pointed. 'Not that pond there.' He pointed in the other direction. 'Has leeches in it. Darned nuisance, too. Must find out how to get rid of them without ruining the water.'

With that he threw a towel over his shoulder and, carrying some clean clothes and a large bar of soap, disappeared towards the creek at the foot of the meadow.

When he came back he combed his hair, made himself a *mate* and, for the first time, sat down. The three of us were talking quietly about nothing in particular when the lad we'd seen earlier – who turned out to be nearly twenty years old, although he certainly didn't look or act it – cantered up, a little dog in his lap. He was Páez's son, and Alvarez soon had him starting the fire for the *asado* in the centre of the floor. The horse, which he'd tethered by the open end of the shed, was the fattest horse I've ever seen, and stood there farting sonorously until the lad moved him away in disgust.

As night fell Páez arrived with his wife and his son's girlfriend, bringing with them a mountain of meat, a tray of tomato salad, and a demijohn of red wine. They set up the grille which, to our amusement, we saw had been made out of a bicycle wheel and a piece of wire mesh cut from bedsprings, and put Páez junior in charge.

Food and drink were two of life's great pleasures for the robust Mr Páez, and he described with eloquent joy some of the great meals he'd eaten and the details of their preparation, keeping a constant watchful eye on his son's work at the fire.

'You're spoiling that boy, m'dear,' he murmured mildly to his wife.

For some years he'd been managing *estancias* for absentee landlords, and now he'd bought this piece of land as an experiment. He was going to split it up into paddocks, and planned to graze sheep there in rotation, apparently not the traditional way of doing things. He still didn't know how large a flock the land would support when used that way, but he aimed to find out. He was a warm, amenable man who believed in earning his relaxation by working hard, and he attributed most of the country's problems to the fact that nobody else seemed to feel the same way. Now where have I heard that before?

'They all want it easy,' he said. 'Give them a golden opportunity, and they blow it.'

He went on to tell us a story, which seemed to bother him deeply, about a large sale of lemons that had been made to Poland, on the strength of a sample shipment. Apparently the producers, whose lemons didn't all measure up to the standard set by the samples, had filled up the boxes with their usual stock, adding a layer of the good ones on top. To their horror, Poland returned the lot.

There was something primitive and deeply comforting about sitting in that dimly lit shed with these kind, hospitable strangers, flickering flames chasing nimble shadows around the wooden walls, washing that wonderful meal down with generous helpings of wine. It was late when we went to our beds, sated and somehow enhanced.

CHAPTER TWELVE

FIESTA CRIOLLA

The sun had turned the tent into a bread oven. From somewhere in the middle distance I could hear the sound of vigorous hammering and sawing. The faithful wife wanted to sleep for just a few minutes more, so I wandered across to the *ranchito* on my own. Alvarez had already tidied up all traces of last night's *asado*, and was now making a door. The kettle was simmering on the embers so, at his instigation, I made myself a morning *mate* and sat down at the rickety table. He came in to join me under the thatch.

He'd been in the army for 21 years, he said, in the cavalry regiment whose barracks we'd passed on the way into Tacuarembó. Originally he'd signed on for 15 years but, attracted by the prospect of a good pension, had decided to stay on for another 15 until, one fine day, he just couldn't stick it any longer. From there he went to work at the *frigorífico*, where he stayed for 11 years, although he didn't like that much, either. He'd realized, perhaps a little late, that he didn't like to be bossed around. But at least he had his army pension. Well, 'got' wasn't quite the word: he'd qualified for it. It would still take another two years to reach him. Retroactive too, in a lump sum, although he'd lose the interest of course. He was going to put some of it into this sheep project, which he'd be taking care of as foreman. That's why he was fixing up the *ranchito*, see, because he'd be living here most of the time.

He has a house in Tacuarembó, but he prefers it out here in the open, with some work to do. He likes to work. Keeps him fit. He likes to keep fit. Look at him: strong, healthy, 53 years old, you know; oh yes, 54 on 29 March. He smokes. It's his only vice. And *mate*. Must have *mate*. Oh, yes, *mate* and cigarettes. Women and strong drink: he can take or leave. He likes them, but he can live without. Right now he earns more money than he can spend, living out here on his own, but if he feels like it, he just goes into town and has a whisky or a *caña* or whatever he likes. Oh yes, he can drink as many as he wants: four, five, eleven. . . . But if he doesn't want to, why, he can go for months without a drink. Doesn't need it, you see. Quite happy not to eat meat, too. He likes it, but vegetables can be made very tasty too, you know. A lot of goodness in them. Don't need meat. Look at him: strong, healthy, almost 54. Mutton's the worst: all that fat. Gets stuck in your veins. Potatoes are good. You can do a lot of things with potatoes. Full of vitamins. And exercise, that's good too. Work is exercise, helps him keep his muscle tone, keeps him fit: he can still whip any young fella who comes looking for trouble. But cigarettes, well, that's his only bad habit. Yes, he knows they're bad for him, but at his age: what can he do? Smoked all his life. Doesn't want to stop now. Make him work as hard as you like, all the hours that God sends, but don't take away his cigarettes or his *mate*, oh no, if you do that, well, that's the end of your workman. Down go the tools and he'll walk into town if he has to. Yup. To get his cigarettes and his *mate*. Wouldn't do that for anything else, mind you, but a man has to have his little pleasures. Even when he knows they're bad for him.

Doesn't care much about money. That's not what makes him work. He works because he likes to, it keeps him busy, keeps him fit. When he's got money he spends it. Or sometimes he saves it. You never know. There might be some left over at the end for his kids, and there might not be. Doesn't really matter. They can work. He's worked all his life. He likes it. Prefers to work alone, though, set his own pace. Other people can never keep up with him. It was always like that in the army. His commanding officer hardly ever gave him anything to do, just left him to it, and everything got done. Everything: building, cleaning, moving, fixing . . . everything. Working with his body, you know. And his tools. Must have his own tools. Doesn't like using other people's tools. They don't know how to take care of them. Doesn't feel right. A man has to have his own tools.

Every headwind we'd ever met paled into insignificance by comparison with what awaited us out on the road. Until it died down, we even had to pedal downhill as well as up. Although it had much in common with the countryside along the littoral of the Río Uruguay, the land seemed more open, more primeval, certainly far less populated.

We came to a ridge, the Cuchilla del Ombú, which had been struck not long ago by a freakish wind that had destroyed a swathe about 200 metres wide. A eucalyptus forest had a broad strip torn out of its heart, and part of a farmhouse had been reduced to rubble. Chickens had died, cows had miscarried, horses had bolted and damaged themselves. The roof had come off the barn, and two truckloads of wool, paid for and awaiting collection, had been spread all over the meadow. Curiously, the farm across the road had been left intact and untouched.

It was gusty and overcast when we met the Río Tacuarembó again, about 70 kilometres downriver from where we'd had our swim. It was a bigger, broader river here, although it moved more sluggishly. Looking down from the high bridge onto a sandbank in midstream, we could see groups of men armed with spades loading sand onto small, horse-drawn carts. The carts, drawn by teams of three, were crossing the shallow channel back and forth to the shore, transferring their loads onto a waiting lorry. These were the *areneros*, the sandmen, who lived in their own small settlement on the outskirts of Ansina, which stood facing us on the opposite end of the bridge.

We stopped at the *comisaría* on the way into town to get our bearings. A group of boisterous policemen greeted us like visiting royalty, offering the use of their shower and suggesting places nearby where we might camp. Our top priority was a cold, quiet drink, so we left the police in charge of our bikes and went off to find a café. It was quite a smart, if modest, little town: the houses and gardens well cared for, and the gravel roads in good condition.

We returned to the station to find that the *comisario* wanted to meet us. He was a dark, stocky, rather severe-looking man in his late thirties, sporting a bushy black moustache. Unlike his men, he was dressed in 'civvies'. He introduced us to his tall, blonde wife Miriam. They lived in a small house behind the *comisaría*.

'Why don't you put your tent up here?' he asked, his wife nodding her head in agreement. 'There's plenty of space. Come on, come and have a look.'

The station had its own *quinta*, where the police grew some corn and vegetables and kept a few chickens. They also had some fruit trees – orange, lemon and fig – and a grapevine across a trellis between the station and the *comisario*'s lodge. A stone table stood in its shade on the gravel. At first I was a little reluctant to accept the invitation.

'Nonono, you're not going anywhere,' he said assertively, 'you can put your tent up somewhere in there, it won't be any trouble and no one's going to worry you. Then you can tell me some more about your trip. We don't often have visitors here. And call me Bacho.'

'Patricia,' interrupted Miriam softly, 'wouldn't the two of you like to freshen up a bit? You can have a hot shower here in our house and then we can sit down for a drink and a chat, don't you think?'

For Patricia the words 'hot shower' have magical properties far exceeding those commonly attributed to the more familiar 'Abracadabra'. Once they'd been mentioned, there was no hope of our going anywhere else.

Although as we travelled it had become almost habitual for us to stop and ask the police for directions whenever we were in any doubt, I had never been able to shake a vague feeling of unease when dealing with them. It is, of course, unfair to make blanket generalizations but the strong arm of the law, especially in Montevideo, had never shown any reticence about complying with the dictates of Uruguay's military rulers in the dark years. I couldn't easily forget the many occasions when I'd been peremptorily flung against a wall and searched at gunpoint for concealed weapons or subversive literature, nor the three days and nights that a friend of mine spent as a guest of the police, on his feet the whole time with a black bag over his head, for the crime of having left home without his I.D. card. Once, as a young teenager, on my way home from a friend's house carrying my guitar, I was ordered to lie on the ground in front of it, and, arms outstretched, unlatch the case, with half a dozen uniformed goons standing over me with machine guns at the ready.

You may understand, then, when I say that even though all those days were behind us now, and our hosts were nothing but charming, I sat at that table with mixed feelings. Since it was an easy, neutral subject, we talked about our adventures and, as I thought the stories might interest Bacho, I mentioned the *comisario* at Palmar, who'd offered us a lift if we could pay for the petrol, and the farmer in Paysandú who had told us about the monthly subsidy he paid his local police chief.

'Lucky police chief!' said Bacho with feeling. 'I wish I had a few neighbours like that in my parish!'

He went on to tell us that rural police stations are deliberately paid an insufficient budget for things such as petrol – which they need if they are going to patrol their patch at all efficiently – and that the *comisarios* are expected to make up the difference themselves, raising the funds from their communities in any way they can, organizing dances, raffles and bazaars. I was curious to know what sort of work the police did in places like this.

'A lot of the work is preventive,' said Bacho, 'helping people patch up their differences before things get out of hand. Some breach of the peace, gauchos getting drunk, that sort of thing. Fights. Some of them can get pretty touchy and they all carry knives, as you know. Illegal gambling. But we have to go softly with that, a lot of influential people involved, people with political clout. Arrest the wrong man and we get in trouble ourselves. Not as much theft here as there is in the city: everyone knows everyone else. Ambulance service, I suppose, getting people to hospital, which is one of the reasons why we need the petrol. Some cattle stealing, but not too much, most of that happens up closer to the border. Around here it's usually some poor wretch trying to feed his family, and you can't really get too tough about stuff like that. Smuggling. We're pretty far from Brazil, but this road here takes you straight to it, and we still have to stop anything that looks a bit suspicious. Catch a lot of gear, too. Surprising. Had a guy full of holes, once: woman shot him with a thirty-eight. Messy business. Bullets the size of grapes.'

Inevitably, the conversation strayed to politics. Bacho made no attempt to conceal his orthodox, right-wing views, which he held in common with all his family and which were predictable enough in a senior police officer, but he surprised us by saying that a cousin of his had been a Tupamaro ('the real thing, not just a big talker') and barely managed to escape to Sweden with his life.

'Caused quite a sensation in the family,' he said. I could well imagine.

When I mentioned our annoyance at having missed the Fiesta Criolla in Tomás Gomensoro, Miriam clapped her hands with glee.

'Well this is your lucky day!' she said. 'There's a Fiesta here in Ansina on Sunday. Why don't you stay?'

As we retired, promising to think about it, Patricia commented that throughout our journey we'd been wanting to camp near a fig tree, so that we could have fresh figs for breakfast.

'Plenty on the tree,' said Miriam.

When we woke up it was pouring, but as we'd decided to stay for the rodeo there was no hurry to get out of bed. We lay there, lulled by the patter of rain on the tent, until well after nine. Bacho and Miriam were already up, waiting in their little thatched house for us to join them for breakfast. The single room served as bedroom, sitting room and dining room. Miriam said nothing as we prepared our *mate*.

'The figs!' said Patricia, suddenly remembering. 'What about the figs?'

'I was just going to say,' answered Miriam. 'I was wondering whether you were made of sugar or something, afraid to melt in the rain.'

Bacho dug out a huge, black rubber policeman's cloak, with a high, Dracula collar. I wrapped myself up in it and, armed with a bucket, made my way to the tree. It was in the middle of the chicken run, and as I gathered the fruit I came across a few eggs which I brought indoors too. The green-skinned figs were small, but beautifully tasty. Patricia and I gorged ourselves.

'Give you a good run for your money, those figs,' said Bacho wryly.

Seeing our fishing rod, he asked whether we'd had any luck, which forced us to admit our embarrassing failures.

'We ought to have some fish for lunch, then,' he said.

He brought a large parcel out of the refrigerator, and unwrapped half a dozen massive *tarariras*.

'Caught these day before yesterday,' he said. 'Maybe this afternoon we can try for some more.'

The rain had stopped and the sun was working hard to dry the ground. In the police station kitchen Patricia helped Miriam to clean and prepare the fish. They were to be cooked over the embers in the hearth built into the wall. Once they were gutted, Miriam stuffed them with herbs and chopped vegetables and then wrapped each one tightly in a carefully greased sheet of newspaper. The oily parcels were then placed onto the warm grille. One of the advantages of being Chief of Police is that you have plenty of butlers: Bacho asked one of his men to keep an eye on the meal, and the four of us went to the zoo. It had been started by a French doctor who'd settled in the town several decades before and, over the years, had built up a collection of local fauna. The zoo had no financial support from the government, nor was it run commercially: the neighbours all chipped in to help with the feeding and maintenance.

We had the shock of our lives when we came to the snakes. Coiled in a glass box in front of us lay a large version of the little snakes we'd seen on Bald Mountain. The skull and crossbones painted on the windowpane was unequivocal. There were more, of all sizes, in other identically labelled boxes. I read the inscription. They were *cruceras*, cousins of the infamous rattlesnake. Deadly poisonous. The sign said that the babies were, from the moment they hatched, just as lethal as the adults. In fact, because their venom glands were young and efficient, a small *crucera* could be even more dangerous than a large one, which might take a few days to replace any poison used in the hunt. Death was slow and horrible, it said, and inevitable unless the antidote was taken within six hours. Patricia and I looked at each other, and gulped as we thought of the careless glee with which we'd wandered about on our hilltop. When we told them the story Miriam, who had a deep-seated 'thing' about snakes, shuddered with horror.

'You're never completely cured, you know,' she said, 'the venom attacks your nerves. It's worst in March, when they go searching for mates. They have no time to hunt, you see, so the poison builds up. An uncle of mine was bitten in March some years ago. He took the antidote, but every March he still comes over all funny. Gets very jumpy and sick. And if you're walking about in the fields,' she warned, 'you should never *ever* walk in close single file. If there's a snake there, the first one to pass frightens it. It strikes at the second.'

Bacho had recruited quite a team for our fishing trip: the four of us, the young Justice of the Peace and his wife (they lived next door) with their two small children, and an off-duty policeman, renowned as the best angler in town. Two blocks away from the *comisaría*, the blue police van broke down. In a flash the bonnet was up and everyone but Patricia and I was under it, with people appearing from nearby houses to join in. Hands reached in from every direction to pluck at cables and tubes. The muffled, conspiratorial mutter of mystical diagnoses and helpful advice, ebbing and flowing in waves, culminated at last in a proud 'Right! That's it! Try now.' Magically, the engine coughed into life, and we were on our way again.

The others looked on admiringly as I assembled the fishing rod. Of course, they had no way of knowing that I had no idea *at all* what to do with it. None of them had rods: they all had *aparejos*: plain, stout lines with a weight and a large grisly hook at one end.

'What'll you use for bait?' asked the judge, sounding like an auctioneer. 'We have a bit of roast udder, some meat, a bit of liver and a banana. Yes, a banana.'

Despite his hearty commendations in favour of the banana, I chose the liver. Lacerda, the fishing champ, had decided to use minnows.

'Ah, yes *che* . . . but you have to catch them first,' said the judge. 'Give yourself more work for nothing . . . ' his voice trailed off.

Lacerda was bringing in minnows like there was no tomorrow. Miriam foul-hooked a small *bagre*. Very small, I noted snootily.

We were at a broad bend in the river. The opposite bank, inside the curve, was washed into a broad beach. On our side the fine sand was piled up in crumbling shelves. I scrambled to the top of one and cast. Lacerda took his minnows and went out of sight behind some bushes around the bend. Bacho and the judge had settled into deck chairs to direct the operation.

'Good for construction work, this sand,' said Bacho, telling us about the *areneros*; 'most of the houses in Tacuarembó are made with it.'

I wasn't having any luck at all. Something kept stealing my bait, but stubbornly refusing to climb onto the hook. I felt a rumbling in my guts. Lacerda reappeared with two more catfish, and walked past to try his luck somewhere else. The rumbling became thunder. Bacho's early morning fig joke began to take on a new, sinister meaning. Feeling the onset of cramps, I realized that I'd have no time to get back to the police station intact, no matter how quickly we went. I drew in my line as fast as I could, made some excuse about wanting to try the spot Lacerda had vacated, and disappeared towards it at a gallop. I didn't get very far. I cast any-old-how in the general direction of the river, saying 'I'm casting now, going to catch something!' very loudly for the benefit of anyone who might be listening and, throwing my rod to the ground, barely got my shorts off in time before my intestines exploded.

My reel started to click, and then to whirr. Oh God, not now! I thought to myself. Heart pounding, I hurried back to it as soon as I could, and struggled for several exciting minutes before landing my prize: a willow branch. Despite a layer of insect repellent, the mosquitoes were having a field day with me here, so I had to return to the others. I didn't need the seclusion any longer, anyway.

'And what did you do with the handkerchief?' asked Patricia in the shower later, once she'd stopped laughing at my misfortune, 'You should have brought it back. I could have washed it for you.'

My wife can be really disgusting at times.

There was to be a dance in town that night. The four of us sat under the vine, sipping our drinks, waiting for it to get started. Bacho was telling us how he'd drifted into the police force after an argument with his father – who had a small farm – over a cow, an unlikely beginning if ever there was one. So bitter was the row that Bacho refused to work with his father any more. He'd finished the first stage of law school when, needing a job, he accepted an invitation to go to officer training school. By now we'd grown friendly enough to be able to talk frankly, and had downed enough cocktails to dare, so I asked him point-blank about torture. It stuck in his throat and he wavered a while, looking for something to say, but in the end he tacitly conceded that for some years it had been standard operational practice in some localities.

'What I've never been able to understand,' I said naïvely, 'is where on earth they found the men to do the torturing!'

He faltered and blushed.

'As I understand it,' he muttered eventually, as though the words tasted unpleasant in his mouth, his eyes not meeting mine, 'whenever they carried out that sort of interrogation they forced all the officers present to participate, so that no one could rat on anyone else.' He coughed and shook himself, like a dog coming out of cold water. 'On the other hand,' he went on hastily, 'the military promised law and order, and that's what we got.'

Police work had been made much easier, he explained, because their powers had been expanded to the point where the courts no longer needed to be so assiduously consulted. My reaction to that was fairly predictable.

'Well, I mean,' he said, 'in places like this when something goes wrong you usually know who did it, and they know you know, too. Hang around trying to collect the evidence, you get nowhere: people shut up, evidence disappears, sometimes even the guy disappears. In those days we just grabbed the man and locked him up, worried about evidence later. We had to have it, of course, but we could take our time about finding it.'

But surely power like that is open to abuse? It's a bit like a loaded gun, whose hands do you put it in?

'Yes, okay, but take illegal gambling, for instance. Whatever you think of the laws about gambling, the law says that certain games are illegal. Take *taba*, for example. (This is a traditional game of chance, played for large sums of money. Rather like dice, it involves casting an object in the hope that it will land with the correct side facing upwards. The object in this case is a cow's knee bone which, when cast onto the ground, must land one of two ways.) *Taba* is against the law, but everyone plays it. There are dens all over town. Think about this: for a population of 3,000 here in Ansina, there are six *taba* dens that I know of. During the *Proceso* I could have marched in there, arrested the owners, and closed the places down. Nowadays I can't touch them. Not because the law has changed, but because they're an important source of campaign revenue for our beloved democratic politicians, who get "contributions" from the operators. What am I supposed to do? I leave them alone: my boss drags me over the carpet. I move in: I lose my job. And apart from that, people jump about and say it's part of our heritage. Hell, I've even seen those same politicians go in there and play the game themselves: "mixing with the people" they call it. Either you change the law or you close them down, you can't have it both ways. In the old days I'd just go in and bust the lot of them, and that's a good day's work done, but now *I* break the law, by leaving them alone!'

But surely that corruption isn't the exclusive domain of crooked politicians. The military, even the police, are known to have dirty hands. Very dirty, in some cases.

'Yes, okay, maybe you're right. In the wrong hands too much power can lead to corruption, but even without all that power, we still have to cope with it. Besides, it's easy enough to point the finger and say 'oh, corrupt, corrupt', but do you know how much some of my men get paid? Twenty thousand *pesos* a month. Man comes along, says to one of my boys "Look the other way, put this in your pocket", what do you think he's going to do? If you want to stop corruption you don't throw him in jail: you pay him enough to feed his family. I'll tell you something worse, listen to this: there's another *comisario* near here who broke a smuggling ring one day, impounded 27 Ford Mustangs being run in from Brazil. He gave one to his boss, one to the circuit judge, another to I forget whom and kept one for himself. He even offered *me* one. The other 23 he sold. And that was just one of his deals. Every time I see him he's smoking a bigger cigar. And he has a go at me for not playing the game.'

Which only proves the point. If the police are badly paid now, they were badly paid under the military, so that hasn't changed. And under the military there was more power and therefore more temptation and opportunity for excess. And to make it even messier, civil liberties were being abused, sometimes quite horribly.

'Yes, okay, but the point here isn't a political one, it's about police work and law enforcement. You think it's easy to enforce the law: put a man in uniform, give him a gun, put him out on the streets and Hey, Bingo! everybody behaves. But it's not that straightforward. Man wants to break the law, he's going to find a way to break it whatever you do. My job, if I can't stop him the first time, is at least to stop him from doing it again. How can I do that when my hands are tied? Tied by the legal system, tied by bleeding-heart-liberal circuit judges who keep finding in the criminal's favour, tied even by the limitations imposed on us that have nothing to do with the law at all. I mean, the things I've told you about and a whole lot of others. How can I do my job when my men are afraid of being shot at, which happens all the time, and won't fire a warning shot themselves because if they do they'll have to pay for the bullet out of their wages? And even if they try, the damned things are usually so old that they won't go off, anyhow! Would you put your life on the line for a system that doesn't help you? No, neither would most people! And then kids . . . Kids! Couple of teenagers around here been raising hell since they could walk. Can't arrest them, can't hold them. Under age. Parents come in, magistrate says release the child into its parent's custody, I have to obey. Damned if they don't go out and steal something else. Can't bust the kid, can't bust the parents, can't bust the magistrate. . . . Who is the law supposed to protect, anyway? I'm a cop. I like to think I'm a good cop. How can I prove it without the tools?'

We never made it to the party.

A stream of people flowed up the road from the village to the farm where the Fiesta was going to be held. The laughing women minding the gate waved our station wagon through. There were four policemen in it, although only one in uniform. Low profile was the order of the day. We jolted over the rutted track and parked by a wooded knoll. Beneath the trees the gauchos were gathering. Dressed in their best, they stood and they squatted in purposeful groups, sipping their *mate* and trying to appear casual and uncaring. Others strode back and forth looking proud and determined, hats pushed down over their eyes, silver hilts gleaming in coin-covered belts. A couple of makeshift paddocks had been set up in the shade. Restless, impatient horses cantered and stamped back and forth in nervous anticipation. The atmosphere was electric.

We picked our way amongst the people and the horses and the dung to the far side of the wood. We took the long route, to avoid the *taba* court scratched into the soil, where men with reams of paper money held in their fingers like fans were tossing the bone. Bacho studiously ignored the game. The field ahead dipped into a shallow bowl, a natural amphitheatre. We found a good spot in full view of the *palenques*, the three tall posts that already had been set firmly into the ground at its centre. Around us, skittish young gauchos in colourful shirts strapped on their spurs and tightened their belts. Behind us, suspended over acres of smoking, glowing embers and tended by burly, perspiring *criollos* in leather aprons, a grille the size of a double bed groaned under the weight of selected delicacies. To one side of us, on the back of a truck, the judges and the commentators huddled around a microphone: rally round, they called, rally round, it's all about to begin.

A pair of dusky, muscular gauchos cantered into the meadow, leading angry, unbroken horses. Swarthy hands by the *palenques* took over, gently blindfolding the animals and tethering them close to the posts.

'And now, ladeees and gennelmen, we begin this Fiesta Criolla with a newcomer here in this beautiful fiellld which our ever-helpful neighbourrr and well-beloved patriarch of this parishhhh has invited us to use. A gallant young blood all the way from Cuchilla del Ombú who'll be teaching a lesson to that mean, angry bay at post number one: just look at her now, look at her pull! And then a familiar face to us all, our friend from Dos Hermanos, will ride that palomino being brought up to post number two. Gennelmen please, take your positions.'

This was the moment the young bucks were here for, now they could start testing their fire. They filtered out from the heart of the wood and ranged themselves on its edge, waiting for the lottery to match each of them up with a horse. The first competitors left their laughing and teasing companions and swaggered across the grass. The *apadrinadores* sat mounted and waiting.

Onto the unsaddled back of the bay went the first. The mare didn't like it: she twitched, pulling against the harness holding her to the post. The brave held up his hand: he was ready to go. In one flowing movement the mare was released, the blindfold torn from her eyes, she was gone, gone, gone: bucking and kicking and galloping hard, desperate to shake the man from her back, racing, racing, racing in earth-eating strides towards the foot of the field. Our man tried his best, his legs locking on, fingers entwined in the mane, his hat in his hand slapping the muscular rump, to find himself suddenly tossed like a nothingness into the air. The godfathers chased, one to each side, reaching one for the horse and one for the man. He struggled across, escaping his mount, set back on the ground by his rescuing friend, embraced by the cheers of the crowd.

Again and again the challengers flew, hung in the air, fell to the earth. The horses resisted, stood on their heads, twisted and turned in defiance. Harnesses snapped, men tumbled off, clutching a handful of mane. Only a minute, you have to stay on for only a minute, you have to wait for the bell. Stuck on the back of a galloping gale that rattles your teeth and tears at your bones, a minute is stretched into years. Sometimes you're lucky, the godfathers catch you, and sometimes they get there too late and you lie on your back in the dust, your body protesting, trying to remember to breathe.

CHAPTER THIRTEEN

THE OLD PIRATE

It was noon by the time we were back on the road heading east. We passed the now empty field where yesterday's heroes had made our hearts pound, and went on through the gentle roll of the land, surrounded by natural pasture: this was cattle country through and through. Our tyres whispered on the road, the spokes humming as they spun through the still, hot air. We made good time and seemed to be barely into our stride when we saw that we'd already come the 50 kilometres we'd planned for the day. A shining white farmhouse stood amongst some distant trees. The heavy wooden gate by the road had been recently painted. It opened easily at our touch. We walked up the sandy track, past a pond decked with lilies where waterbirds waded and dipped for their food.

At the hub, on his way to the stable, we met a tanned, handsome gaucho with a bushy moustache, wearing pale brick-coloured *bombachas* and a faded red-checked shirt, riding bareback on a beautiful *café-con-leche* mare. He was slim and unusually tall.

'That's the man you want to talk to,' he said with a shy smile, 'Tomás, over there.' He pointed to a man stretched on a blanket under the *paraísos*.

Tomás sat up as we walked past the barn towards him. He was also very tall, with a broad, honest face and laughter in his eyes. His clothes, too, were faded but spotlessly clean, although his boots looked as though they'd been through the war. His spurs rang like miniature bells as he stood. There was silver inlaid on his belt and on the hilt of his long knife. The holster was empty, but a large, ebony-handled revolver was thrust through his belt on the left. He greeted us warmly, with a firm, lingering handshake, and rolled a cone-shaped cigarette while he heard us out.

An older man, a bit on the scruffy side, with a bushy grey beard and a flowing mane of grey hair, who'd sat listening quietly on a stool nearby stood up, brought the wooden stool across, and set it down next to Patricia. He wore a pale blue *guayabera*, baggy tan trousers and black rubber boots. With no further ado, he worked his way into the conversation. He was Torres, and he was a *kilero*. So what's a *kilero*?

'You don't know what a *kilero* is? Well,' he drawled, 'it's a man who does kilos. Like me.'

Kilos of what?

'Kilos of anything I think I can sell.'

He turned his pale, almost transparent green eyes on me. Beneath heavy black brows speckled with grey, they were startling.

He was a smuggler of the old school, bringing kilos of this or bottles of that draped across his saddle, from Brazil. One would have thought that nowadays, when contraband thundered across the border by the lorry load, small-time work such as his would hardly be worth the trouble. But he had more strings to his bow, plenty of tricks up his sleeve. Not the least of those was his skill at manipulating the *campesino*'s hospitality. In the few hours we were on that *estancia* together we saw him quietly putting his talent to work. Not that he was in the least bit sly or secretive: on the contrary, he was refreshingly, roguishly open about his shocking behaviour. First he collected a sackful of figs from the trees that grew near the barn, having first sweet-talked the sack from the cook. He knew a woman, he said, a few leagues away, who made wonderful jam. If he took her the fruit, who knows? she might give him a jar or two. While he was gathering figs, he found a few eggs in the grass. He picked those up too, and once he'd made up a dozen he went back to the cook, and had her hard-boil the lot 'for the trip'. The parcel went down on the grass, next to the figs. Then he went to work on Tomás: is the *patrón* coming today, or is it tomorrow? Tomás didn't know. But he might, said old Torres, you never can tell. Is there enough meat, just in case? No? Well, don't you think you should slaughter a sheep? It wouldn't be nice for the boss to turn up and find there was nothing to eat, now would it? Well now, since you've already killed it, and have so much meat, do you think you could spare me a quarter? The front end will do. It went next to the figs and the eggs.

China, the cook, came to meet us. She was a short, fiery woman, dark, sinewy, strong, with a vital air of no-nonsense about her. Constantly on the go, she stopped several times on her way from one task to another to exchange a few stories or to pull old Torres' leg. She scolded him without shame for having no shame, but seemed fond of the old rogue nonetheless, and we could see that she found him amusing.

The *estancia* mechanic, in charge of the tractor and truck, also came up to see who we were. His name was Bonanza, he was brown as a nut. He sat down on a stool with his *mate*. Torres, ever the dreadful old pirate, an unfailing eye for the main chance, sat down beside him and started to fidget with a battered red and white plastic transistor radio, casually telling whoever was listening that radios like this are the devil to come by, gets all the stations, runs on these little batteries, see? I'd hate to be parted from it, a wonderful thing, but if you insist. . . .

'No one's insisting, put it away!' said Bonanza.

'But China, she's interested, aren't you my dear? You see, Bonanza, you see? China here knows when something is good . . . '

'Oh Torres!' she snorted, leaning against the bole of a tree, 'Nobody wants your silly old radio!'

'Now don't be so negative,' Torres replied, 'why, these young people here, they're very keen, I'm sure they've never seen anything of quite such good quality. . . . But I understand. It's just as well, really, that I don't want to sell.'

He started to tell us of his marvellous Arab, a *fabulous* horse, famous the length and breadth of the land. Tomás and Bonanza chuckled with amiable scorn but the pirate went on, undeterred. So highly regarded, in fact, was this horse, that he'd been persuaded by people who knew about these things to enter it in a couple of forthcoming races to be held in the village nearby. Of course, all the quality would be there, come to look at him ride. The word gets around, you know what I mean? A guaranteed winner, he said, a sure thing to lead by a length. If we had any money to spare we should go to the race and bet on his horse. We'd be glad that we had when he came in ahead. Not really a bet, if you're not a gambling man, look on it instead as an investment: you can't lose. Well, if we couldn't be there, he'd be happy to take our bets *now*, as a special favour, in strictest confidence of course, and lay them down on our behalf. We could collect our substantial winnings at the Bar Nuevos Rumbos, a very sophisticated establishment outside Las Arenas. We'd like it, *he* was there quite a lot, the boss was a very dear friend and associate of long standing, like this they were, so close. *He* knew what was what, and he'd be betting a little bit too.

Patricia and I had long been on the lookout for a photograph to bung on the cover of the book we were meant to be writing and, as Tomás and his men slipped into the saddle a few moments later, we thought that a picture of them on their horses with us on our bikes might be just what we needed. They had that casual, comfortable style that makes the gaucho on horseback so special to see. I told them what we had in mind. From one moment to the next they were completely transformed, suddenly stiff and self-conscious, posing and preening and fixing their hair, sitting up straight, faces like stone. It was as though some Hollywood casting direc-tor had asked them to star in a film. They were hamming it up something awful, smoothing down their moustaches, tilting their hats, trotting and wheeling and looking intense. Torres, of course, not wanting to be left out, had sprinted off to the stables to fetch his Magnificent Arab.

'What about my truck?' asked Bonanza, 'I can drive past in my truck, if you like . . . '

'Ay, Bonanza!' exploded Tomás with a laugh. 'Everyone's tired of looking at trucks! It's people on *horseback* they want.'

He tugged on the reins, making his mare lift her head and tread back-wards, a delicate, high-stepping dance.

China took charge of the camera just as Torres returned with a moth-eaten blanket thrown over his shoulder, trying to look debonair, astride a razor-backed, flea-bitten, foul-tempered nag, with a green plastic clothes-line for reins. Shergar, 'e weren't.

Tomás and the men, on the other hand, were mounted on beautiful beasts. I commented on it, and asked whether they had very many. 'Well . . . ' said Tomás, 'we have quite a few, but it's hard to tell you exactly how many. The herds just move around free, you see. I guess we have somewhere between five and seven hundred, all told.'

But Torres wasn't a complete villain. Throughout the afternoon he'd been muttering that he had to leave early, to pick up a calf for China. It seems that a *tropilla* had passed by the gates the night before and, following tradition, China had let the *troperos* camp on the *estancia*, and had given them something to eat. One of the cows had calved in the night. Since taking the newborn animal with them would slow the herd down, and probably mean that it would have to be carried across someone's saddle for most of the way, they too had followed tradition and left it behind as a gift. This was the calf that Torres was going to bring back. Reluctantly, making a great deal of fuss, he saddled his Fabulous Arab and left. Not long afterwards he returned with the news that the calf was nowhere to be seen. To my shame I must confess that I thought he'd decided to keep it for himself.

An hour or so later, approaching across the fields from a different direction, we saw Torres returning again. He was cursing and swearing fluently at the bawling brown and white calf that lay draped across his saddle in front of him. It was a beautiful little animal, female, and desperately hungry. It cried and whined and bleated and lowed, sounding more like a rusty hinge than a calf. With a professional eye, China poked and inspected the orphan.

'Good milker, this,' she said approvingly, of the Holando-something-else crossbreed. 'I'd better feed the poor little wretch before it falls over.'

Although pleased with her new acquisition, she was distraught at the prospect of yet another hungry mouth in her care. She already had a husband, she said, and two children, and now a two-month-old baby, as well as two orphan lambs, and as if that weren't enough, she also had to cook for four gauchos with hardworking appetites. And the owners, whenever they came to stay. And feed the chickens at some time in between. Her life was a constant round of preparing food for something or someone.

We put up our tent in the meadow behind the corrals. The ground fell away in front of us towards a lagoon. It was fed by a little *cañada*, lined with a miniature forest of shrubs and small trees and a couple of tall, improbable palms. We could hear something splashing about in the water – *nutria* perhaps, or *lobitos de río*. Cattle and sheep grazed on the prairies around us.

That evening, when the men had come back from the fields, we sat sipping *mate* together in the rapidly fading light. They talked softly and unassumingly about their lives. The 5,000 hectare *estancia* was one of three the same size, the result of subdividing the original estate amongst two brothers and their mother. Although conditions here were relatively good, the only shower the farmhands had was cold and their toilet was the great outdoors. ('Be careful if you're planning to pick any figs,' China had warned, 'The men do their business under the tree.') They were expected to provide their own boots, saddles and winter ponchos: this cost them two weeks' wages for the first item (boots rarely lasted more than four or five months) and a month's wages for each of the others. But they liked it out here on the land, they couldn't really get used to life in the cities.

'I lived in the town once, for seven or eight years. Had everything: house, refrigerator, nice clothes. Couldn't stand it. Too noisy, nearly went mad. Had two bicycles too, nice ones, Lygie. Gave them away to my brothers, and came back out here. More peaceful. A man can hear himself think,' said the man in the red shirt.

'I spent a few years in Bagé,' (Brazil) said Tomás, 'it wasn't too bad.'

'Yeah, but you didn't stay there, did you?'

'In the end it's always the same,' they explained. 'A young man goes into town, looking for work, trying to improve his standard of living, but sooner or later you learn that it's no better there than it is here. It's a shame, though. A lot of young men are still leaving the countryside, looking for work. Very few of them left in the *campo*.'

They had to laugh when they realized that, although only in their early thirties, they were talking like old men.

China came out and took us back to the kitchen for dinner, a solid, rib-sticking stew. When we walked back to our tent the men had all gone to bed, so we followed suit. In the middle of the night we were woken by neighing and snorting and the thunder made by the hooves of some of those 500 horses, who seemed to have chosen our field for a moonlit parade.

Something was snuffling and flubbing its lips. Whatever it was, it was close. I dragged myself out from under a curtain of sleep, expecting to find something unexpected in my bed. There was only Patricia. As my mind cleared I realized we were in a tent, and the noise was happening outside. I stuck my head through the flap. A palomino stallion was grazing in the groundmist an arm's length away. The sky was black and filled with stars, paling through a million shades of blue into a thin, yellow line on the horizon. Against it stood the silhouette of the palm trees and, hanging above them in the void, the crescent of a Muslim moon.

We wandered up to the kitchen for a *mate*, and hung the dew-drenched tent on the clothes-line to dry. The orphan calf, confusing the billowing folds for its mother's belly, rummaged around underneath it in search of a teat. China offered us some meat for the trip, but we asked her whether we could have a few hard-boiled eggs instead. She gave us a dozen.

Not long out of the gates we went through the village of Las Arenas and, just beyond it, passed the Bar Nuevos Rumbos, which Torres had recommended. It lived up to his description as much as had the 'Fabulous Arab'. Almost at Las Toscas we passed a *tropilla* on the move, and wondered whether the orphan's mother was amongst the herd. In the village we tried without success to buy some fruit or vegetables, settling instead for *galletas* as hard as roofing tiles and a packet of *yerba mate*. But what we really wanted was fruit, so after several failed attempts Patricia gave up being honest and liberated an armful of apples from an orchard.

At the *bañados* of the Río Negro, as we rode across the eerie marsh towards the bridge, through the trees draped with Spanish moss we saw a truck racing across the fen about half a kilometre away, on a parallel course to ours. We met it again just beyond the bridge. The back flap was down, revealing boxes and cages and nets. An extremely unpleasant looking group of men, armed with rifles and pistols and long, wicked knives, barely controlling a pack of angry dogs, were splashing and yelling in the shallows. We slowed down for a closer look, but something in the openly hostile way they responded to our curiosity made it eminently clear we weren't welcome. They were poachers. The licence plate on the truck identified them as Brazilian poachers. Not content with raping and pillaging their own wildlife, they had now come to Uruguay for more of the same. A nation which has no respect for itself can hardly be expected to have any respect for anyone else, certainly not a small, poorly guarded neighbour. The history of the relationship between the two countries, regardless of its merits, is a litany of such abuse. It's almost as though the Brazilians have never recovered from being unable to annex Uruguay. Sickened and angry we continued on our way, praying for the safety of the egrets, herons, spoonbills and storks that we could see strutting about in the wet, marshy fields, and for all those other little creatures that we couldn't see.

Our bicycles had given us such little trouble, despite the punishing routine, that it was only a matter of time before things began to go wrong. Sure enough, as we pedalled gaily along, I heard something ping in my back wheel. At first I thought it might have been a stone but, stopping to check, I discovered I'd broken a spoke. Predictably, despite a bagful of tools, I lacked the very one I needed. The closest town was Melo, about 40 kilometres ahead. We decided to stop for the night and try to get there in the morning. Facing a tidy hamlet of houses made of mud and straw, a track led away from the road through a eucalyptus forest to a distant farmhouse. We turned into it.

Wrought-iron railings framed the long, tall windows, and vivid lilac and crimson bougainvillaea climbed the walls to the red-tiled roof. The family was away, but the foreman, a stocky chap with a dark, earnest face, wearing a beret pushed rakishly onto his eyebrows, immediately gave us permission to put up our tent. At first shy, he was soon telling us how he'd been on the estate 'since he was little'. Everything had been just fine until a year ago, he said, when the *Señora* decided to take up beekeeping. He'd discovered that he was allergic to bee stings: one bite was enough to make him keel over in a cold faint. He waved his arms about as he told the story of how he'd only just managed to get off his horse the first time he was bitten. The hives, he scowled, were at the foot of the meadow – we could see them glowing white in the middle distance – and he now gave them a wide berth. He lived in dread of a calf or a lamb straying into the woods nearby, in case he had to go in and get it. Even honey put him off.

'I suppose I should look on the bright side,' he said, 'bee stings are supposed to be a good cure for rheumatism. We'll see how true that is this winter. Not that it'll make any difference, 'cause even if they are, I'm not likely to let myself get bitten again!'

Belkis, Manuel García's wife, was one of life's surprises. A bustling, exuberant woman, with bright henna hair cut very short, she wore large gold gypsy hoops through her ears. She bubbled with laughter and stories as she showed us around the little house in the hard white light of a butane-gas hurricane lamp. There was no electricity in their cottage, except for a single line brought across from the *casa grande* to keep the refrigerator going.

'You have to meet the *Chico Loco* before you go,' insisted Belkis next morning.

The Mad Boy turned out to be a tame *nutria*. It was only some years after adoption that the family discovered that the Mad Boy was really the Mad Girl, but by then the name had stuck. I'd never met a *nutria* before, and was surprised at how tame and friendly the animal was. She loved to be petted and tickled under her chin. The problem was that once you started, she wouldn't let you stop. Not that we complained: her pelt was magnificent to touch. Considerably larger than a domestic cat and an altogether different shape, rather like an oversized guinea-pig, she had the funny, box-shaped head, with eyes, ears and nose ranged along the top, so typical of all the indigenous rodents; the little *watereá* and the larger *carpincho* (which is as big as a sheep) being the two extremes of size. She had large, square, carrot-coloured incisors and webbed, leathery feet. Although she was free to come and go, she spent most of her time in a pen, where the Garcías had built a small pool. In her younger years, she'd been allowed to sleep in daughter Paola's bedroom, but Manuel had stopped that after a memorable night when the *Chico Loco* had gnawed her way through one of the little girl's bedposts, and almost brought the whole thing crashing to the ground. As we left, Belkis pressed a parcel of 'something to keep you going' on us. In it were some hard-boiled eggs, a few tomatoes and some lamb steaks.

A sign in the bicycle shop window said it was closed for lunch, so we sat down on the doorstep to wait. A large, burly man in his sixties, wearing gaudy Prince of Wales *bombachas*, extricated himself from a car and wandered over.

'Going far?' he asked amiably, settling onto the doorstep next to us.

'Montevideo,' I said, taking up his jocular tone.

'You're not going to get any closer just sitting here,' he said. 'What happened, *che*? Wear yourselves out?'

'Bust a spoke,' I answered.

'*Y yo que culpa tengo?*' he expostulated, spreading his arms wide, a grin opening his craggy face. 'I saw you on the road last Sunday,' he added.

'Must have been Monday,' I said, 'near Ansina. We weren't cycling on Sunday.'

'You sure, *che*?'

'Sure I'm sure . . . '

Just then the door behind me swung open and I fell backwards into the shop, flat on my back at the feet of a very large woman.

'Surprise!' she said. 'Is my old man giving you a hard time? Ignore him. He's dreadful.'

The Andrades had run the shop together since heaven-knows-when and she was as good a mechanic as her husband, a former cycle racer. Grandparents now, they were only minding the shop for their son and heir, who was laid up with a painful case of varicose veins. Mrs Andrade took us around to the yard at the back and opened up the tool chest. A short while later the son limped out to join us. He was as corpulent as his parents.

'Half the trouble,' he muttered. 'Too fat. If I weren't so fat, my legs wouldn't give me so much gyp. Can't find a diet that works. Not that I could stick to it if I found it, mind you, but it would be nice to know one existed.'

While we were there, an estate agent wandered by from his office next door. His opening salvo was along the lines of 'Oh, so you're cycling along the main roads, are you? That's all wrong. You won't see any of the real Uruguay that way. You should have taken the back roads . . . '

It was inevitable that someone, sooner or later, would find fault with what we were doing and how we were doing it. I'd thought I was prepared for it, so I was surprised to find myself so disturbed by his attitude. I couldn't be bothered to debate or explain it. It had already occurred to us that off the main roads we might find more places 'untouched by civiliz-ation' but, having seen and travelled along a few of those backstreets, we'd decided against them for the health of our bikes. In any case, the dividing line was thin. Still, his comment rankled.

Very soon after leaving Melo we entered the foothills of the Cuchilla Grande, a range of hills running in a shallow crescent towards the distant coast. It's not as high as the Cuchilla de Haedo in the north, which we'd crossed some days before. Or was it weeks? How long ago was it, exactly? Time had begun to blur, and the days to lose definition and slip into each other. It was as though we'd been on the road forever. We'd settled into a routine of travelling, making camp and breaking camp, the smell of horses and the smell of us. Those quiet conversations over *mate* and pestilent hand-made cigarettes squatting underneath the trees with the gauchos, the continuous wrestling with the heat, the hills, the bugs and the dust had all become our new reality. Although we still had a long way to go, I suddenly realized that we were now officially on the return leg of the journey. I didn't like the idea. I didn't want to 'go back'. Our life had become simplified, our difficulties immediate, easy to identify and easy to solve. I wasn't looking forward to rejoining the old reality, where we would quickly lose that clarity and soon be tangled up in all the complications of an urban life. All those gauchos who'd summed up their distaste for cities with the phrase 'too noisy' were now speaking for my heart, too. I remembered as though it were yesterday how I had felt when, coming from Montevideo, I arrived in Europe for the first time: the claustrophobic enclosures, the barricaded lives, the cut and fenced-off countryside without a single corner where a person could stand and see neither house nor highway. My eyes had grown accustomed to gazing over never-ending distance: no windowless, hermetic walls, no traffic lights, no faceless men in suits. Even sleepy Montevideo seemed too busy to me now.

Pedalling through the sharply cut and intricately folded hills, we found an *estancia* on an east-facing slope, from where we hoped to see the sun coming up. The *capataz*, a brown, wrinkled man wearing a floppy, broad-brimmed hat spoke softly, his language full of bits of broken Portuguese. He was from Rivera, he said, as he led us across the paddocks to a place where we might pitch our tent. The meadows fell away from one to the other in broad terraces down the sharp incline. Rocks the size of trucks thrust up through the soil, littering the fields. We found our spot behind the stable, where the lowest terrace ended and the hillside tumbled down into a deep ravine. On its opposite side another hill rose up before us; cattle and horses grazing across its stony, shrub-entangled face. Braga, the *capataz*, pointed out a tap rising incongruously from the ground.

'You can get water out of that,' he said, 'comes from the well up by the house.'

As we were setting up the tent, the hands came in from the fields. They unsaddled their horses and rinsed them down in the stable yard, led them through the gate into the neighbouring meadow, and then gathered curiously around us, solemn, taciturn, arms crossed.

'You all from around here?' I asked of no one in particular, once we'd shaken hands all round. My eye settled on a young chap with a thick, handlebar moustache, wearing a wide-awake hat, the thong around the back of his head.

'Nope,' he answered.

'Well, from somewhere nearby, then . . . ' I went on.

'Nope,' he said again.

'Oh. So you come from far away . . . ' I prompted lamely.

'Yup.'

He nodded, turned, and strode away, spurs jingling. That was that. He'd had his conversation for the day, and was glad that it was over.

I woke up around midnight, soaked in perspiration, feeling hot and feeling cold, feeling so sick that I wished I were dead. I lay there in the dark, trying to catch my breath, hardly daring to move for fear I would explode. Nausea rose in waves, making me shiver and shake. I suddenly knew I had to get out, whatever the cost, for fear of an accident in our clean little shell. I barely made it out of the flap in time to throw up on the grass, and then I had to squat right where I stood as my intestines heaved and spat. It all happened too fast: I'd had no time to be careful. I limped through the moonlight to the tap which now seemed miles away to rinse myself off, stopping every few paces, doubled up with cramp. I had to make a few more stops on the way back to the tent, and all through the rest of the night I was in and out like a jack-in-the-box.

When dawn eventually broke I was exhausted and all my body ached. In another excursion into the meadow in the hesitant, early light, I found myself surrounded by a ring of curious, pensive horses. By then I couldn't have cared less who stood about and watched: it could have been the President and all his blessed Cabinet for all the difference it made to me. I noticed that I was squatting amongst clumps of *carqueja*, the magic weed that Jaime had shown me so many moons ago, and ripped up a handful, just in case.

It took ages to dismantle the tent and make our way through the fine drizzle back to the house. The *capataz* and his son were collecting ill and wounded sheep into a corral for treatment. When I explained what was wrong, young Braga rushed off to the kitchen and brought back a jug of boiling water. I drank two cups of *carqueja* tea, one after the other, with my fingers crossed. I was feeling very weak.

On the way here I'd noticed that my brakes had done the damage that the roads had failed to do. They'd worn a groove on the sidewall of my rear tyre so that its profile was lumpy and uneven, which made the bicycle wobble. While I sipped the tea, Patricia and I replaced it. We carried a very hi-tech spare which folded into a neat little packet. Not quite as tough as the Michelin, perhaps, but it would have to do. Behind us, Braga father and Braga son were practising their gory medicine on an endless succession of sheep. It never ceased to amaze us how badly the animals could hurt themselves, and still survive.

We had to stop again along the driveway before we reached the road but my body was now almost empty and I only had a meagre, painful heave. Or perhaps the *carqueja* was already beginning to work. And so began a very difficult day. Since then we've wondered often what might have brought the sickness on, but we could find only one thing that I had done which Patricia hadn't, and that was to drink a cup of water from that tap in the stable yard. It still seems to me too violent a reaction for that to have been the cause, but we couldn't identify anything else.

Progress was slow and laborious. I was determined to be bluff and brave and show of what stern stuff I was made, but I couldn't even fool myself: the shallowest inclines defeated me and I had to get off to walk my bicycle up, stopping every few paces to rest. As usual, Patricia was far more patient and understanding than I would have been, even letting pass the golden opportunity to tease whenever I lay down on the verge to whinge and complain.

After what seemed an eternity we cycled into Arbolito, a little village nesting in a hollow in the hills, another battlefield in the constant struggle for power that tore at the country in the nineteenth century. We pulled up at a wooden-fronted *almacén* and went into the gloomy, old-fashioned store. An antiquated cash register and a balance with large, polished brass trays stood on a marble-topped counter by a glass-fronted cabinet holding cheeses and hams. The shelves against the wall behind the bar were laden with boxes, packets and tins. I slumped onto an unsteady bench at a worn wooden table, while Patricia asked for a litre of Coke, as much for my thirst as for its bowel-binding properties. We sat there in the half-light watching the locals come and go, some of them stopping for a beer or a plateful of steaming mutton stew, while a few small children played noisily around us on the dusty concrete floor, pretending to be cyclists in our honour.

The landlady surprised us with a tale about another couple, also on bicycles, who'd passed this way some months before, apparently on a long-distance tour such as ours. They were French, she said, describing them. We'd heard a similar story at a previous stop some days ago, although on that occasion we were told the couple had been English. Both accounts coincided on one point: the travellers had spoken no Spanish. How sad, we murmured to each other, to think of all that they had missed by not speaking the language. And how brave, we thought, or foolhardy, to have undertaken the journey none the less.

We were too tired and in no state for public relations, so we camped on an anonymous hillside that night, just beyond the town. The next morning, as we were leaving, we stopped for a few minutes to watch an ostrich with eight young. The chicks, by now about the size of long-legged turkeys, went instinctively into the sort of evasive manoeuvres we'd seen adult *ñandú* doing before. It was still a new trick for them, and it was very funny to see them tearing about as fast as they could, running in circles, crashing into each other and their guardian, who kept a constant eye on us without participating himself.

Although still a little weak, I was feeling very much better by then, and only had to get off the bike to walk up the steepest of the slopes. For several hours we seemed to be surrounded by ostriches with young. We guessed that by now the eggs we'd seen in the nest at Los Macachines must have hatched into just such a flock. We felt a sudden desire to see Jaime again. Coming out of the Cuchilla we had a couple of exhilarating downhill runs – spokes ringing as they sliced the air, tyres humming on the tarmac – which were enormous fun. On one in particular, a long, practically straight glide into a valley, we got up to the extraordinary speed of 74 kilometres per hour. On another, we were able to prove what Miriam had said about travelling in single file. I was coasting along a couple of metres in front of Patricia when I saw what looked like a dried branch lying in the middle of the road. I shifted my weight to one side to avoid it, only to realize at the very last minute that it wasn't a stick at all but a very large snake. Yelling out a warning to my wife, I whizzed past its nose at a hell of a lick, turning my head just in time to see the startled serpent rise up in alarm and strike at one of the panniers on Patricia's bike. It was an unsettling moment.

Our hunger was demanding attention, so we stopped at a diminutive hamlet for supplies. There were two shops in town: one was closed for good, and the other closed for lunch. The place was deserted. On the principle that we'd probably find another shop somewhere further along the road, we ate the last of our apples and set off again. The hills now behind us, the landscape became increasingly flat. For what seemed like interminable kilometres we cycled across a bleak and windswept plain, which was occasionally stained a deeper green by patches of marsh. We were coming into rice-growing country. Perhaps it was our mood, but we felt that the land here held out none of that inviting warmth and promise which had embraced us further north. It all seemed somehow harsher, and not nearly as friendly. Since the land so often defines the men who live on it, we wondered what sort of people we'd meet.

BANG! Pssssssssss . . . puncture. The first. It was my replacement tyre that had suffered. In the shade of a twisted *tala* we mended it, batting away the *tábanos*. Continuing south, we began to worry because we were getting steadily closer to Treinta y Tres, and we knew that *estancias* near cities were smaller and less likely to be as hospitable as those further away. To make matters worse, we hadn't found a shop yet and still had no food.

At the crest of a ridge we saw what looked like quite a large, smart estate surrounded by eucalyptus trees, so we turned into the gate and made our way up the drive past a herd of cows. The track curved around the woods, to approach the house from the opposite side. The elusive, magnificent perfume of unidentifiable herbs hung in the air as we drew near. From the back, the house looked even grander than it had from the road. The track ended in a broad yard in front of a large stable. A small gate led into a garden and on towards the house. We took our bikes into the cobbled barn, and rested them against the spotless, whitewashed wall. Dozens of branding irons hung on the walls with ploughshares, sickles and hoes. In the corner, on the clean-swept cobbles stood a gleaming, four-wheeled carriage, its polished wooden spars resting on the floor.

'There's something wrong here,' said Patricia, as I looked around.

'What do you mean?' I asked, intrigued.

'No smell.'

'Well, it's clean . . . they're tidy people.'

'It's *too* clean. There haven't been any animals in here for years.'

Armed with this new wisdom I looked around again, and she was right: it *was* too clean. It wasn't a stable, it was more like a farming museum. We followed the path to the flagstone courtyard at the centre of the U-shaped house. Ferns and flowers stood in terracotta pots around the walls. An untidy pack of small, overweight dogs raced out of the building to meet us, yelping and yapping and wagging their tails, uncertain how to behave. Alerted by their barks, an olive-skinned woman with more than a hint of Indian ancestry, poked her head around a curtain. We smiled and nodded and took a step forward.

'There's nobody here,' she said flatly, her eyes nervous and afraid. 'They've all gone to town.'

There was a tart finality about this information. Taken aback but undaunted, I went into our Famous Writer Routine, ending, as usual, with a request for permission to put up our tent somewhere on the estate.

'Oh no,' she said, shaking her head vigorously, 'certainly not. I'm afraid you can't. The boss will take a belt to my hide if I say yes. He never lets anyone stay.'

Not having been refused anywhere before, I somehow couldn't cope with what she'd said.

'Are you sure?' I asked her lamely. She was.

Almost a word at a time, we elicited the information that the boss was not expected back from town before half-past seven or so, at least another two hours away. If we wanted to wait, well, we could, but we'd have to wait outside the gate. We were joined by a young lad with no front teeth, white crusts of dried saliva at the corners of his lips and, by the look on his face, very little brain, who stood with his shoulders hunched up and his hands plunged into his pockets. He wore a battered beret slapped flat on top of his head like a stale blue pancake. I asked whether the foreman was about.

'Oh no, no foreman!' scoffed the woman, 'Not any more, not since the *patrón*'s father died, only this boy here,' she added, with unconcealed derision. 'It's a small *chacrita* now, not the *estancia* that it used to be.'

'Yeah, right,' said the boy simply, nodding his head slowly, his empty eyes betraying no indication that there was anyone at home behind them.

'Could we at least have a glass of water before we go?' I asked. 'Cycling is quite thirsty work.'

She took my request literally, and came back a moment later carrying one glass of water. I stood in silence holding it, waiting for Patricia to return. She'd gone to the barn to fetch our canteens, expecting we'd be able to refill them.

'Is he a very bad man, your boss?' I asked mischievously.

As I had expected, I was flooded in a torrent of disclaimers and denials. The lady doth protest too much, methinks.

'Then why are you so afraid of him?' I couldn't resist asking.

'He's said to me lots of times: "Not even my brother; if I'm not here, don't let anyone in". He's the boss. I'm just an employee here. I can't do anything for you.'

She was growing ever more agitated. It was unfair to make her any more uncomfortable, she was only doing what she'd been told and it plainly didn't please her, so we left, full of curiosity about the *estanciero*.

Further down the road we stopped to talk to a man and a boy on horseback, who were taking some cattle across the road from one field to another. We stopped to talk to them. Their clothes were clean but very old, and both of them were barefoot. The man was probably my age, but looked a great deal older. A hard life had cut deep grooves into his face. He smiled shyly, and we saw that his front teeth were capped with gold. There were no more shops until Treinta y Tres, he said. We were welcome to camp on his land, but he was really only the caretaker: the farm didn't belong to him. He lived there with his family, and together they barely scratched a living from the ground. He was sorry but, however much he would have liked to help, he had no food that he could sell or give us. Perhaps a piece of pumpkin, but even then he wasn't sure. That was very bad news indeed: we were getting really hungry, and had nothing left to eat except the remnants of a jar of honey that Belkis had given us.

From the road the farm buildings seemed verging on the derelict, but with the sun on its way down we were no longer in any position to be fussy. Just as we were opening the gate, a little red car full of people turned into the track behind us. The driver, a man with greying hair, a large moustache and glasses put his head out of the window and gave us a broad smile. A pert woman seated next to him stooped so that she could see us through the windscreen, and waved a manicured hand.

'I hope you live here,' I said, 'because we don't, and I can't tell you anything about it!'

The man laughed: 'I live here,' he said: 'come on in, I'll meet you at the house.'

With that he accelerated and drove away, while we closed the gate and followed.

We reached the house to see the family being greeted by a screeching, grunting, barking, miaowing, clucking, quacking cluster of farmyard animals.

'Of course you can stay,' said Mr Duarte, 'and don't worry about food. Yvonne here will take care of you, won't you my dear?' he added, introducing the foreman's vivacious wife.

Spotting a sister of the spirit in the coquettish Mrs Duarte, Patricia dispensed with the formalities and, wading through the chickens and the pigs, zeroed in on her with lethal accuracy.

'Doña Tota,' she said, getting straight to the point, 'could we please have a shower?'

Doña Tota laughed and said of course.

She bustled off indoors to open up the house which, close up, looked even more seriously in need of attention than it had from the road. Patches of damp had risen waist-high up the flaking walls, and the room she led us into smelled musty and long-closed-up. The shower hung over a shallow, square, tiled pit in the bathroom floor, and the plaster was peeling from the walls. But, as far as possible, everything was clean and tidy, probably thanks to the formidable Yvonne. We had a splendid hot shower, gazing through the open window at the pigs wandering loose in the field, snorkelling about in the grass near the house. They wore curious triangular collars made of three sticks tied together so that the ends extended just enough to stop them from fitting through the fence.

Soaped and scrubbed till we shone, we sat on a wooden bench in the courtyard, luxuriating in the wonderful sensation of wearing clean clothes again. Yvonne was hanging some laundry on the line, and Patricia asked whether she might do some washing too. Together they drew some water from the well and filled up the old stone basin in the yard. The Duartes, who had only come to bring some feed for the animals and generally to check on things, had left again, insisting that we make ourselves at home. Patricia pummelled and lathered our filthy clothes and we pegged them on the line helped by Fernandito, the foreman's son. He also helped me with the tent.

'No, no, not over there,' said Rocha, his father; 'the grass is covered with arsenic. I just dipped the cattle this morning, and that's where they stood around afterwards. You don't want to wake up dead in the morning.'

No, I agreed, we didn't. We moved the tent closer to the house.

Our duties done, we carried some chairs out of Rocha's little house and set them in a circle by the door, and as the sun went down we sat there and had a very civilizing drink (our special and by now perfected recipe: grappa 'sours'). Yvonne brought out a little breadbasket, lined with a white linen square, and passed it around. On slices of coarse-grained home-baked bread, she'd put wedges of home-made cheese. It was delicious. She explained how at Santa Olga they had a few milk cows, just for their own consumption, you see, and they often had more milk than they knew what to do with, so Yvonne had put her ingenuity to work, done some experimenting, and now here it was.

'She's a clever old thing,' said Rocha, 'always full of ideas.'

He was a short, stocky man, with a slow, deliciously impudent drawl and a mischievous gleam in his eye. He was bald as an egg up on top, which he covered with any one of a selection of caps, worn at jaunty, improbable angles. He also wore a disreputable hand-made cigarette stuck permanently in the corner of his mouth.

'Some years ago,' he said, 'when I was working construction in Treinta y Tres, she baked a cake so I could take a bit with me for lunch. One of the guys there really liked the look of it, so he asked me to bring him a slice the next day. By the end of the week everybody wanted some.'

'Well,' interrupted Yvonne, 'it was a nice idea, but we weren't rich, you know. I couldn't be baking for the whole crew. I asked Rocha if he thought he could sell it.'

'So I explained to the boys and said that if they wanted to, they could buy some. And when they said yes, well, I told Yvonne to get cooking. Three cakes a day we used to sell.'

'Yes!' said Yvonne, laughing with glee. 'Remember the shirt? He used to send signals with his shirt.'

'We were living near the building site, see. I took one cake with me in the morning, already cut into slices. When it was nearly finished, I used to hang my shirt – I had a red T-shirt, like this one, but red – I used to say to the guy in the service lift: Pepe, I'd say; Pepe, take my shirt up to the top and hang it from the scaffolding.'

'I could see it from the house. I'd look out of the kitchen window, and when I saw his shirt I knew it was time to bake another cake. And then I'd take it, still warm, to the construction.'

'Yes, the guys all used to ask: Rocha, how come your wife always knows when you've run out of cake? They never caught on.'

'And the *milanesas*? Remember the *milanesas*?'

'Oh yeah, that was another one! I was out of work at the time. Friend of mine had a little bar, and I'd gone in to say hello. A man came in, said he was hungry. My friend didn't sell food. He didn't cook. I said: hey, let me take care of this. Can I take care of this? Sure, said my friend, so I said to the guy that I could get him some *milanesas* if he wanted. The man said yes, so I ran all the way home and got Yvonne to make a few up . . . '

'No, you only wanted one or two. I said you'd better take more, just in case . . . '

'Well, yes, but anyway: I stopped at the bakery on the way and when I got back to the bar, I gave the customer a nice, big *milanesa* sandwich. And then everybody wanted one. Sold them all. Did that for some time, too,' he said, laughing.

He'd had all sorts of jobs: construction worker, farmhand, labourer in the rice paddies and in the packing plant, waiter, even. And how had he come to be working here?

'Oh, well, that's a good story,' he said with a rascally grin. 'I used to know Duarte, see. He used to come in and eat in a restaurant where I was working as a waiter. He didn't know my name, but we were good pals, always joking, calling each other *tu*, none of this *usted* business. And then one evening some years later – I was working somewhere else by then – I was walking home and this car stops next to me. Guy sticks his head out to ask directions, and it was Duarte. He recognized me, and we said hello and all that, and then he told me he was looking for a guy called Rocha who lived around here, did I know which house? Sure, I said, I know the house. What do you want him for? Well, it seems that Duarte was looking for a foreman, and wanted to offer this guy Rocha the job. Oh do you, now? I said. And why him? Well, someone had told Duarte that this Rocha was a good worker. He'd met the man's wife, see, and she'd told him to come around one evening and talk to the man himself. Did I know her? Yeah, I know her, I said. Duarte said she seemed to be a good woman. Oh, she's okay, I said, easy to get along with. Oh, you know her well, then? What about this man Rocha then? You know him? What's he like? He wanted my opinion, see, before he went to talk to the guy. Oh, he's okay too, I said. Hard worker. Easy to get along with too. Well, imagine, old Duarte just couldn't wait. Come on, he said, take me to meet them, sounds like just the man I need. It was a scream. You should have seen the look on his face when I took him to my house, and kissed my wife hello, and he realized that I was Rocha! He called me all sorts of names, but he gave me the job.'

We dined indoors, at a worn wooden table. The fare was plain: lamb stew with rice, but it was the best we'd had yet. We could easily understand why Yvonne's cooking had been so successful. It was a modest little cottage: kitchen, which also served as sitting room; dining room, where Fernandito slept on a mattress on the floor, which they brought out and stored away afresh every day; and a bedroom for Rocha and his wife. They also had their own bathroom, with hot and cold running water. The floor was bare cement all the way through, and the thatched roof was blackened on the inside with smoke from the wood-burning stove.

Although it could have done with a fresh coat of paint and a little bit of work on the masonry, Yvonne kept it impeccably clean and tidy and it felt very much like a home.

The next morning dawned crisp and clear, but quickly misted over. As we were getting up, Rocha rode past us bringing in the cows to be milked. We settled onto the bench in front of the cottage, and had a morning *mate* with Yvonne.

'Why don't you stay another day?' she asked out of the blue, voicing a question we'd both been thinking.

It seemed an excellent idea to me: I could settle at the table in the courtyard and spend a few quiet hours catching up on my notes, which again had fallen ages out of date. They had become a millstone round my neck: I either 'did things', thereby giving myself material, but no chance or time to write it down; or I wrote, and thereby 'did' nothing.

Fernandito came to check on me from time to time as I sat there on my own. Yvonne came up to feed some scraps to the scrawny kittens, who had to contest every mouthful with a pair of large, extremely aggressive roosters. She startled me by producing a whip made from a piece of string with a plastic bag at one end and a stick handle at the other, with which she lashed at the roosters to keep them at bay while the kittens ate up their food.

When I wandered around a few hours later to see what they were up to, I found Patricia and Yvonne making gnocchi on the dining-room table and gossiping away for all they were worth. Yvonne was vivacious and talkative, generous and yielding of build. Her black curly hair was cut short and her dark eyes sparkled in a mobile, expressive face.

'We shouldn't be making gnocchi,' she muttered in a rich, resonant voice, 'they're so dreadfully fattening! And look at me: *look* at me! Oh, dear, I'll just have to go on a diet tomorrow. Ooh, but I like food too much . . .'

We commented over lunch about how glad we were to have been refused permission to camp on that other *estancia* up the road.

'Oh, him again!' said Rocha meaningfully. 'The guy's a rat. He doesn't even like his neighbours to visit him on horseback, 'cause of the grass the horses eat!'

It seems that the man was deeply embittered at having lost so much of the original family estate, a loss which the family had brought upon themselves by sheer bad management.

'All that land was his before,' said Rocha, waving an arm generally northwards. 'They lost the lot. Had to sell. Couldn't run a farm to save their lives. Too busy screwing around in politics. Didn't make much of that, either.

Capataz up the road, friend of mine, had a couple of cows stray into the man's fields, once. He wouldn't give them back. Said he was too busy, *capataz* should come again some other time. Went on like that for days. In the end my friend just rode in, separated out his cows, and rode them out. He got his own back in the end, when the same thing happened the other way around. My friend had the old bastard come back every day, asking for his cows. The old rascal was getting so pissed off he even asked me to go and get them for him. No chance. Then he turned up with all his old friends from the police, all loaded up with guns, can you believe it? He still didn't get his cows back for another three days, though. The *capataz* was too busy!' Rocha chuckled with delight as he imagined the scene. 'Great neighbours. . . . No, he never lets anybody camp on his land. In fact, if you'd met him he probably would have sent you over here!' Which, oddly enough, was just what Duarte had complained about the day before. 'Always open my doors,' he'd said, 'I believe a man should share the things he has. I don't mind people coming here at all. I just wish that scoundrel up the road wouldn't send them all to me, though. I'd prefer it if they found their way alone.'

The Duartes weren't really farmers. Doña Tota had inherited the *estancia* from her father and, although they enjoyed it and it was reasonably profitable, they didn't really 'work' it, preferring instead to simply draw the bounty from the generous land with as little effort as possible. It was sad, in a way, because the paddocks and installations were visibly suffering from neglect.

CHAPTER FOURTEEN

HAVE I EVER TOLD YOU ABOUT THE DAY I CAUGHT A TARARIRA?

At first we were a bit wary about the unpaved road to La Charqueada, but we soon discovered that it was a prince amongst such roads. Beautifully smooth and flat, it made a satisfying hiss beneath our wheels as we glided along down an avenue of eucalyptus. They belonged to a variety we hadn't seen before (one of 32 in the country, I'm told): shorter, with a bushier crown and thicker, corkier bark. The road swelled here and there, but by and large the terrain was now practically flat. There wasn't a single car to be seen, which was by no means exceptional: we hadn't seen many cars at all in the course of our travels. In fact, I've seen more cars in six minutes at Hyde Park Corner than we'd seen in the last six weeks. It was wonderful not to have them coughing their noxious discharge into our lungs and puncturing our peace with their clatter. The air tasted as good as champagne. Sometimes I wonder about progress. As someone I once knew used to say: Every silver lining has a cloud.

But if there weren't many cars to share the road with us, there were quite a few cyclists. Many of them seemed to be carrying guns, evidently off for a bit of Sunday depredation. In a perfect little hollow, where the road dipped towards a wooden bridge, we met just such a group of eager hunters, four rather desperate youths on bicycles. Between them they carried an assortment of bulky, anonymous sacks, a rifle in a case and a complicated cage. They told us they came from Treinta y Tres. The cage, which had a single *cardenal* in it, was a trap. The bird in the trap was the *llamador*, the caller, whose song would lure other birds in. As for the gun, well, they'd shoot anything they found. Hare, *nutria*, or perhaps a capybara. Even when I was a boy the *carpincho* was still common in rivers and streams, where they lived in family groups, wallowing in the shallows, feeding on roots and sprouts, nursing their abundant young, purring and muttering to each other. Now they're very rare and hardly ever seen, thanks to the grotesque extent of over-hunting. In many parts of the country they're already extinct, and wherever they still survive they are under constant threat from all those so-called sportsmen. Idly, I asked the lads whether or not it disturbed them to pursue and kill such rare, defence-less animals.

'*Y, qué se yo? Qué se le va a hacer?*' ('Hmph! How should I know? What can one do about it anyway?') one of them answered with a shrug and a grin which I felt like pushing straight into the back of his head with my fist.

Hunting fever had taken hold, they were on their way to kill something, they didn't care what. I drew what consolation I could from the fact that they looked clumsy enough to frighten any prey away before they found it. We rode on in angry, sullen silence. They weren't unique. I felt encased in sorrow as I recalled that some of my old Uruguayan friends, who profess the greatest love for their country, are amongst the hunters guilty of the decimation of its wild life.

In the broad, shallow basins the ground was marshy and wet, and through the trees we began to see the emerald glitter of rice paddies. The trench-like gutters along the verges of the road were filled to the brim with water. The road was like an island, running straight across the marsh. Even if we'd wanted to, we wouldn't have been able to leave the road or find a dry place for the tent. Although the sun was hard and hot, the air smelled of wetness and decay. We stopped from time to time to climb up on a dyke or peer into a pond full of frogs and tadpoles. Glued onto the stems of reeds just above the waterline we found clusters of small, fuchsia-coloured eggs like brilliant pink and crimson caviar. They were snails' eggs. The adults, which we also saw, were the size of tennis balls. Hearing a tremendous thrashing and splashing in one of the paddies, we discovered a family of *nutria* having a frenetic, boisterous party, and prayed that the hunters behind us wouldn't have such luck.

There was water everywhere. By a complex system of ditches and dykes, some of the flooded fields were higher than the road. We even found a little stream which flowed beneath it although on either side, behind retaining walls, it was a good half-metre above street level. Facing upstream from this curious bridge we watched a kingfisher dipping nimbly for his food. Downstream the banks were dank and overgrown: the tunnel through the forest looked very jungly and mysterious. A little further on we passed a chapel, ruined and abandoned in a field near the empty shell of what once had been a monastery.

We began to tire and wish that we could stop and set up camp, but the road went on and on and ever on across the marsh, cutting through damp, gloomy forests that held out no invitation. Often we saw what looked to us just like a normal, grassy field, with cattle grazing placidly across it, only to discover that the grass and the scrub concealed a shallow pan of water. Occasional palm trees punctuated the endless shimmering plains. There were no houses or buildings to be seen.

We passed several chapels, abandoned and overgrown, even one that had been converted into a barn. A donkey stood in the doorway, and chickens pecked and scratched at the ground around him. I made some facetious crack, which Patricia didn't like, about the building at last having been put to sensible use.

I was baptized a Catholic at my own instigation, at the ripe old age of ten. When I was very young, my mother and I went to live with her two sisters – who weren't much older than I was – and my grandmother. I can't remember my mother ever saying anything to suggest she was even aware that religions existed, but her two sisters, on the other hand, became real head-banging fanatics the day they hit their teens, and thought it was great fun to parade about draped in lace mantles and rosary beads, looking pious at the drop of a hat. With all the goodwill in their teenage hearts, they tried their level best to get me interested in catechism classes and going with them to Mass, but it never really worked. Their much-beloved nuns, who taught in the convent at the corner of our street, and to whom I was brought to be sanctified, either terrified me or bored me half to death. One of them gave me a booklet once, with the stern instruction that on its blank pages I should draw a little flower, a petal at a time, to commemorate each occasion I'd been 'good'. I got a little too absorbed in the artwork and, completely overlooking the moral dimension, quickly filled the booklet with garish, improbable bouquets. The next time I returned to see the nun I asked her for another book, because the one I had was full. She gave me a ferocious fire-and-brimstone glare and told me 'Little boy, *nobody's that* good!'. It rather put me off the whole idea.

Although it was supposed to have been secular, we had a fair bit of religion shoved at us at school, mainly in the form of morning prayers and daily readings from the Bible. In late adolescence, when I was given the 'honour' of reading in assembly, I chose a passage from Ecclesiastes, which greatly impressed my form master who was unaware that a band called The Byrds was then using the very same passage in its current top ten hit. But I digress. Much before that, when all my peers were busy being well-brought-up little boys and girls, an important topic of playground conversation centred on the question 'What religion are you?', launched and argued in much the same tone as another important topic: 'What's your favourite football team?'. The answer never really mattered, provided you had one, unless your inquisitor was bigger and tougher than you or backed up by a group of similarly minded friends. The football favourite changed from year to year, depending on which team looked poised to win the Cup, but the religion issue was set as if in concrete. Most of the kids were Catholic, natural enough in a predominantly Catholic country, and most of the rest – it being an English school – were Anglican or Protestant of some sort or another. The other faiths (Jews, Mormons, Muslims, that sort of thing) were represented by the children of diplomats and foreign businessmen. Not having one myself, I was getting heartily fed up of being unable to participate in the debate about whose Church was the best, so with that in mind I took my complaint home one afternoon. I explained to my mother that I didn't much mind which she gave me, but she'd better give me a religion quick because I felt left out. My request seemed to puzzle her but, as mothers do, she promised to see what could be done.

'Do you really want to?' she asked. 'Oh well, all right then.'

While she consulted with her sisters I carried out my own research. By then my mother had married again, to a not very orthodox Jew. I thought about that one for a while, since it had rarity value, but when I discovered I'd have to be circumcised first I got rid of the idea pretty quick. No one was going to take a knife to *my* plonker! Although one of my best friends was a Mormon, the Mormons were out too, because they couldn't drink tea or Coke or tell rude jokes. And the Islamic faith was out because my Egyptian friend Hassan hadn't brought me a present on my birthday. So almost by default and much to their delight, I followed my pious aunts into the Catholic Church.

One of them was to be my godmother, and her brother, my godfather. We ran into a temporary technical hitch because my uncle was away in Indonesia at the time, (where, by coincidence, my Dutch father had spent most of the war as a guest of the Japanese, in the local Nippon Disneyland) so we had to find a stand-in for the ceremony. My aunt volunteered Mariano, her Costa-Rican boyfriend. After the priest at the local parish church had chucked some water at my head, we went back home for chocolate cake. Mariano gave me a plastic chess-set in honour of the occasion, which I thought was jolly nice of him, and when my uncle eventually returned from Indonesia he brought me a polished pewter beer mug, which I thought was pretty decent too. All things considered, I'd done pretty well out of being baptized. Except that now, fully equipped to answer the vital question and enter the debate, I was never asked it again!

More through necessity than choice, we ended up cycling the 82 kilometres to La Charqueada. The houses were small and square and single-storeyed and didn't differ very much from one another, although later, when we went exploring in the town, we found that on the backstreets only some were made of brick, the rest being made of wood, clay or straw. The Río Cebollatí is a big, muscular waterway, about the size of the Thames at high tide, except that instead of cutting through London it cuts through a dense, matted jungle, sometimes flowing between high, sandy cliffs, sometimes carpeted with rippling *camalotes*, floating miniature islands of lilies and other river plants. The town was set back from the bank, which here fell in a perpendicular drop to a narrow strip of beach.

Between the houses and the low cliffs there was a park, complete with little stone barbecues for campers. Further downstream, beyond the last houses, the road petered out into a footpath and the bank grew wilder again. The shadows were lengthening fast and the light was tinged with violet and mauve when, on a grassy knoll overlooking the river, amongst old *talas* festooned with Spanish moss, we pitched our tent. From the cliff-top we watched a boat approach along the crumpled gold leaf water from the east, straight into the last rays of the setting sun.

As the sun went down, clouds of mosquitoes – the bane of our lives – rose from their hiding places full of energy and appetite. Patricia promptly leapt into the tent and zipped the netting shut, leaving me to go to the Parador on the other side of the track, about 500 metres away. We wanted to have a little drink before retiring, but were short of the ingredients. For some reason I had a sudden craving for a cigarette. I couldn't really bring myself to scrounging one off the innkeeper, even though he seemed a pleasant chap, so I bought a packet. When I returned to the tent and she saw what I'd done, Patricia was furious. With extraordinary – although not always successful – self-control she'd tolerated me having an occasional smoke but *buying* cigarettes was quite beyond the pale. She had a jolly old go at me for it, too.

Next morning we went into the Parador for some hot *café con leche* and asked Walter, the landlord, whether he knew of a boat on which we might spend a day on the river. He could think of three: one belonged to the *Prefectura*; another was the tourist boat we'd seen in the evening, which belonged to the *municipio*; and the third belonged to the *Co-operativa de Pescadores*, the fishermen's co-operative. Had he known sooner, he'd have woken us up. The municipal boat had left an hour before, headed for the Laguna Merín, and we could have hitched a lift on her.

The *Prefectura* was on the waterfront looking out across the gardens onto a sodden, moss-covered wooden pier. The *Prefecto* was an articulate, highly strung young man. Although he would have loved to take us for a spin, he couldn't help. The only craft he had was a Zodiac inflatable, and it was in dry dock because of a puncture. He had the glue, he said, bought at great expense from the French manufacturers, but he had a problem: there were strict instructions on the pot not to use it when the humidity exceeded 40 per cent because, if it was damper than that, the glue wouldn't stick.

'I've been waiting for ages!' he said with an expressive shrug of his shoulders. 'And I'll probably have to wait for ages more. Just look at it!'

We looked. The weather was by no means promising. The air was thick and sticky, and heavy clouds were collecting on the horizon. The irregular, unseasonal weather which had been following us around for days was clenching its fists into a lulu of a storm.

'Let's try the fishermen's collective,' he said.

We followed him out of the office to the warehouse that the fishermen used as their headquarters.

'*Gordo!*' he called, '*Che, Gordo, estás ahí?*'

A very large, very hairy and very smelly fisherman sauntered out of the gloom with his thumbs stuck in the waistband of his straining blue trousers. From a faded red T-shirt several sizes too small, a generous belly overhung his belt. He had an unkempt, reddish-brown shock of hair, with exuberant mutton-chop sideburns to match. His chin was thick with bristles several days old. This was the Gordo Vizcaíno, Head of the collective. Sure he could take us, he said, once he knew what we wanted, but it would have to be tomorrow. He needed to check with the others first just to see if the boat was available, but otherwise it was no trouble at all. He promised to call at the Parador in the evening, to let us know.

'I think you'd better check with the municipality too, just in case,' the *Prefecto* said softly. 'You never can tell with these guys.'

It seemed a shame not to go out with the *Gordo*, such a colourful chap and probably a mine of local information, but there was something persuasive about the tone of the advice.

The *Intendencia* was just around the corner, on the main street. We found Mr Furtado, the Mayor, a square-jawed, raw-boned, angular man, on the steps in front of the modest Town Hall. The only thing we really had against the *Stella Maris* – the municipal boat – was that we couldn't afford the fares they normally charged for the excursion. There was no point in beating about the bush, so I told the man our problem straight away.

'I'll see what I can do,' said Furtado. 'But it'll have to be tomorrow. The boat's already out today.'

Well, that suited us just fine. We shook hands on it, and agreed to talk to him again that evening. Which left us with the day off.

The breeze had strengthened into a gusty, changeable wind that lifted the dust from the ground and flung it in our faces. The sun tried bravely but without much success to break through the gathering cloud. Something about the backstreets made us feel uneasy, as though some dense and brooding presence lurked just out of sight. La Charqueada was unlike any of the villages we'd seen so far: shadows seemed gloomier and corners somehow darker. The people were furtive and the children hid from our eyes. The entire region is so steeped in superstition and unusual lore that if someone had told us that a witches' coven held regular meetings in the town, we wouldn't have been surprised.

'It'll be hell in the tent tonight!' said Walter truculently, when we returned to the Parador. 'Why don't you move into one of the cabins?' he waved an arm in the general direction of the thatched, whitewashed lodges.

'Don't worry: it's on the house,' he added, seeing our hesitation.

An odd-job man who was painting the outside of the cabin Walter had chosen for us, stopped working to chat as we appeared. He was vivacious and voluble, with a lively, moon-shaped face.

'I hear you want to go fishing,' he said. 'Good river for it. You can catch stuff casting from the bank right here. I do.'

He went on to tell us how sometimes, when he was out of work, he depended on what he could catch to keep his family fed. Occasionally, especially in winter, he would take a *carpincho*, which kept them going for about a week.

It was one thing to theorize about a man hunting to feed his family, but quite another to be confronted with the real thing. Idly, I mentioned the 'hunters' we'd passed on the road coming into town. He laughed.

'They won't catch a thing. Not like that,' he said flatly. He then described what it took nowadays in these parts to track and bag the rare and elusive capybara, painting a vivid picture of wading for hours in the swamps on cold winter nights, the icy water up to his chest, carrying a torch and a single-shot .22 above his head.

We didn't have the temerity to ask, but it was even money that he was one of the dispossessed we'd heard so much about, who wasn't above taking the occasional sheep from one of his more fortunate neighbours.

When dawn finally broke, the sky, grumbling in its guts and spitting out sparks, was like a metal plate from horizon to horizon. We walked down to the pier. A grizzled, reptilian old man was stamping his feet on the deck of the *Stella Maris*. A sort of river bus, the wooden craft looked like a smaller and more primitive version of the excursion boats cruising the canals of Amsterdam.

'You ready?' asked Ricardi gruffly, once we'd introduced ourselves.

With such rotten weather we hadn't really expected to find anyone there, so we hadn't brought our things with us.

'No, no,' he said morosely, 'this won't stop us. We can leave whenever you like. I'll just have to go and get the boy out of bed if you still want to go.'

Well, of course we still wanted to go, so we agreed to meet here again in a few minutes. We hurried to the cabin, pulled on our lightning-proof jackets, grabbed what baggage we needed, and hurried back to the boat, stopping at the Parador on the way to pick up a Thermos of hot water for our morning *mate*. Humberto, 'the boy', was almost as old as Ricardi but, boyish and irrepressible, his *nom de guerre* was well deserved.

The diesel coughed reluctantly into life and we nosed away from the pier, turning in midstream to head downriver towards the Laguna Merín. We hadn't travelled very far when the squalls began again, throwing abrupt handfuls of rain against the windows and veiling and unveiling the wild and tumbled banks. The forest, flattened by the greyness of the light and further dimmed by isolated tendrils of mist, looked ancient, primeval and mysterious. We huddled on our benches in the boat, sipping *mate* and nibbling bread and cheese, and wondered whether the landscape had even changed at all since the days when an estimated 20,000 *Arachanes* in settlements all around the shores of the vast Laguna Merín had the region to themselves.

'River wasn't always so wide,' said Ricardi, a calloused hand resting lazily on the wheel. 'Not even when I was a boy. Eats more of the bank away every year. All sand and clay, see.'

We could see what he was talking about. In places the forest came right into the shallows, water lapping at the trunks of trees, draping debris in their lower branches.

'Used to be more animals, too,' contributed Humberto. 'Full of *carpincho* when I was a boy. Don't see many now.'

'There were less snakes before, too. A lot more snakes now,' said Ricardi.

Snakes, by which first and foremost he meant the deadly *crucera*, were a fact of life in these parts, so much so that a full-blown tradition had grown up around them. Local folklore has it that a snakebite can be cured using a combination of two plants that grow on the forest floor. I'm still kicking myself for not having written down the names – it shows how bad I was at keeping up my notes! Apparently one of them, a shrub, has very fibrous branches encased in thick, corky bark. The first step is to take one of these branches – or even just the bark – and tie it around the affected limb. So, if you get bitten on the foot, for example, you tie it around your ankle or your leg.

'A sort of tourniquet,' I said. 'You can do it with anything, can't you?'

'Oh no,' said Ricardi. 'It has to be that plant. And you don't put it on tight: it just has to go all the way around so that the ends touch. Provided the ends touch, however loosely you tie it, the poison can't get past.'

The second step involved another plant which, from his description, sounded like a lily of some sort.

'It has big, fat leaves. Very juicy stems. White flower, shaped like the head of a snake. If you look inside it, it's brown. The markings are like the teeth, like the mouth of the snake. It stinks. It really smells awful. Like something dead and rotten. Worse, even. You need the flowers. Or the seeds. You put them in a bottle of *caña*. You have to keep it ready, of course, because it has to stand in the dark for at least a month. When you get bitten, you tie that little branch around there and drink a big glass of the *caña*. Works every time. You might feel a bit sick, but you don't die.'

'And it *works*?' I asked, incredulously. It sounded too far-fetched for me. The *crucera* is a killer.

'Course it works!' he snorted with unconcealed contempt. 'Why, there's an old lady lives in that straw house we just passed a few minutes ago.

She grows vegetables and things. Seventy-two years old, she is. Been bitten three times in her garden, and cured herself that way every time. Doesn't have any hair left, but she's alive.'

Then there was the story of the woodsman who'd been felling trees when a *crucera* bit him on the toe.

'He chopped his toe off, just like that, didn't even stop to think about it. He's still alive, too.'

'Some people even *eat* the goddam things!' said Humberto, in disgust.

'What, *toes*?' I asked.

'Nah, *snakes*!'

'Not any more,' contested Ricardi, 'Not since old what's-'is-name died.'

Old what's-'is-name had lived on the outskirts of the village, in a wooden house he'd built himself, raised up off the ground on stilts. Snakes lived underneath it, and one of his favourite party tricks was to call them by whistling in a special way.

'He fed them on scraps. It was like they knew him. They never bit him, anyway. Sometimes, when he was down on his luck, he'd sit on the doorstep and call them, choose a big one, kill it and eat it. You have to know how, of course. He showed me once. You've got to measure the width of your hand behind its head. You cut that bit off and throw it away. The rest you can eat. No! I never ate any! I'm not crazy, you know. . . . One day, God knows, maybe he was drunk or over-confident or something; he didn't cut enough off. Terrible, it was. Blew up like a balloon. Big like this, he was. Saw him before he died. Hands, his fingers, his face, all his body, he just got huge, all swollen up. Horrible pain. Nobody could do anything for him.'

Ricardi had lived here all his life. So had his father. Grandfather was Italian, from the old country. When he was a boy, eight years old, he followed his dad into the woods to make coal.

'Lousy job. Lousiest job in the world. Did it for years. To do it properly you need about 40 cubic metres of wood, 16 or 20 good-sized trees. Takes a couple of men at least a week to cut them down and chop them up to the right size. Then you've got to clear the ground, big patch. You plant a stake in the middle, small tree trunk, that sort of thing, then you start putting the wood down around it, like the spokes in a cartwheel. You build it up. Have to leave a few spaces for it to breathe, but you just build it up, as high as you want. Then on the outside, to about a metre, you put turves, you know, like peat, and then, over the rest, grass and leaves. On top of all that: earth, packed on, for insulation, always leaving a few holes. That's the oven, takes another ten days to build. Then you take the middle stake out, put in some fuel, and light a fire in there. Have to take care of it, feed it all the time, make sure it burns evenly and that you don't get any flames. Pig of a job. Hot. Pray it doesn't rain. If the wind changes, you have to close up some of the breathing holes and open up others. Eight, maybe ten days later, you let the fire die down. If you did it right, you've got coal. Sometimes it goes wrong, the whole thing's lost, all your work's wasted. You've got to be careful when you open it, because it's so hot in there that sometimes the whole thing catches fire. You've lost it all. Have to start again. Got a better job now. Easy. Work for the municipality. But the pay's no good. I've never lived in a stone house, you know that? Straw. Thatch. Have to rebuild it every seven or eight years, depending on the weather. That's no fun either, gathering thatch. All day long up to your knees in the water. You've got to go into the *bañados*, where the reeds grow. You grab an armful, like this, like a baby, and then you bend over and cut them off at the bottom with a knife. You never know what's living there until it's too late, usually. Full of snakes.'

The weather had deteriorated so much that going into the *Laguna* was out of the question. Even in the relatively sheltered mouths, the wind had whipped the water into waves. The two men debated for a while about where we might stop and try to fish. In the end Ricardi took us to one of his favourite places: a secret, isolated spot in the sheltered lee of the bank, where the forest walked into the river. He let the boat glide the last few metres into the lush, flowering *camalote*. Humberto tossed a rope around an overhanging willow branch and tied it fast. With the engine off, the silence was absolute: the river sucking at the hull, the drizzle beating on the glass and the branches overhead clicking in the wind only made it richer and more tangible.

Humberto, who grew steadily more bouncy as the morning progressed, brought a box of tackle out of a locker, muttering that if he'd known that we were going fishing he would have brought a rifle or some better bait. The bait I could understand, but why the rifle?

'Oh, we could shoot a bird and use its guts,' he said. 'The fish love 'em.'

He baited a light, toylike line with a crumb of cheese and flicked it about in the water.

'Here minnow, heeere minnow minnow minnow . . . ' he crooned.

Bang! The first was on the hook. In a minute or two he'd landed half a dozen.

'Right. That's the bait. Now for some *tararira* . . . What about you, Ricardi, what are you going to do?' he asked over his shoulder, fastening two of the little fish onto a large and vicious-looking pair of hooks at the end of a stout *aparejo*. In the bottom of the box the older man had found a forgotten hook already baited with a piece of bird gut, and was threading it onto a similar line.

'I'm going to get some *pintado*,' he said flatly, casting far out into the middle of the river. 'Wish I had some worms. Worms are best,' he went on in his gravelly, funereal voice. 'These have had it.'

He held up a glass jar with what looked like half a dozen bits of dried twig in the bottom.

'Been here for days, Hm. . . . Maybe I can resuscitate them a bit,' he grunted and, hanging over the side, scooped some water into the jar and put it down on a bench.

'And you chaps, what about you chaps?' asked Humberto.

Patricia and I were still wrestling with our fancy rod and rummaging through our collection of hooks. We'd given up trying to look as though we knew what we were doing.

'What are you going to use as bait?' asked Ricardi from the grave.

'Well, I don't know, to tell the truth. I thought we'd try with *mortadela* first,' I said.

Ricardi coughed behind his hand, his equivalent of laughter. Humberto's open guffaw was more easily recognizable.

'No no, mustn't laugh,' he stopped himself, 'you never know. Have to try everything once. Always something to learn.'

'You'll have to wait a long time if you want to learn about fishing from us!' I said.

Just then the older man's line twitched, and started to run out. He grabbed it carelessly and gave it a single dry, solid tug.

'There,' he scowled, and started hauling it in hand over hand.

On its end, firmly hooked but fighting bravely, hung a glistening *pintado*, a type of catfish with a tan, polka-dotted back, hence the name. It has very sharp barbs on its side and dorsal fins which, if wrongly handled, can cause extremely painful wounds. With the smooth ease of long practice, Ricardi grasped each poisoned spur between his fingers and snapped it expertly off at the base, before taking the hook out of the fish's mouth. The side barbs, which he showed me, were like shards of hacksaw blade. The dorsal one was like a mattress needle.

'Hurts like hell if you jab yourself with these,' he said, throwing the bits into the water. 'Nothing you can do about it, either, except wait for the pain to stop.'

He dropped the *pintado*, which was about the size of a big trout, into the catch net hanging over the side.

Humberto whooped with joy, 'Now we're getting somewhere!' he crowed, rushing out onto the deck to bring in his line, which had run right out and was tugging at its mooring. Seconds later he landed a very large, very ugly and very vicious-looking grey, bullet-headed fish. Its bear-trap mouth was rimmed with awesome pin-sharp teeth. This was the famous *tararira*.

'Yes, ladies and gentlemen, this is getting interesting,' said Humberto, carefully keeping his fingers out of the way of its jaws as he picked the fish off the hook and dropped it into the net. 'Now I'm beginning to enjoy myself!'

He did, indeed, seem to be having a wonderful time, even though for him and his partner, fishing wasn't a sport at all but an essential skill: 'no catch, no food' was for both of them a rule of iron. He rebaited his hook and cast again. Ricardi, in the meantime, had landed another two *pintados*. One of them was small so he threw it back, but not before breaking off its barbs – 'So that I won't get hurt the next time I catch it' was his explanation. For ages he kept bringing them in, expertly recycling the same piece of bird's gut until one of them ('Greedy bastard!') finally swallowed the bait.

Patricia and I had tried with mortadela, cheese, compacted bread and even a fillet of minnow, but although we'd landed tons of waterlily roots, we hadn't even had a nibble.

'Here, let me see that,' said Humberto gently, checking the hooks and the line. 'Do you always set it up this way?' he asked with surprising tact.

I told him I did, but that he needn't be shy about changing it because I'd never caught a thing.

'Okay,' he said simply, and set it up his way.

'Here, Humberto, maybe you can use some of these,' murmured Ricardi, holding up the jar.

Like dried peas, the crumbs of worm had absorbed the water and swelled up until they looked almost respectable and lifelike. Humberto had changed the weight on my line and added a second hook, and onto both hooks he now threaded a reconstituted worm.

'Over the side!' he said, 'Try now.'

Well, now that I had a fighting chance, I went outdoors and onto the roof of the deck house. Whizzzz . . . plop! I settled down to wait in the fine drizzle. The rod was very light and sensitive, and I was very new at this, so when I felt the first soft knocking on the line I guessed that it was just another root and let it lie. The second knock was a distinct tug. Too excited to say anything, and too afraid of being mistaken, I started reeling in without a word.

'What's that?' called Patricia from below, 'Why are you reeling in so soon? Have you got something? Huh?' Her head appeared out of the window beneath me. 'What's going on? Oooh, *look*!' She clapped her hands, 'A *fish*! It's a *fish*!' Just breaking the surface was a *pintado* locked onto one of my hooks. For some reason I could still feel something pulling, so I kept winding the handle until there, lo and behold, a second *pintado* appeared. Two hooks, two fish. Now *I* was having fun. Pandemonium. The boat was in an uprorar as we celebrated my success.

'Not a virgin any more, not a virgin any more!' hollered Humberto, stamping his feet on the deck and doing a little dance. Patricia was jumping up and down, clapping her hands. Even Ricardi was chuckling. I just stood on the roof of the deckhouse, striking a pose and feeling aloof. Ernest Hemingway, step aside.

While Ricardi helped me get them off the hooks and into the net, Humberto dragged in another two *tararira*, and lost one.

'I'm done with rabbits,' I said, 'I want a tiger, too.'

'It'll bust your line,' said Humberto, wryly shaking his head.

'No, no, no,' I said, 'show me how to set it up.'

After all, I'd seen Spencer Tracy do it in *The Old Man and The Sea*, and Henry Fonda in *On Golden Pond*, I knew all about this stuff.

'Come on, come on, come on, we gotta do it!'

We'd run out of *mojarritas*, the minnows, by then.

'Me, me!' demanded Patricia.

Pretty soon she was bringing them in like a purse seiner.

'One here and one here, like this,' said Humberto.

Back on the roof of the deckhouse: whizzzzz, plop, silence. Drizzle. Nothing happened.

'You have to be patient,' advised Patricia, her arm through mine.

From down below we could hear the soft sound of Ricardi's snores. His dinner secured, he'd fallen asleep on the bench.

I felt some twitches and some gentle tugging, but every time I reeled in the line all I found was that my bait had disappeared. Down to our last *mojarrita*, I cast once again. Wait. I huddled deeper into my jacket. It wasn't really cold, it was just that sort of day. The rain was coming down in earnest, but I wasn't going to give up now: I just put on my hood and stayed where I was. A distinct thud, like a head-on collision, came down the rod into my hands. Then it went slack. Having watched Humberto do it I sat perfectly still, hardly daring to breathe, and prayed that it would come again. Then there it was, a firm – and this time constant – pressure. I gave a single sharp tug and waited for what seemed an eternity. Without any warning the reel started humming, line began to fly out as though I were tied to the devils of hell. At that point I started to worry. Whereas Humberto was using a cord as thick as a hawser, all I had was a light, four-kilo line. I'd seen the look on his face as he lent me one of his hooks, a look that said 'I'll never see this one again!'. Judging by the pull from whatever had it in its mouth right now, I began to wonder myself.

Something broke the gunmetal surface out in midstream. It was a *tararira* all right, and it was no baby. It was headed towards me, so I started turning the handle. It leapt clear again, very much closer, close enough so that I could see that it was trailing my line. But then it turned and raced away once more, rattling the reel and bending the rod. By this time I was making such a racket up on the roof that everyone came out to have a look.

'Be careful, it'll bust your string,' warned Humberto.

Like hell it will, I thought. Ricardi rolled another cigarette and stuck it in the corner of his mouth.

'Come on, come on, come on . . . ' said Patricia through her teeth, clenching and unclenching her fists.

Little by little I brought the fish alongside.

'I think you'll have to help me,' I said to Humberto, my rod bent like a hairpin.

'Here, over here,' he said from the stern.

Reaching out he grabbed the hair-thin line and gingerly lifted the *tararira* clear of the water. It looked big and mean but somehow disappointing, somehow not quite big enough to merit all the work that had gone into bringing it ashore. There it hung, now moving, now eerily still, several kilos of angry, recalcitrant fish. Keeping respectfully away from that snapping jaw, Humberto disengaged it from the hook.

It was raining far too hard by now to stay there any longer, so we brought the net inboard, disentangled ourselves from the *camalote*, and headed back towards the town. The palm trees on the cliffs were being bent and whipped by the wind, the sky hanging like a heavy hammer overhead. Visibility was very near no good at all, and the temperature had dropped. I couldn't give a damn. I'd caught a *tararira*.

We tied up at La Charqueada. Humberto asked whether we wanted the fish we'd caught, visibly hoping we didn't. We invited them to have a drink, but they were in a hurry to get home. Hand in hand, walking on air, Patricia and I stepped ashore. We walked through the village to the bakery, where the woman tried to overcharge us for a Coke. We let it slide. We couldn't give a damn. We'd caught a *tararira*.

CHAPTER FIFTEEN

A SHORT WALK IN THE ROCHA MARSH

There being no bridge, we were going to cross the river by barge. It travelled back and forth a couple of kilometres upstream from the town. Just after eight we left the Parador, weaving our way through the maze of puddles and slime that the dusty road had become. After falling all night, the rain had stopped, and the morning was hot and clammy. The humid air stuck in our chests and made our skins itch.

Half an hour or so later, we found that the track through the rice paddies down to the landing stage was a soupy, treacherous mess, far too muddy for cycling. As though the rain had not already done enough, some of the paddies had overflowed the retaining dykes and dumped an even greater flood onto the road. The mosquitoes, which usually spend the daylight hours sheltering in the grass, had nowhere dry to stop and rest. We could hear their thin obnoxious humming as they swarmed and swirled in a torpid grey haze at knee height. Desperate for a place to stand, they fastened themselves onto our clothing and our bags in such thick, scummy layers that they looked like knitted covers. From time to time we stopped to sweep them off by the gritty, greasy handful. For some reason – not that I was complaining – they were in no mood to feed, but even then Patricia's face was pale and strained.

From the crest of a low ridge we looked down onto the Río Cebollatí. So close, and yet so far: between us and the bank lay a ski slope of slimy black clay. Laughing so hard we were in danger of falling over, we slithered down it together, holding each other up, taking the bicycles one at a time. As at last we rolled the second one on board the flat, rusty barge, a voice called out from the opposite shore.

'No, no, not on the barge! Don't put them on the barge!'

It felt solid enough beneath our feet, but for a moment we wondered what was wrong: perhaps the wretched thing was about to sink. . . . The voice was rowing towards us in a wooden boat.

'Not on the barge!' it called again, and we realized that the young man in charge of it intended to take us across in the rowboat.

He was a big, strapping fellow. While he and I, splashing and grunting, manhandled the bikes into the bow of his precarious craft, Patricia rinsed her feet in the shallows.

'Come on, Patita, let's go,' I murmured. 'We're ready.'

'No need to hurry,' interjected the boatman, 'let her wash her feet if she likes.'

I felt chastized.

'Not that it'll do much good,' he added. 'It's worse on the other side.'

Patricia stood up with a jerk. 'What do you mean, "worse"?'

'Well, *worse*,' he answered with a shrug. 'Mud and clay, for about five kilometres. You won't even be able to wear those,' he said, pointing at our rubber flip-flops. 'You'll lose them. They'll get sucked off your feet.'

A look of deep suspicion spread across my wife's face as she clambered hesitantly into the rowboat. The boatman pushed us off the sand and leapt aboard. With long, powerful strokes he pulled across to the opposite bank, and helped us carry the bikes over the narrow beach, through the thick and matted treeline and onto the road.

It was flat and smooth, like the road to La Charqueada, surfaced with a mixture of sand and clay which probably was hard and firm when dry. Wet, however, it was a nightmare, exceeding beyond measure the boatman's dour prediction. I think we tried the first three or four paces with our sandals on, but we soon grew tired of leaving them stuck behind us in the glue so we dispensed with them altogether and trudged on barefoot. The mud squelched up between our toes like chocolate toothpaste. Pushing the bikes was hard work. One moment they'd stick fast, buried up to the panniers, and the next, they'd slip and skid out of control as though on ice.

The air was thick with the smell of animals and rotting vegetation. Without fences to contain them, cattle strayed across our path and stopped to watch, inquisitive and unafraid. The track was strewn with their dung, which mixed in with the warm soup sucking at our bare feet.

It seemed to take forever to reach the village of Cebollatí. At the heart of a rice-producing region, it was larger than La Charqueada, with more houses and even one or two paved roads.

We stopped to buy some fruit at a corner stall. As I paid for our purchases, I noticed that Patricia had disappeared. One of the lads caught my eye and grinned.

'She went in there,' he said, pointing to a doorway in the wall. I found her in the garden, rinsing off her feet with water from a well.

The main street petered out at the junction with the highway, marked on our map as paved but in reality so abominable it paled every awful road we'd ever seen. Strewn with coarse, black, razor-rimmed gravel, it was hard to tell where one pot-hole ended and another began. It was flanked on either side by flat, bleak, never-ending marsh and the ditches, little rivers, were clogged with rushes and papyrus. The sun couldn't make up its mind: sometimes it shone and sometimes it didn't.

We'd only advanced a few kilometres when I had my first puncture. Fortunately there was no traffic, because there was no verge to which I could retreat while I patched the tyre. Sitting by the flooded ditch, I made my first repair. Another few kilometres, and yet another puncture, again the rear tyre. This time I took the precaution of changing them around, putting the tougher Michelin at the back. It seemed as though we'd only just started off again when a sibilant hiss announced another flat. Same tyre, now on the front. It hadn't punctured, though: my second patch had come unstuck. I replaced it. The afternoon wore on. The third patch, too, refused to hold. I changed the inner tube. Then *that* punctured. Betting heavily against each other as to how long it would last, I gummed on another patch. It didn't last a hundred metres. I thought I might be doing something wrong, so this time I studied the procedure step by step, even reading the instructions – 'find hole: patch it' – trying deliberately to be more careful. Then I remembered that the *Prefecto* in La Charqueada hadn't been able to mend his rubber dinghy because of the damp. I looked around. We were in the middle of a flooded plain, and the air was as close to 100 per cent moisture as you can get without it actually pouring with rain.

We thought it best not to place too great a strain on the weak repairs, so we began to walk. It didn't make the slightest bit of difference. Another two patches later, seven in all, I gave up trying to mend the leaks. I had no choice: I only had one patch left, and I didn't want to waste it when I knew it wouldn't hold. Perhaps, if we could light a fire, I could somehow dry the rubber out enough so that my last patch would stay on but, short of lighting a fire in the middle of the road (assuming we could find something dry to burn in the first place!) there was nothing we could do. The gravel tore at our shoes, the afternoon wore into early evening. There were still no passing trucks to give us a lift.

Although as usual we were covered in insect repellent, when the light began to fail my wife began to fret. Soon her buddies the mosquitoes would rise up again like marshland Draculas and start to hunt. She put on her knee socks. A little while later she peeled off her shorts, put on her Portuguese Army surplus trousers and some more repellent.

Splashing across the fen towards the road, from the first trees we'd seen for ages, came a battered green Land Rover. We met it at the fence. It was full of woodsmen. No, there was no house there, although even if there *had* been, there was no dry route across the soggy desolation.

'There's an *estancia* on the right, just a little further up,' said one of the men; 'it's dry there. The owner's quite a decent chap, I'm sure he'll let you stay. You can patch up your bike in the morning, if it gets drier.'

We found the gate. The driveway climbed a gentle slope towards a wood.

'Why don't you cycle on ahead,' I said to Patricia, 'before it gets too dark. I'll walk up behind, and meet you there in a couple of minutes.'

She didn't like the sound of that at all but she did it just the same, pausing only to put on her jacket. The mosquitoes were starting to rise. As she left I heard a horn blow behind me: the woodsmen. One of them came running towards me.

'Here!' he said, out of breath, 'I found this in the glove compartment. I'd forgotten I had it. Maybe you can use it.'

He handed me a puncture repair kit. It held a single, solitary patch and a tube of glue.

'Good luck!' he called over his shoulder, already jogging back to the Land Rover.

It took me about ten minutes to get to the top of the driveway. In the gloom amongst the trees I saw the vague outline of a house, and made my way towards it. As I crossed the neglected, broken cattle-grid, a vague, uneasy feeling settled over me. It increased when I saw the house: the shutters were all closed and the paint was cracked and peeling. Patricia's bike was leaning against the fence, but she was nowhere to be seen. Empty liquor bottles were scattered about everywhere in the long, untidy grass. I whistled 'shave and a haircut'. No reply. Dropping my bike where it stood, I walked through the gate, whistling again. This time the reply – 'two bits' – wafted through the dusky air. Telling myself that if she could whistle she must be all right I relaxed, but not much. A moment later she came around from behind the house, looking tense and distraught. I didn't need to ask.

'Let's go,' I said, taking her arm. As we left, a cloud of mosquitoes rose from the weeds.

'Oh God, it was terrible!' she said, her shoulders shaking, as we walked back to the gate, 'I've never *seen* such awful people . . . '

For a moment I thought she might cry.

She'd found the foreman and his family, and from her description they sounded like extras from a horror film: dirty, hostile and covered in sores, living in degenerate, mephitic squalor. She hadn't even bothered to ask whether we might stay, so keen had she been to get away.

We should have guessed, I thought, as we walked towards the gate. We should have seen the signs. This, for example: the bleached carcass of a sheep, every bone in place, lying in the middle of the track, in exactly the same place where it had fallen down and died, how long ago? The broken wire, the fallen cattle-grate, the neglected house. Hindsight is a marvellously useless thing.

The last pale glow of sunset was slipping from the western sky as we reached the gate. We'd been travelling for twelve hours. With almost religious reverence we squatted in the dust and tried the patch the *leñador* had given us. It didn't hold either. There was nothing we could do but soldier on, driven halfway nuts by the sound of the mosquitoes in orbit around our heads. Never in our lives had we seen so many, not even at Playa Agraciada. It sounds a paltry thing, just a few little insects, but the constant whine as they tried to find a repellent-free landing site had our teeth on edge. Restless, jumping things splashed about in the ditches. Legions of frogs coughed into life and launched their hoarse serenade. A veil of cloud concealed the moon. In the gloom a large white owl sailed as silent as a ghost from fencepost to fencepost, following us down the road. Somewhere in the darkness, dogs began to bark. The only lights in the coal-black night were the wan orange smudges cast at our feet by the bicycle lamps. The heat was overwhelming. Buried in her Barbour and long trousers, Patricia was perspiring heavily. Vaguely remembering 'tips for survival', I began to worry that she might dehydrate.

'At least the mosquitoes can't get me,' she said with a shudder.

We no longer cared so much about hitching a lift, we were far more concerned about finding fresh water (surrounded by it, and not a drop to drink . . .) and a dry place to pitch the tent.

Ages later we saw the yellow cones of headlamps in the distance. Just as suddenly as they'd appeared, they were gone again, behind some darker shape. A hill? A wood? We couldn't tell. They reappeared about fifteen minutes later, coming straight towards us. I signalled with the torch. The car pulled up a few metres away, trapping us in the light of the high beams. The driver was nervous, as though afraid that we might stick him up. No, he didn't know the neighbourhood, no, he didn't have any water. In a hurry to be gone, he put his foot down to the floor and roared away. Over the next couple of hours, two more cars raced past, ignoring our signals, before the third one stopped. It was a station wagon, piled high with gear, a family crammed into the cab. The driver, a portly young man with a beard, recognized our plight at once and, despite the boy's protestations, snatched a bottle of fizzy lemonade from his son's clutching fingers and handed it across. Patricia stuck it in her mouth and tipped the bottom up towards the sky. She'd been perspiring heavily inside her coat, which she still refused to take off despite my pleas. I was only wearing shorts and a singlet, but even *my* tongue was swelling with thirst. The man was some sort of magistrate in Cebollatí.

'San Luis is more than 30 kilometres away,' he said, 'but if you can keep going just a little longer there's a turning up ahead, and if you follow that, you'll find a police station on your left. Good lads, there.'

Having heard similar recommendations before, I took his with a pinch of salt. I asked him to repeat it several times, but when he left I was still wondering whether he'd said the turning was two or twelve kilometres ahead. In Spanish, the words are very similar: *dos* and *doce*.

'What did he say?' asked Patricia.

'Oh, just a little further,' I lied.

In the hope of attracting less mosquitoes, we switched off our lights. My wife was burning up inside her coat and, obsessed by now with dehydration, I persuaded her to take it off. She tried without it for a while, but the little vampires of the night just wouldn't leave the girl alone. She put it on again. At last we reached the crossing. Oh thank heavens, it was two and never twelve! We turned left.

We couldn't see, but we could hear that the flooded fields on either side of us were full of cattle, lowing and splashing restlessly about. And then we understood why the cars had all slowed down along this stretch: silhouetted by approaching headlights, we saw that the road was crowded with cows. Driven half insane by the mosquitoes in the marshes, they'd broken down the fences and come to where the ground was dry. Now, before the slow advance of the approaching car, the herd was moving solidly towards us. Ditch to the left, ditch to the right, a million cows up ahead. I hoped the driver had the sense not to accelerate or blow his horn, which might trigger that enormous mass into a stampede. Stopping where we stood, Patricia's fingers locked onto my arm, I signalled with the torch, hoping he would see and understand. Eventually the car broke through the herd and stopped beside us. Miracle of miracles: the driver had a demijohn of water in the boot. We filled up all our bottles and poured the rest straight down our cracking throats. He was a young lad, the editor of a weekly news-sheet published in Lascano.

'But be careful you don't miss it,' he said of the *comisaría*, 'all the lights were out when I drove past just now.'

It took us almost two hours to get through the herd, hoping all the time that the owner wouldn't find us there in case he thought we were trying to steal his cows. We tried everything we could think of to get past them. If we walked slowly, then so did the cows. If we hurried, making noises in the hope that they would separate and let us through, they just galloped a few paces further on and stopped again to wait. The cattle in the neighbouring fields, as though afraid that they might miss the party, rushed to join those already on the road, dodging past us, brushing us aside in their frantic haste to join their pals. Patricia nearly had a heart attack when a small, complaining calf stuck its head up in between her handlebars, looking for a teat, only then to realize its mistake and, in its hurry to escape, tearing the bike out of her hands. We became so familiar with them that we began to think we could recognize individuals by their behaviour. One, in particular, constantly threatened to charge, only to surrender and canter away at the very last minute.

By the time the last dozen cows had let us through and fallen far behind we were filthy and exhausted, although glad to be walking across the moonlit marsh on our own once again. The sky had cleared: the Milky Way was strewn like luminous confetti across the black, and in the light of the opal moon we could see bats flickering back and forth amongst clusters of palm trees. A fine dew began to fall, condensing in beads on the bikes. On the sluggish air came the pungent smell of pigs. A small black and white dog, tail wagging, appeared out of the darkness.

'We've gone past it, I just know we have,' murmured Patricia.

The dog trotted on ahead, looking back from time to time.

'He'll take us there, don't worry,' I said, trying to encourage the two of us.

As soon as I'd said it, the damned thing disappeared and left me with my theory in my lap.

We were just about to surrender when, just like the promised land, we saw the station looming in the moonlit mist. The little dog was sitting by the gate. It took us a few minutes to wake the sleeping policemen. Two of them, looking dazed and confused, came to the door with a hurricane lamp. The youngest of the two looked us up and down and grinned, and invited us in. The other hovered about in the background, looking deeply suspicious. We could almost hear him thinking. Having considered for a while, he made his decision and looked me straight in the eye.

'*Documentos?*' he challenged.

Trying not to look too closely at the grass, we pitched our tent in the back yard amongst the pigs and chickens and ducks that had woken up and come to see what we were doing, just in case we dropped something they could eat. It was half-past two in the morning. Nineteen hours it had taken us to get this far. Filthy and stinking but far too tired to care, we collapsed into our beds.

CHAPTER SIXTEEN

SMUGGLERS

Hot.

Sticky.

I opened one eye and looked at Patricia. Her face was streaked with grime. Recollections of the day before filtered slowly into my waking mind. Walking, walking, walking. My feet hurt. Had we really walked so much? My hands were grey. There was dirt under my fingernails. Patricia stirred.

'Ooh . . . ' she sighed, long and drawn out, arching her back. 'I've just had the most awful dream . . . ' she murmured, lacing a bare leg over mine.

'It wasn't a dream,' I answered. Her eyes flicked open.

'I was afraid you'd say that. You're filthy.'

'Seen yourself lately?'

'Those bloody mosquitoes . . . '

I pulled on my shorts and stepped out through the flap for my first proper look at our surroundings. We were in the middle of a scruffy, weed-choked yard, between a tin shed and the back of the police station. In the shed there was a broad-rumped Chevrolet Impala that once had been black. On a wooden bench by the open kitchen door, sat one of the cops, drinking his *mate*.

'Good morning,' he said, 'slept well?'

Not long enough, I told him, stretching my stiff muscles, but otherwise fine. A large sow and a handful of chickens scraped about in the bare soil near the tent.

'Think we could have that shower now?' I asked.

'Sure. It's right there,' he said, leaning forward and pointing with his cigarette towards another open door. 'I'll pump some water up into the storage tank.'

'No, no . . . ' I protested, 'let me do it.'

I followed him to the covered stone well.

'I have to feed it first,' he explained.

He slipped off the hose leading to the storage tank on the roof, and poured some water from a battered bucket into the assembly. He gave the handle a couple of cranks, and then let me take over. I pumped until my arms ached. I intended to stay in that shower for the rest of my life.

Armed with all our soaps and towels, Patricia and I stepped into the bathroom. Like an angry dragon, the living stink jumped out of the drains and punched me in the face.

Patricia coughed. 'My Lord . . . ' she choked.

The smell was so thick and dense that two strong men could have picked it up and carried it into the yard. A lidless toilet bowl, encrusted with the dirt of years, stood in one corner. Facing it was a small washbasin. From the opposite wall, high above our heads, protruded a short length of twisted lead pipe: the shower. Set into a drainage hole in the centre of the floor, clogged with nameless debris, was a metal grille. The small, dark room had no light or windows: we'd have to trust the cops and shower with the door open. Not that we could have closed it without suffocating.

The water was ice-cold, but after the initial shock it was like heaven on earth. We stood under the jet facing upwards with our eyes closed, as if in pagan prayer. Carefully, Patricia unwrapped our sole remaining bar of soap, and handed it to me. I was just working up a lather when it shot upwards, as though fired out of my hands, and, twisting in mid-air like a slow motion salmon, nose-dived straight into the filthy toilet bowl. Our eyes met. There was nothing we could do but laugh: neither of us had the courage to attempt a rescue. Luckily there was a sliver of police soap on the washbasin.

Scrubbed and scraped, we slumped onto the bench. My feet were bruised and sore, and where they had been exposed by the canvas *alpargatas* they were covered in tiny red pinpoints. Patricia had been wearing leather tennis shoes with sturdy rubber soles, so she hadn't suffered as much from the broken road, but the fiendish mosquitoes had found the ventilation holes in the leather and, even through her thick socks, had themselves a feast. Like living adverts for the brand, both her feet bore perfect replicas of the manufacturer's trademark.

By one of those strokes of good luck, the sergeant, who lived in a shack at the foot of the field behind the police station, had a packet of Brazilian tyre patches. Perhaps more suited to the climate, the adhesive held at once. With *that* problem at least taken care of, we settled down by the road in the shade of an osier with Richard, the younger of the two policemen, to wait for a truck. No power on earth could have persuaded us to walk. It was two hours before the first one came along. It was an old, brown, Chevy pickup truck without a bonnet. There were three young men in the cab and another two in the open back. Richard flagged them down and, leaning on the windowsill, kepi pushed onto his eyebrows, held a murmured conversation with the driver. Of course they'd take us, yes of course, officer. They seemed to be in a tearing hurry to please. As we were loading the bikes onto the truck, the other policeman appeared, carrying an empty butane gas container. Without wasting time on hellos, he banged it onto the gravel.

'If you get the chance, could you pick up a refill for us?' he asked, 'and a litre of fly spray?'

Yes sir, of course sir, three bags full sir.

He held out some money, folded into a wad, which he tried to press onto each of the lads in turn. None of them would touch it, but they jostled each other for the privilege of loading the bottle alongside the three they already had.

Patricia got into the cab with the driver, I climbed into the back with the other four and, with a crash of gears, we lurched off. My companions were friendly, likeable rogues. They were smugglers, on their way to Chuy, where the border between Brazil and Uruguay runs down the main street. Armed with a shopping list and a pocketful of money, they were headed for the Brazilian side. Today's orders included a refrigerator, a colour television, small electrical goods such as liquidizers, irons and hair driers, and a selection of foodstuffs and domestic goods, as well as refills for the three – now increased to four – bottles of butane gas, all of which were cheaper on the other side. They explained, in case I'd missed the point, why they hadn't accepted the policeman's money. He knew what they were, and what they were on their way to do. The gas and the fly spray were his tithe, his fee for not looking too closely into the truck on their return. Had they accepted his money, it was as sure as eggs is eggs that he would search and fine them as assiduously and meticulously as the law provided. It was all part of a day's work, and fully accounted for in their 'overheads'.

We stopped at 18 de Julio for customs inspection. Our driver went into the shed alone. While we waited, a large, brand new Peugot sedan, coming from Chuy, its suspension down to the ground thanks to the weight it carried in the boot, drew up and stopped alongside us. The driver, dressed like a Marbella golfer, got out and walked into the shed carrying two large jars of instant coffee. Moments later he came out again, red-eared and sheepish, only to enter once more with a bottle of whisky and a carton of American cigarettes. The duty officer had disdained his initial gift, telling him bluntly that he'd have to do better in view of the cargo he carried. Our driver came out with the news that the 'fee' for fridges had gone up to 15,000 pesos (about £20) but, since they were steady customers and, not knowing about it, hadn't worked the increase into their profit margin, they wouldn't have to pay it *this* time.

About two kilometres beyond the customs post the engine coughed and died. Out of petrol. With much amiable yelling and waving of arms, two of the lads were elected to hitchhike somewhere for fuel. Of those who stayed behind, one was a soldier on leave and another was a plain-clothes policeman. Besides this little smuggling operation, he was visiting

Chuy on unofficial business. He couldn't collect enough 'tax' in his present position so he'd applied for a transfer into the local force, a job which, with its opportunities, tips and backhanders, was far more rewarding. He wanted to see how his application was coming along. You see, he explained, there were a couple of people currently in the Chuy force who were cramping his career, and he might have to get them out of the way. It was nothing to worry about, just a minor detail: all he had to do was set them up and let them incriminate themselves.

Along with the petrol, the others brought the news that a police booth by the road on the way into town was manned, and someone they knew was on duty. If he saw us, he'd want his bite. So, approaching Chuy, we lurched off the road into Brazil, jolted across a field to the end of a backstreet, and drove into the town along that.

The smugglers let us off in the forecourt of a petrol station on the main street, not only the frontier between two countries, but also the dividing line between two worlds. The Brazilian side was an anthill of activity: large, gaudy bazaars overflowing with multicoloured, eye-catching merchandise. Shoppers and gawking day-trippers – most of them Uruguayan – jostled each other and haggled with aggressive, loud-mouthed shopkeepers. Everywhere we went, someone had something to sell. We were accosted from all sides by hawkers noisily thrusting their wares at us. The pastoral tranquility of the countryside was gone; we were back amongst the predators. Wanting to get some patches, we went looking for a bicycle shop. On a little sidestreet we found four.

We were surrounded with pavement cafés but Patricia, overwhelmed by the bustle and noise and feeling an odd loyalty for 'poor little Uruguay', preferred to cross the street and find a café there. In Brazil, all the streets were paved; here they were cancerous with sharp-edged pot-holes and bare, eroded earth. The place was a dump. We found a bar on the main street, and settled at a pavement table with a bottle of mineral water. As we finished, the waiter brought the bill: 300 pesos. Since the price had usually been somewhere between sixty and a hundred, I asked him whether he was sure. It was hardly the sort of establishment where one might pay a little extra for the privilege of being there. He didn't answer, going instead to fetch the proprietor from another table, where he sat drinking with his insalubrious pals. He was a medium tall, unpleasant-looking man; bald on top; dank, oily hair hanging limply over his ears; and badly in need of a bath and a shave. His few remaining teeth were brown and twisted.

'Yes, fine, one mineral water: 300 pesos,' he said, his voice laden with challenge.

'Don't you think that's a bit expensive?' I asked mildly.

'Sir, I don't question your business, please don't question mine,' he retorted with unconcealed hostility.

'That's not a very positive attitude . . . ' I said, surprised.

'I'm a businessman, this is my place and I take whatever attitude I please!'

Unsurprisingly, I didn't like his answer much. Normally I'll walk a mile to avoid a fight, but somehow I found myself being drawn into the sort of puerile argument which would have run aground very quickly if it hadn't been for a comment he made, probably in honour of my fair hair, as though it proved something. It was this:

'Uruguay for the Uruguayans!'

If he was a sample of the sort of Uruguayan he had in mind as worthy guardians of the country I was born in, I thought, I'd rather feed it to the pigs. I was about to tell him so in no uncertain terms when we were rescued from any further escalation of the conflict by Patricia.

'You're a very rude man, *señor*,' she interrupted indignantly, 'a very rude man indeed! I hope you choke on this money!' She threw a handful of coins onto the floor and, nose in the air, tugged me along by the sleeve. 'Come on, darling,' she said, 'we're leaving.'

We had to cycle a couple of squares before our anger wore off. Even now, as I write, I can feel my temper boiling up again. I wish I'd hit him. I really do.

On the way out of town we stopped at the telephone exchange to ask for a few spare parts from 'base camp'. The people in the queues around us all looked as unpleasant as our pal the barkeeper. We couldn't leave Chuy fast enough. Heading west towards La Coronilla, on the coast, we had the wind behind us and raced over the tarmac at a spanking pace. There was more traffic than we'd seen for weeks. We were back in civilization, back amongst the hurried lives. It made us feel agitated and keen to get off the road. For added incentive a storm was piling up on the horizon, layer upon malevolent layer of black and purple cloud in growling, precarious towers that threatened to collapse at any minute.

The wind was high when we reached the shore. The sea was a disappointing chocolate brown. 'Iodine,' the coastguard said. The public campsite was neat, but far too busy. We longed for the peace of the open savannah. On a backstreet we found the local council and went into the office to ask for advice.

'Well,' said the only person there, 'there's an open field next to the police station, by the woods. But it floods every time it rains. With the storm that's coming, you'll drown! Just wait a minute,' he said: 'Would you mind? I'd like to check something.'

He darted out of the office, leaving us there. A few moments later he came back.

'There's a hotel just down the road, Las Palmas.'

'I'm afraid our budget no longer runs to hotels,' I cut him short.

'No, no. The owner, that's him over there, drinking *mate*, he's invited you to stay there as his guests.'

'*Qué tal, muchachos?*' said the landlord, a *latino* Pickwick in a bright yellow bathing suit and gaudy, floral shirt.

'*Querida,*' he called to the chambermaid, 'give them number thirteen. Make yourselves comfortable. Talk to you later,' he said with a grin, slapping me on the back as I passed.

We followed the *querida* across the lobby and into a grassy courtyard. The rooms led onto a gallery around it, canopied with corrugated sheets of translucent green plastic. As though timed to the split second, no sooner had we leaned our bikes against the wall outside the door to number thirteen, than the skies opened up with a bang. I don't know who does the P.R. for the Uruguayan weather, but the advertisements before the storms have no equal anywhere. First comes the darkness, thick like the inside of a boot, then a crashing and walloping and flashing of lights and only then, once you're thoroughly impressed, do you get the rain. At the Hotel Las Palmas we got no raindrops as such: we got jets as thick as your finger squirting out of the sky.

Number thirteen was barely larger than the double bed, and halfway through redecoration: the carpet was out, in its place only a few glue stains on the tiles. The walls, a battlefield encrusted with the flattened cadavers of bugs, were in need of a new coat of paint. But the bathroom was impeccable, the shower was hot and the bedclothes were clean.

We'd picked up a few things to nibble on, and we still had the bottle of *Caña* which we'd bought so many years ago in La Charqueada. While the windows rattled and the thunder crashed we spread out on the bed and had a feast.

'I'm thirsty,' I said, halfway through the celebration; 'how about a glass of water?'

Patricia held the glass out through the window, underneath the stream cascading off the roof. In a second it was full.

'You cheated,' I accused, 'do it again.'

She did.

We strolled to the bakery to get some fresh croissants for breakfast and, much to our surprise, the girl there tried to keep the change. Had we not been short of cash and counting every penny, we might never have noticed. We'd lost the habit. For weeks we'd been travelling as if inside a protective membrane, sheltered from the greed and the haste of consumer society. Now we were back on the front line, on the tourist-rich strip along the coast, in the fairground, solidly amongst the 'marks'. Next to the bakery there was a butcher's shop. Above it, an undertaker's parlour.

Their signs projected together from the building. Shades of Sweeney Todd.

La Coronilla is a small holiday village. It's far from opulent, perhaps because of the brown ocean which, we learned, was a more or less permanent feature. After longing for so many weeks to bathe in the sea, the rich cocoa was a disappointment. We consoled ourselves with the fact that the weather was overcast and stormy, and we couldn't really have enjoyed the beaches anyway. We spent the day strolling on the sand, getting caught in the occasional cloudburst, and dipping hesitantly in water clogged with jellyfish.

The sky was still grey when we left next morning, heading towards Punta del Diablo, a fishing village further along the coast. On the way we stopped to explore the Fortaleza de Santa Teresa, an evocative and handsomely restored stone fortress built on a hill by the Portuguese in one of their many invasions.

As the sun wore away the sullen grey clouds, our enthusiasm mounted and when, halfway along the dirt track leading to Devil's Point, the highway now far behind us, we caught our first glimpse of the perfect blue Atlantic up ahead, our excitement was uncontrollable. At last, the ocean, and a proper colour this time! Just as we rounded a bend, a vaguely familiar large white station wagon roared past us and screeched to a dusty halt. The back was full of pretty, suntanned girls, looking just like an advertisement for some exotic cocktail. The cab door opened, and who should drop onto the road but our old friend Jaime! He was in town visiting his girlfriend, Manuela, whose parents had a beach house in the village. Meeting them was all we needed to complete the promise of the day. Everyone talked at once: we didn't know which story to tell first.

'Tell me later,' said Jaime, 'tell me later!'

He explained how to get to the house, and roared off ahead.

Once upon a time Punta del Diablo was just a humble cluster of fishermen's thatched wooden shacks, but the spot was far too beautiful to remain unnoticed for very long. The discerning few had already started building glamorous chalets up on the rolling dunes. So far, we were pleased to see, the new houses all echoed the rustic flavour of the place, and everything was still splendid chaos as urban planning had not yet regimented the buildings or the streets. Inevitably, perhaps, we wondered with some foreboding just how long that character could last, as we recalled the rape of the Mediterranean coasts by the heartless, mass-market tourist industry. But we weren't here to get depressed and anyway, Devil's Point was too lovely to allow it.

As we made our way along the sodden, rutted streets, only now beginning to dry out, an overpowering odour of fish, mingled with something reminiscent of wet dog, closed in around us like a clamp. It took us a while to realize what it was: in the yards, rank upon rank of salted fish, the famous *bacalao*, hung out to dry in the sun. In a festive cluster at the foot of the stone and concrete wharf, we caught a glimpse of the wooden stalls where long-haired artisans sold quaint, colourful trinkets made of sharks' vetebrae, sea shells and turtles' carapaces.

Manuela's parents had their thatched white stucco house halfway up a dune, looking out over the perfect bay. We stood by the gate and gaped at the tumbling emerald sea, crested with racing white horses. One of the things we most wanted to do while we were here was to go out on a fishing boat and spend the day out there. The wooden craft, painted brilliant oranges and blues, were drawn up on the sand. Impatient and unable to wait, we wandered through the town looking for a skipper. We found one, at his 'other' job as a builder, working on a house. He'd be happy to take us along, he said, if the sea calmed down enough to let him sail, but we'd have to clear it first with *Prefectura*.

The coastguard were quartered in a pretty little house right on the beach. Well, said the officer on duty, if the captain says it's all right, then I suppose it is. But no women. He was adamant that Patricia couldn't go. The men went out to work, he said, they could do without any dangerous distractions. I tried to explain that Patricia was unlikely to try to sunbathe topless or dance the conga on the wheelhouse, but he refused to budge. Take it or leave it, he said.

We spent the rest of the day on the beach with Jaime and Manuelita's family, being sinfully, deliciously lazy. In the evening we set up our tent at the top of the dune behind the house, with the magical, intoxicating view spread out at our feet.

CHAPTER SEVENTEEN

IN WHICH WE GO TO SEA

The weather wasn't good enough for the fishing boats to sail, so we didn't have to put the coastguard's resolution to the test. Instead we were on holiday, so we spread out on the beach, swam, played volleyball, and wandered off on endless walks. We dug for clams and *tatucitos*, a sort of salt-water beetle, grey and prehistoric, that lives in the sand at the water's edge. 'They make excellent bait,' said Jaime. The next bay, to the east, was a magical, untouched wilderness. The forests that came down to the dunes were all part of the Santa Teresa national park, a nature reserve.

Playing about in the breakers, I was just getting ready to dive through a wave, when I felt a twang in my right calf. The muscle went directly into spasm. Sitting on the sand, trying to rub some of the ache away, I realized that we might not be able to leave next morning as we'd planned. It was a dreadful shame, but there was nothing I could do: we'd just *have* to spend another day in paradise. We managed to talk Jaime into staying on as well. In the late afternoon, with me limping along in the rear, we went out on the rocks at one end of the bay to try our hand at fishing. We didn't catch a thing, not even a cold.

The following morning, rubbing the sleep from our eyes, Patricia, Manuelita, Toto (her younger brother), Jaime and I stumbled in a daze onto the rocks to try again. We sat there sipping *mate* and munching on our sandwiches, totally ignored by the fish. Jaime handed his rod over to Toto, and disappeared amongst the boulders.

'I've got a bite,' said Toto.

'Yeah, yeah, just like yesterday!' murmured his disbelieving sister, recalling all his teasing of the day before.

'No, really, I *do!*'

Jaime, coming back, didn't believe him any more than we did.

'It's going to get away!' the boy pleaded.

Something in his voice made us all look up. The rod was bent double, the reel was racing, and Toto was being dragged across the rocks. Jaime lunged as with a bowstring twang the heavy line snapped apart, sitting Toto hard onto the stone, an astonished look on his face.

'What on earth was *that*?' we all exclaimed as one.

'God knows,' said Jaime, 'but it was big, and now it's gone!'

Over dinner the night before we'd assured everyone that we were going to catch a ton of fish, which Patricia had promised to make into *Ceviche*. Confronted yet again by our inadequacy as anglers, we did the only thing we could have done: we cheated. On the way back we stopped at a fisherman's house to buy the basic ingredient.

'What were you using for bait?' he asked. 'White fish, eh? Probably a shark, then. The only thing that takes white bait. Or a manta ray. I caught one there a year ago. A hundred and twenty kilos, it weighed. Needed several of us to get it out of the water. The cartilage is on the wall in the restaurant around the corner.'

Indeed it was. A massive beast. We went to have a look.

Early next morning we loaded ourselves onto Jaime's station wagon, and continued west. Beyond the Laguna Negra, at the crossing with the road towards Aguas Dulces, on the coast, Jaime and Manuelita dropped us off. Even though the sky was grey again, we were determined to go to sea. Had we not just come from Punta del Diablo, we would no doubt have been delighted with Aguas Dulces, but the memory was still too fresh and we found the busy streets a disappointment. Hardly pausing for a look at the houses built on stilts along the beach, we headed out along an earth road towards Valisas, birthplace of the Gordo Vizcaíno, who we'd met in La Charqueada. It was a bleak place. Whatever beauty its broad beaches might have had in fairer weather, was spoiled by a howling gale. We had a little conference by the side of the road. La Paloma, a small city on the coast, lay 60 kilometres further west. We'd already done 30. Can we get that far today? We don't really want to stay here, do we? No, we don't.

Patricia took the lead and we set off, the wind pushing us along. Every now and then we caught glimpses of the distant sea, but for much of the trip we cycled through pine forests and open, deserted plains. I was worried about our tyres on the gravel road, but we managed to reach the tarmac, at about the halfway mark, without incident. We made the trip in record time: barely two hours after leaving Valisas we were standing in the harbour at La Paloma, in front of the Port Authority. After our last experience with the coastguard, we thought it best to go straight there in case we needed special clearance, or had to arrange now for a trip the following day. Twenty minutes later we were chugging out of the harbour into mountainous seas in a small orange boat.

The *alferez* on duty in the *Prefectura* had acted surprised when we told him that, although in the end we hadn't gone because of the weather, Patricia had been refused permission to sail.

'Nonsense,' he said. 'When would you like to go?'

We muttered something about whenever it was convenient.

'Fine. How about right now? This man's just about to leave. What do you say, Teo?'

Teo, standing at the counter next to us, looked up and grinned. He was tall and fair-haired, tanned and weather-beaten.

'Love to,' he said. 'You ready?'

We bundled our bicycles into a microscopic prison cell, grabbed our jackets and followed him to the quayside. Nodding at the pier was a large, powerful fishing craft.

'Oh, not bad,' I said.

'No, no, not this one. The next one.'

Well, the next one, although smaller, didn't look at all bad either.

'No, no, not that one either. The next one.'

Next one? Next one where? There didn't seem to be a next one. We clambered across the deck and there, on the water far below us, bobbed the *Paraná Hum*. But it was too late to turn back now, so we lowered ourselves on board the tiny wooden boat. Teo's 'crew' was there already: a burly, bearded, *far-from-Ancient* Mariner and a friend who was coming along for a spot of sport.

'Sport?'

'Yes, after we've cast the nets we're going to try to catch some shark.' Patricia paled and retreated deeper into her coat.

As soon as we passed the harbour wall the boat began to kick. The waves were enormous. Coming out of nothing they towered overhead, picked us up like driftwood, and held us for a moment in midair before dropping us into a bottomless trough and starting all over again.

'Now don't be sick,' I warned my wife; 'you don't want them to think you're a cissy.'

She fixed her eye onto the horizon and, clutching on with both hands, stood as motionless as possible in that tossing, ruptured sea. At Teo's request we were standing in the microscopic hold astern, the deck level with our waists, a scant arm's length from the seething water.

It took about half an hour to reach the chosen spot. Teo switched off the motor, and he and his crew began casting out the nets. Without the thrust of the propeller the boat began to drift until we were broadside to the sea, which changed the motion of the boat to a disconcerting pitch and yaw. Although unsteady on her feet, Patricia was bright and cheerful.

'You see?' she said, 'I didn't get sick!'

The first hint I had that something wasn't quite as it should be, came when the smell of diesel began to clog inside my nose. From there it dropped into the pit of my stomach and in no time at all I was feeling distinctly ill. Sailing straight into the sea I'd been fine, but now, with this belly-churning side-on wobble, I wished we were back on terra firma. I hung on to the gunwales and hoped that no one would notice. My wife was chattering away about how she'd avoided seasickness by concentrating on a single point on the horizon, and wasn't this exciting, and I wonder whether they'll catch any sharks this afternoon and heaven-knows-what endless torrent of cheerful yap, when she looked across at me for my opinion. She stopped in mid-flow, the sudden silence clear and fragile as a soap bubble.

'You're greeeeen!' she crowed, hooting with laughter. 'Seasick! My Jacques Cousteau, are you feeling ill?'

Had I dared to let go of my grip on the deck I would have pushed her overboard.

'Shuddup fer chrissakes, jus' shuddup!' I snarled through my teeth. 'It'll pass in a minute, jus' leave me alone!'

'Oh, my Captain Ahab, my old sea dog!'

I searched for an oar so I could beat her over the head with it. Teo and his pals stopped working for a moment and looked towards us.

'You okay back there?'

'Yes, yes thanks we're fine, we're quite all right,' I said, hoping they'd believe it and wishing it were true.

They had a kilometre of nets to put out. It felt like fifty, but eventually they finished and we were on our way again. As soon as we'd escaped that fiendish roll I started feeling better. We cast anchor close to the rusted, jutting superstructure of a centenarian wreck. They baited hooks the size of gaffs and then Milton, Teo's friend, poured a demijohn of sheep's blood mixed with sugar – to stop it from coagulating in the bottle – into the sea to draw the sharks. Although the boat still tossed about, the anchor kept us pointed into the waves so the movement wasn't so uncomfortable.

'Don't worry,' said the burly crewman in a deep, sonorous voice, 'I still get seasick too, sometimes.'

For a long time nothing happened, except for the occasional slip of our mooring. Then Milton got a bite. His reel began to whine.

'I've got him, I've got him!' he bellowed with excitement. 'A big one, boy-o-boy, I bet you it's a white!'

A few tense moments later a look of disappointment swept across his face as he landed a *corvina*. Not quite the giant white he'd been hoping for, but at six-odd kilos, still a handsome catch. No, no, he was disconsolate.

'You have somewhere to cook it?' he asked. 'You take it.'

We'd been talking of how much we wanted to barbecue a fish. The sea was getting steadily rougher and our anchor kept slipping, so Captain Teo said he thought they'd better call it quits and head back into port.

Back on the motionless pier, Teo asked where we were planning to stay that night. To be honest, we hadn't really had a chance to think about it.

'Well, you can come to my house then, and put your tent up in the garden. I've got a *parrilla*, we can cook up the beast for dinner.'

He was telling us how to get there when another skipper joined us on the quay. He'd caught a *corvina* too, he said, just now, right here in the harbour. It was even bigger than Milton's. He didn't want it either, so he donated it as well. Now we had *two* of the beauties to look forward to. He was an *Argentino*, this other skipper, by the name of Page. He told us he was descended from a Captain Page, a Virginian who, as an officer in the Confederate Navy during the Civil War, had deserted with ship and crew and sailed to Argentina. There he'd become a Captain in the Argentine Navy and, said our Mr Page, the first – perhaps even the *only* – man to sail his ship along the inland waterways from Buenos Aires all the way to Bolivia.

Magdalena, a short, stocky woman, gave her husband a quick, mildly quizzical look as he introduced us and said he'd invited us to put up our tent in their garden, but she was obviously used to having him surprise her and immediately welcomed us in. Two enormous dogs uncurled themselves and gave us both a thorough sniff. Songbirds chirruped and fluttered in aviaries amongst the bushes and papyrus plants.

We'd only just settled down at a table on the back porch when the telephone rang. It was the coastguard: they wanted to see Teo in their office at once. He seemed terribly concerned about the urgent summons, and hurried indoors muttering mysteriously to his wife before going back to the port. For a moment we worried that it might have had something to do with our sailing on his boat, but Magdalena, trying unsuccessfully to hide her agitation, assured us that it didn't.

We stayed on the veranda with her and her daughter Gabriela until, unable to contain herself a moment longer, Magdalena told us that her thirteen-year-old son Daniel had been arrested. In the decaying cold room of an old, abandoned warehouse in the harbour, he and some friends had discovered that the walls were lined with sheets of white polystyrene, the sort of stuff that's used for packaging and insulation. They were peeling off and falling to the floor. The sight of such abundance going to waste while they were suffering from an acute shortage of surfboards had been too much to bear, so the boys had helped themselves to a sheet or two. They'd been trimming them to size, prior to trying them out on the beach, when a zealous watchman had found them. Instead of giving the boys a thick ear and sending them home, he'd dragged them by the collar into the harbourmaster's office, and filed a written report. Magdalena, a gentle, profoundly conventional woman, was deeply embarrassed about what we might think of the way she brought up her children. Yes, she accepted that boys will be boys, but this was going a little too far! It wasn't the sort of thing they were used to, the kids went to good Catholic schools, had a good education, how could Daniel do this?

Some time later, unannounced, the lad arrived. He leaned his bike against the wall and came straight across to kiss us both hello. He was obviously feeling sheepish and ashamed, and retired at once to his room. He certainly didn't look like a hardened criminal. He was followed closely by his father, head hung low with embarrassment. Teo tried to put a brave, paternal face on it, but he was haunted by visions of 'what if . . . ?' What if the warehouse had collapsed, as it threatened to do at any minute, and the boys had been trapped inside? What if they had hurt themselves? What if the watchman had shot them by mistake?

Next morning it was raining again and Teo had already gone to sea to bring in the nets. Magdalena and Daniel were preparing for their day in court. We cycled to the harbour to greet the returning boat and inspect the catch.

'Only 200 kilos: not very good,' said Teo in a sombre voice, but to us it seemed a marvellous selection.

There were even a couple of shark in the net. He selected a few *pargo* for our dinner, and handed them to me to clean. He and his friend Jorge, a dark, bearded man with an aquiline nose and almond-shaped eyes, who looked just like a bedouin, were going out hunting that afternoon. They'd be taking the dogs. With a bit of luck they might catch a *mulita* or two, which we could bake in their shells and have for dinner instead of the fish.

Catching that *tararira* had whetted our appetite. Despite, or perhaps because of, our failures at Punta Del Diablo, we wanted to have another go at sea fishing, so we suggested to Daniel that we go together. Patricia's philosophy was that if we wanted to learn how to fish, we ought to try it with someone who knew what to do. He considered the proposition shyly. The magistrate had given him a hearty chewing-out before she let him off, and he was still smarting.

The shadows were long when we set off, taking Daniel's shortcuts through fields and people's back gardens on our way to the 'good spot' on the beach. Patricia brought up the rear. Daniel fixed his clear blue eyes on me.

'Is she always that slow?' he asked anxiously.

'Always,' I said.

'Even when you had to walk all those kilometres with your bikes?'

'Even then.'

'Pajarito!' he whistled softly.

About 100 metres off the shore the waves were breaking on a line of rocks. Along the beach stood a row of people fishing. We cast out and while we waited Daniel scurried off amongst the fishermen, poking in their buckets and asking what they'd caught. He returned with the news that they were biting further down, so we reeled in and moved along.

The high water line was littered with seaweed and clear, translucent spheres like ping-pong balls. They glowed like Christmas ornaments as they caught the sun's last golden light. They were eggshells, some said of manta, some said of snails.

The bait which Daniel had rescued from the freezer had seen better days. The little fish stank and grew slimy as they thawed.

'Here's a good one,' he said, grinning from ear to ear and wrinkling his nose as he fastened it onto the hook with silk thread; 'nice and smelly!'

We hadn't come as well equipped as our neighbours, who lounged about in deck chairs at folding tables, sipping cocktails or *mate*. My line went slack. Thinking that the waves had moved it, I brought some of it in. I didn't think there was anything there, but I consulted with our expert just in case. Daniel fingered it gently, and tweaked it once or twice.

'Nobody there,' he declared.

It slackened again, and I was just about to wind in some more when the reel started racing.

'I think you've got something,' said Daniel solemnly, as though there were still a doubt. As the reel went on whining he started to jump up and down. 'Yes, yes, you've got something now!' he crowed. 'Don't let it get away, whatever you do.'

For several minutes the fish and I wrestled until, to our surprise, a receding wave revealed something brown flapping in the shallows. Whatever it was, it was fairly big. Daniel sprinted over the sand towards it. Another wave came in and, with a powerful wrench, the fish headed out to sea again: the line broke as though it weren't even there. The boy and I looked at each other in silence for a moment.

'Well, they're biting all right,' he said diplomatically. 'We'll try again.'

'It was huge,' he said excitedly as he baited another hook, 'the biggest on the beach. No one else has one that size! I bet it was a black *corvina*.'

I thought it might have been a small ray.

I broke the line twice in fudged attempts at casting.

'Let me try this time,' Daniel said with a smile, too polite to say frankly what he thought of my skills.

With carefully selected bits of rotten fish he took control. He'd barely taken in the slack when Zip! the line ran out. His eyes opened wide and a look of joy spread across his face.

'This one won't get away,' he said. 'Just wait and see.'

He played and teased it for all it was worth until at last he landed his exhausted prize: a golden, glistening *corvina*, about a kilo big. The boy was so delighted he seemed to be on fire. At least one of us had performed honourably. Night was falling, and with the sun the warmth was gone, so we headed back to the house. Daniel's young cousin Diego was there, a vivacious lad with a wicked sense of humour. He couldn't stop laughing and teasing Daniel about his run-in with the law.

'Don't worry about your dad,' he advised, 'he'll be over it by now. And if he's still mad, I tell you what – you just say it was the normal sort of thing that boys get up to. Tell him it was kid's stuff! *That's* what you should say.'

They wandered off together to collect some firewood.

It grew later and later, and still no sign of Teo. Magdalena was getting quite worried when Jorge's wife arrived with Teo's dogs.

'I've brought you these,' she said darkly, 'the rest will be delivered in the morning.'

Magdalena looked surprised.

'The rest? What rest? What do you mean?' she asked.

'Your husband and mine,' growled the woman, looking heartily fed up.

Magdalena sat up straight. 'What are you talking about? Where are they?'

'They're in jail,' the woman said. 'The police will let them out tomorrow morning.'

'Oh God!' moaned Magdalena and slumped onto the table, burying her face in her hands. 'Why are they in jail?'

'For hunting illegally on somebody's land.'

Magdalena folded like a paper doll and began to cry. Diego was laughing so hard he almost fell off his chair.

'Well, he can't yell at you now!' he howled at Daniel.

'Well, you'd better light the fire,' sighed Magdalena, 'I'm going to see what I can do.'

Distraught, she got her handbag and walked to the *comisaría* again. It wasn't very far, and she wasn't gone for very long.

'They may let him out tonight,' she said, disconsolate, as she laid the table.

Teo, Jorge and a third man, a naval officer, had gone off on their *mulita* hunt, as planned. Somewhere, on a country road, they split up. While the other two climbed over a fence into a field, Teo, who'd discovered that his dogs were no damned good at hunting, had stayed in the road. The owner of the field saw the other two and called the cops who, with unprecedented alacrity, descended in force and arrested them all.

Poor Magdalena tried hard to act normally, but she couldn't meet our eyes.

'What will you *think* of us!' she sighed. 'And now you're going to put it in a book. What will people say? We've always been respectable, nothing like this has ever happened before . . . '

We couldn't comfort her, no matter what we said. The last two days had been a bit too much for her. Gabriela, mortified, went indoors to hide. During the night Teo was allowed home in his wife's custody. He'd already put to sea by the time Patricia and I dismantled our tent the following morning.

We'd decided against Punta del Este. A graveyard through the winter months, during the summer it claims to be the most sophisticated resort on the continent's Atlantic seaboard. Whether that is true or not I leave for others to debate; but if absurdly high prices are any sort of index, the rumour may be true. Littered with palatial homes, the setting is undeniably beautiful although rather spoiled by the plethora of high-rise apartments: the pandemic disease of the fashionable holiday haunt. As one would expect in such a place, the seasonal population is grotesquely pretentious; Punta del Este has a fairly high ratio of pains in the arse per square metre. Gorgeous some of them may be, and scantily dressed if you're lucky, but they're still obnoxious.

We stopped at a petrol station in Rocha to enquire whether Ruta 109 was as bad as we'd been told. The pump attendant insisted it was worse. Unable to resist the challenge, we set off towards it. At a bridge on the outskirts of town the paving ended abruptly, as though cut by a knife. Ahead of us, snaking its way into the hills, lay just the sort of road we'd learned to 'love'. We decided to try our hand at hitchhiking: a daft decision if ever there was one, since there wasn't a single car to be seen. We were beginning to think we'd put down roots when a tractor rumbled over the bridge, drawing a trailer piled high with farming equipment and furniture. There were two young lads on board: Tato and brother Tatín, old boys from The Christian Brothers, my childhood school's arch-enemies at rugby. They were only going 25 kilometres into the hills, but if that was good enough they'd be happy to take us. Anything was good enough provided we kept moving, so we shifted some of the load and stacked our bikes on top. Patricia rode shotgun on the tractor, high up on the mudguard, while Tatín and I climbed aboard the trailer.

Unlike other parts of the country, the landscape at the southern end of the Cuchilla Grande is chopped and broken. The valleys are small and deep and the climbs are sharp. Scenic it certainly was, with clouds like continents hanging in the perfect sky. Tato threw the tractor at the twisting road, scored and rutted from years of heavy rain, threatening more than once to turn us upside down. As we got out at the parting of our ways, the lads assured us that the local 'country folk' were friendly and hospitable and were sure to let us camp on their land, maybe even give us food. Being from Montevideo, they obviously felt under no such obligation themselves.

Since it was impossible to ride, we started walking. The going was slow and pretty rough. The sun was almost down before we spotted, on a distant hilltop, the outlines of a farm. In answer to our call, a middle-aged man, sloppily dressed and impossibly dirty, ambled out from a corral where he'd been attending to his flock of sheep. Masticating the end of his hand-made cigarette, he said he couldn't possibly allow us on his land. It wasn't his anyway: he was just the caretaker. I mean, what would the owner say if she turned up unexpectedly and there we were, on her estate? Since he'd also let slip that the owner was living in France, her sudden appearance seemed highly unlikely, but we were in no mood for debate.

At least – although he took some persuading – he agreed to let us fill our bottles from the well. As we were leaving he suggested we camp in a field halfway up the next hill, over there, by the woods. It wasn't his either, but the owner was away and probably wouldn't mind finding us there if he returned.

CHAPTER EIGHTEEN

THE FINAL PUSH

We were woken by the bleating of sheep and the muffled voices of men. I stuck my head out of the tent and saw nothing. The world was hidden in a thick, grey fog. Somewhere in the eastern sky there hung a pallid glow, but a couple of metres away from the tent even the grass disappeared. We could hear the clicking of hooves as the flock rushed past, but we couldn't see the animals or the shepherds.

It took another hour for the mist to melt away, leaving only the occasional cloud trapped in the cup of a valley. If we were glad that once again we could see where we were going, our joy was soon dissipated by the arrival of thousands of .22 calibre *tábanos*. Any satisfaction we drew from the ease with which the slow-moving fiends could be killed, was tempered by the fact that we couldn't kill them all. We needed both hands to steady the bikes as we pushed them up and down the steep, rutted hills, and we couldn't stop moving in case the flies settled. But even while we moved, some of them managed to land, so then we had to stop to fight them off and, once we were still, of course more landed. However slow they were, they settled on our bodies in such numbers that while we were killing one, another bit. Patricia, who'd been so proud that until then the *tábanos* had never 'got' her, was soon in a filthy temper. Without question the insects were the most difficult part of the entire trip. We could cope with the heat, the bad roads, the rains and the hills, but the bugs nearly beat us.

By late morning the temperature had risen to 41°C. In the valley beyond a particularly strenuous climb, we found a stream cascading down a miniature fall into a pool.

'I have to wet my feet, at least!' I said, kicking off my *alpargatas*, by now tattered beyond description. They'd had a strenuous couple of months.

Sitting on a rock, my feet in the water, the temptation was too great: I stripped and let myself slip into the clear, icy pool. I could almost hear it hissing as my body sank. Patricia, ever fearful of the horseflies, turned down the invitation to join me.

'Come on,' I urged, 'they're gone now.'

I was wrong. Very soon they found us, and got to work again. Rest had become an impossible dream. We pushed on.

We arrived in Aiguá in mid-afternoon, glad we hadn't waited for a passing truck: except for Tato's tractor we'd had the road to ourselves for two days. The small town stood on the banks of a stream in the middle of a plain ringed by the hills of the Cuchilla Grande. A few large old townhouses, their glory long since faded, hinted at Aiguá's wealthier, more active past. We followed the stream, looking for a suitable spot to put up the tent. The ground was flooded and the woods were infested with mosquitoes. We went back into town.

On a corner we found the police station, and stopped to ask directions there. I was just leaning my bike against the station wall when a preening sergeant strutted out onto the pavement.

'Hey, you,' he said, hitching his trousers up over his belly and trying to sound important, 'don't put it there, it isn't right.'

I wasn't in the mood. I gave him my best filthy look.

'You're right,' I said, 'My bicycle might get dirty.'

We had a little chat about democracy and citizens' rights and being civil to harmless travellers, with me doing most of the talking. Sheepishly, he offered Patricia the police station shower.

'No thanks, I'd like to get clean,' she replied, smiling sweetly. Sometimes that girl makes me very proud.

'You've got a real mean streak, you know,' she said to me later, as we headed for the town hall. Perhaps someone in the council would be more helpful.

We found two cleaners and a uniformed doorman in one of the offices. The councillors were all away. The doorman telephoned the Mayor, to ask whether we might camp on council land. The answer came back: No. It looked as though we'd have to cycle on. As we were leaving, the doorman scurried out of the building and, in a conspiratorial whisper, directed us to where he lived. He'd meet us there in a few minutes, he said.

Across the road from his modest home stood a little house. Manuel was taking care of it for a friend and, in his friend's absence, used it as a warehouse. A horse was tethered on a long chain in the back garden. The ground was rough and so littered with stones and dung that there was no clear space big enough for the tent. Indoors, the little shack smelled like a barn: sacks of grain and chicken feed were stacked to the ceiling. He led us into the bedroom, chaff crunching underfoot. A lumpy mattress lay on an old iron bedstead, covered with a wrinkled sheet.

'For this, we turned down Punta del Este?' murmured Patricia.

'You can sleep here, if you like,' said Manuel. 'The sheets are clean: I've only used them once or twice.'

He patted them down and tugged at the corners.

'I think it's terrible the way the councillor wouldn't let you on his land. People should help each other. I couldn't let you go. I know what it's like, when you've been travelling all day. The shower's over here.'

We followed him into the bathroom. It was far from clean, but it didn't stink too badly. Patricia and I knew at once we couldn't stay, but at least we could bathe before moving on.

About half an hour later we crossed the road to where Manuel, now out of his uniform, was sitting on his doorstep drinking *mate*. His young wife, a buxom, sturdy country girl with a clear, porcelain skin, was nursing their baby beside him. Thanking him, we shook his hand and got back on the road to Minas.

It was late afternoon, and the sun was quickly dropping towards the horizon in front of us. We'd have to find a campsite soon, before it got too dark. From the edge of the plain the road began a winding climb into the hills. It was a steady, constant slope, not too steep but tiresome nonetheless. For kilometre after kilometre the upward angle never altered or relented, giving us no pause.

On a stony crag up ahead, we caught occasional glimpses through the trees of a mysterious building, perched alone and moody on the heights. Sullen stone walls gave it the appearance of a cannery or abattoir, although it couldn't have been either of those in such an inconvenient, isolated spot. However odd, we knew that it would have to be our destination. At the gate, hot and sweaty all over again, we hesitated. The building looked abandoned, almost haunted. Our hesitation was cut short when a mongrel collie limped into view on the weed-choked gravel driveway, wagging its tail in greeting. Happy and clean, it had to be a good omen. Looking again, we saw some clothes hung out on the line.

Beneath the trees in the courtyard lay the broken, rusted remnants of tables and chairs. Close up, although it retained its institutional, prison-like gloom, we recognized that once upon a time the building must have been a restaurant. It commanded a spectacular view of the valley far below, with the town of Aiguá at its centre. The street lights came on as we watched. A whimsical lad in his late teens or early twenties, wearing a fingerless leather archery glove on his left hand, came to the door. Yes, of course we could put up the tent, he said, wherever we liked. As we hurried to do so before the light failed completely, he told us the place had been built by the municipality as a Parador, but the business had gone bust some years ago. His father, a policeman from Minas, had been given the job as watchman, and moved in with his family.

As we finished building our house Rosita, Rafael's mother, appeared at the window. She hung on the sill, chatting softly, offering fruit or home-made bread. A little while later, on a clattering, smoking motorbike, her husband Eleris roared up the drive. He seemed pleased to see us, and stayed in the courtyard talking until we retired.

The spectacular sunrise we'd hoped for failed to materialize. As I stood and stretched in front of the tent, rubbing the sleep from my eyes, Eleris came walking towards me carrying a Thermos of hot water for *mate* and a basket of home-made bread.

'Here, for your breakfast in bed!' he said with a grin, before going back indoors.

The dog stayed with us. He had a very nasty sore on one of his hind legs, the remnants of a wound he'd suffered in a fight, which had then become infested with maggots. Eleris had cured it with the same stuff we'd seen used on cattle.

The family were gathered in the cavernous kitchen when Patricia and I went in to brush our teeth. Rosita pleaded that we stay another day. She so seldom had guests. We could have lunch together. She wore cumbersome metal leg braces: she'd been crippled by polio when a baby. Mournfully she explained that although she loved her mother, who had recently died, she still blamed her for the illness. She had good reason. Her family had been living in the country, not far from Minas which, at the time, was suffering from a well-publicized polio epidemic. Rosita's aunt had asked her mother whether she might take the newborn baby into town, so that her relatives could see the child. Disregarding the danger, the mother had agreed.

'How *could* she?' asked Rosita. 'How could she take that risk with her baby?'

She didn't like it much up here on the hill. She couldn't get around very well, and missed being able to chat with her neighbours and visit her friends as she'd done when they were living in Minas. But Eleris was fed up with being a small-town cop on the beat, taking orders and being pushed around. When he was offered the job as watchman out here, where he could plant his own vegetables, keep a few chickens and a couple of cows, and breathe the fresh air, he'd leapt at the chance. He'd inherited a couple of the cows as orphan calves, and reared them by hand. The animals were comical to watch: their sense of bovine identity had somehow come adrift, and they behaved more like pets than cattle, following Eleris about wherever he went, constantly nudging him with their big, wet noses so that he'd pat them or tickle their chins.

We realized how poor they were, and yet how generous and kind-hearted, when we sat down to lunch. Rosita had spread out a spotless white tablecloth, on which she presented the modest meal beautifully and with imagination. The starter was a rice salad: cold boiled rice with home-made mayonnaise. The hot main course was pimentos from the garden stuffed with rice, and the dessert was rice pudding with stewed figs. It was all they had, and they shared it with us. For us it was a banquet.

The next day was grey and overcast. We left in mid-morning, struggling through the broken hills against a stiff and surprisingly chill wind which nonetheless failed to dent our high spirits: we were nearly at the end of our journey. *Nothing* could beat us *now*.

An hour or so later we saw some intriguing movement on the tarmac ahead of us, and stopped for a closer look. It was an enormous tarantula, brown and hairy, the size of a saucer. From a safe distance, lest it jump at us, we watched it walk cumbersomely across the road.

It was after midday when, ravenously hungry, we reached Minas at last. We scoured the steeply raked streets of the hillside town for a restaurant, but none of the places we saw really demanded our attention. In despair, we stopped to ask a man's advice. His prodigious, straining belly identified him plainly as someone who took food very seriously.

'Best place to go on a Sunday,' he said, 'is the Parador Salus. Jolly good food, and plenty of it. Cheap, too.' What more could we possibly ask for?

We grunted past an army barracks and up another long, miserable hill until, lo and behold, a signpost by the road pointed us towards the Fuente Salus. This is where Patricia's favourite mineral water springs from the ground. We followed the long, gently curving road past the bottling plant to the Parador high up on the ridge. The parking lot was full of cars and the inn, looking like a fancy country club from the pages of a magazine, was bustling with activity. Crowded tables spilled out of the restaurant onto the broad, tiled terraces, shaded by red and white striped canvas awnings. The air hummed with the sound of clinking cutlery and the smell of Sunday lunch. The doorman helped us store our bicycles in the boiler room, and we went up the stone staircase into the building. With a bang we were back in civilization.

We stood awestruck on the parquet at the whitewashed arch leading into the wood panelled bar, feeling distinctly out of place in our grubby shorts and baggy, faded shirts, struggling to remember how we should behave. We settled gingerly onto the tall, unfamiliar stools and feasted our eyes on the cosmopolitan selection of bottles on the mirrored shelves, trying to make up our minds.

'I want a Luton Airport,' whispered Patricia, meaning a Campari and orange juice.

The white-shirted bartender, bending ever so slightly at the waist, squeezed the fruit out in front of us and littered the wooden bar with tiny dishes of olives, roasted peanuts and minuscule slices of salami, making us feel more urban by the minute. There was too much to choose from, I couldn't decide.

'I want a whisky and a beer,' I said in the end.

We'd done it. We'd cycled right around the country, more than 2,000 kilometres of majestic, intoxicating, wide open spaces. Those nine weeks felt like nine lifetimes, the days already merging into one another in a blur of faces and places and events. All those never-ending roads that had lain perpetually before us, stretching across the vast landscape towards yet another unreachable horizon, now, as if by magic, lay behind us; one could almost say: within us. We felt elated, exhilarated, yet somehow sad and disappointed, sorry that our adventure was coming to an end. We'd grown accustomed to the gypsy life and the simple certainties of the pilgrim. We still had a last stretch ahead of us before the official end of the journey but somehow, sitting at that civilized, universal bar, ragged and dishevelled, grins so broad they threatened to crack open our faces, we knew that in reality it ended here. The rest was a formality.

With isolated words and broken, uncompleted phrases, the shorthand compiled as we travelled, we nudged each other's memories and conjured up visions in mid-air. We chuckled and groaned as we remembered, cradled in a warm, bitter-sweet yearning for all those sturdy, wonderful people whose lives we'd invaded only to be received with kindness and generosity, again and again, whatever the means of our hosts. Their hospitality had been the stuff of legend.

It hadn't always been easy. We'd worked harder than either of us had ever worked before and yet, once the first days were passed, the effort had become part of us, a fact of life, even, dare I say it, enjoyable. It had been a wonderful education, too: we'd learned about ourselves and each other, about our weaknesses and strengths, about how to share and how to function as a team. A lifetime of getting-to-know-you had been crammed into days. *Après* this, the *déluge*.

Patricia, once upon a time a fragile, hothouse flower, was an altogether different woman now. The work had been twice as hard for her, but somehow she'd found the strength to keep going, and when she hadn't found it she'd invented it. It there's a hero to this tale, she's the one.

One of the waiters, a bustling, stocky chap wearing a starched white coat and a pencil-line moustache, came into the bar to tell us our table was ready. We followed him into the dining-room, very conscious of our weather-beaten, dilapidated appearance, me trying to conceal the toes that protruded through the canvas of the *alpargatas* I'd bought on the second day out, so very long ago. Not one of the noisy families around us paid the slightest attention.

It was time to celebrate. The set menu was a monstrous, five-course meal. We had it all, washed down with far too much wine, and barely made it upstaris to the room we'd reserved. It was a proper room, with a proper double bed and matching furniture. It seemed like years since last we'd seen anything like it. We closed the wooden shutters on the afternoon sun, and collapsed. We stayed at the Parador for that day and the next, going for lazy walks in the forest, visiting the centenarian spring that fed the bottling plant, and just sitting on the terrace, feeling deeply impressed with ourselves.

Then the final push. In a single, muscular pull we covered the remaining 109 kilometres to Montevideo. It took us a mere four hours although the last, through the towns on the outskirts of the sprawling city, was rather tough. Unable to break completely our habits of the last couple of months, we stopped at a market we passed on the way to my mother's house for some *asado* and a bottle of wine.

When at last we got there it felt odd and somehow disconcerting not to have to scout about for a place to pitch the tent or somewhere to draw water, or hack about in the undergrowth collecting firewood and clearing a spot for the fire, or any of the hundred other little chores that had become second nature. The energy we'd learned to hold in reserve for the business of camping at the end of every day, now surplus to requirement, sent us stumbling about the house, tripping over the dogs and the furniture, looking in mirrors, admiring the chocolate cake decorated with white sugar bicycle wheels my mother had baked for us, and taking turns to stand on the bathroom scales. Between us we'd shed 22 kilos, most of it from around my middle. No wonder my shorts kept falling off. Throughout all this my poor mother followed us from room to room, trying to get some sense out of us, wanting to hear the whole story in fifteen minutes, congratulating us for having successfully completed our expedition and saying she could hardly believe we'd done it.

'*First* expedition, mum, *first* expedition.'

Because, you see, we already knew that we'd have to go on another one.

GLOSSARY

aduana	customs; customs house
aijuna	interjection – contraction of *ah, hijo de una gran puta* (oh, son of a great whore) no longer used blasphemously, usually indicative of surprise or dismay
Ahí tá	Contraction of *ahí está* – there it is
a la buena de Dios	At God's mercy, any old way
alameda	grove of poplars
alférez	ensign; second lieutenant
algarrobo	carob (tree)
almacén	general store
alpargatas	espadrilles, canvas shoes with rope soles
ANTEL	National Telephone Company
apadrinador	second, as in duel; sponsor; protector
aparejo	traditional fishing tackle consisting of stout line, hook and weight, no rod
apereá	small indigenous rodent *(cavia aperea Erxleben)*
areneros	sandmen, in this case men who work collecting sand
arroyo	stream
Artesano	artisan
asado	barbecue, meat roasted over hot embers (If you've never eaten one in Uruguay, you've never eaten one)
asado de tira	cut of beef (short ribs)
avestruz	ostrich; in this case *ñandú*
bacalao	cod; in this case dried, salted cod
bagre	catfish
bajada/subida de las penas	descent/ascent of sorrow

bañado	fen; marsh (literally 'bathed')
barranca	cliff, bank, embankment
bichos–son bichos preciosos	creatures/they are beautiful creatures
Blancos	one of two main political parties
boina	beret
bombachas	gaucho's traditional baggy trousers
buenos días	good morning, good day
buenas noches	good night
buenas tardes	good afternoon
cabaña	cabin; in this case cattle ranch, stud
café con leche	coffee with milk
camalotes	floating islands made up of lilies and other river reeds
caminera	as *policía caminera* – highway patrol
camino	path, track, route
campesino	countryman, farmer, planter
campo	fields; countryside
canejo	exclamation, 'dammit!' or similar
caña	liquor distilled from sugar-cane, similar to rum
cañada	creek, brook
capataz	foreman
carnicerîa	butcher's shop
carpincho	capybara
carqueja	*eupatorium bonifolium* – medicinal leaf
casa grande	large house; main house
casero	houseboy, houseman, rural butler
ceibo	type of flowering tree; national flower of Uruguay
Cerro Chato	flat hill
ceviche	Peruvian dish of raw fish marinated in lemon juice
chacra/chacrita	small farm; on a large estate, the vegetable garden
che	deformation of *oye* (listen) used colloquially to add emphasis, similar to English 'hey'
chorizo	sausage
colita de cuadril	cut of beef (taken from thigh)
Colorado	one of two main political parties
comadreja	type of weasel
comisaría	police station
comisario	chief of police
consultar	consult, enquire
Co-operativa de pescadores	fishermen's co-operative
corvina	ocean fish similar to bass

criollo	creole, native born to foreign (European) parents
crucera	extremely poisonous snake called 'of the cross' because of pattern of markings on skin
cuadras	85 x 85 m (area measurement)
defendiendo la patria	defending the homeland or fatherland (Patriotic mottoes of this sort, worn around the hat-band, are traditional devices and do not imply affiliation to a specific political party nor even that the wearer is particularly interested in politics.)
de ninguna manera	in no way, definitely not
documentos	documents; i.d.
domingueros	'Sunday people' – tourists
dorado	'golden'; *Salminus Maxillosus*, a type of river fish
dormilón	sleepy head, in this case a bird so named
dulce de leche	caramel confection made of milk and sugar
especial	special
Espinillar	as *caña*, but a higher grade, better quality
espinillo	thorn tree
estancia	estate, ranch, farm
estanciero	farmer; owner of estate
estás ahí?	are you there?
facón	originally a specific sort of knife, now used generically for any gaucho knife
fideos	noodles, pasta
fogón	hearth
frigorífico	refrigeration plant; also meat-packing plant
galleta	biscuit (*see below*)
galleta de campaña	'country biscuit'; a sort of sea biscuit, really a type of multi-leaved bread
gaucho	around Río de la Plata – Argentina, Uruguay and southern Brazil – roughly equivalent to the North-American cowboy (The word comes to Spanish from French *gauche*, meaning rough)
gente importante	important people
goiabada	jam made from guavas, which sets hard in bricks, typical in Brazil
Gordo	fatso
grappa/grappita	liquor distilled from grape seeds and skins, as in Italy
guayabera	long, sort-sleeved shirt with pockets, worn untucked
hacendados	cf. 'hacienda' meaning estate owners

hasta mañana	'until tomorrow' – farewell
helado/heladero	ice-cream (lit. 'frozen')/ice-cream vendor
hornero	oven-bird (*furnarius rufus rufus*)
humildad	humility, modesty
ibirapitá	indigenous tree
lagarto	lizard
legua/league	5 kilometres
leñador	woodsman
lobito de río	type of otter
loco	lunatic
mate	tea made from leaf of *ilex mate*
matorrales	thicket, undergrowth
matungo	derogatory term for horse; nag
meseta	plateau
milanesa	Wiener schnitzel
milhoja	flaky pastry; *mille-feuille*; lit. 'thousand leaves'
molidos	in this case exhausted; literally, milled or ground down
molino	mill; windmill
mulita	armadillo
municipio	municipality, town hall
nacional	national; locally manufactured
ñandú	South American ostrich
ñanduceros	ostrich hunters
novillo	heifer
Nuestra Señora de las Mercedes	Our Lady of Mercy
Nueva Capilla	New Chapel
nutria	aquatic rodent, considerably larger than domestic cat (fur exceptionally well regarded in garment industry)
ombú	indigenous tree; grows the size and age of oak; national tree
ONDA	Greyhound bus company
pajarito	literally 'little bird'; used as exclamation of surprise: 'Good Grief!'
paisano	man of the countryside, countryman
palmar	palm grove
pampero	wind from the pampas
paraíso	literally paradise, in this case name of an indigenous tree
pargo	ocean fish not unlike grouper
parrilla	grille, particularly as used in barbecue; brick/stone structure for accommodating same

parrillada	usually describes the event of barbecueing or the product thereof; party focused on grilled meats & delicacies; also used as generic term for restaurants specializing in that style of cooking, i.e. meat roasted over hot embers
pasando el repecho	just past or beyond the hill
patrón	boss (male)
patrona	boss (female)
pensión	cheap hotel, as in France or Spain
peso	exchange rate at time of trip; approximately 500 pesos to the pound sterling
picho	pooch, dog, mutt
pingo	horse, implies good, brave, worthy
pintado	painted, spotted – in this case fish of catfish family with large black polka-dots on back
pirincho	native bird
pituco	dandy
Policía Caminera	highway patrol
porquería	rubbish, dreadful
Portuñol	dialect spoken on Uruguayan/Brazilian border, comes from *Portugués-Español* (Portuguese-Spanish)
Prado	annual agricultural and traditional fair, held in Montevideo every Easter
precioso	precious, beautiful
Proceso	literally 'process', euphemism used to describe years of military dictatorship in Uruguay
quinta(s)	smallholding, vegetable or fruit plantation
quintero	worker or owner of *quinta*
quiste hidático	cystic disease caught by humans via the faeces or fluids of dogs fed on the infected internal organs of sheep
rancho	ranch; in Uruguay modest house, usually thatched, made of mud, wood or straw
repecho	slope, incline (upwards)
Salus	mineral water, from spring of same name
sandía	water-melon
Señor/Señora	Mr/Mrs
Sub-comisario Duque a las ordenes	Sub-commissioner Duque at your service (deputy-sheriff)
taba	traditional game of chance
tábano	horsefly
Tacuarembó	only Uruguayan province to retain its Indian (*Guaraní*) name, meaning 'river of *tacuara* canes'
tala	native tree, vaguely similar to bay

tararira	large, black river-fish
teros	native bird the size of seagull, nests on ground, extremely aggressive in defence of territory; national bird of Uruguay
timbó	very large native tree of jacaranda family
tolderías	teepees; Indian village
tortas fritas	literally fried cakes; a traditional type of domestic pastry
tropa/tropilla	herd of cattle on the move under gaucho supervision
truco	traditional card game in which cheating is legitimate
tu	second person pronoun, familiar form of address
usted	second person pronoun, formal form of address
y yo que culpa tengo?	and what fault of that is mine? Why blame me?
vacas	cows
venga p'acá	contraction of *venga para acá* – come here
zafreros	seasonally migrant labourers

INVENTORY

HIM

– Bicycle – Raleigh Randonneur
– 4 Karrimor Corniche panniers
– Tent – Wild Country *Nova* & pegs
– Two sleeping bags – North Face *'Chrysalis'*
– *Camera Case*: 35 mm camera; 70–210 mm zoom lens; 28–85 mm zoom lens; 12 rolls film; 4 filters; compass; thermometer; wire saw; sharpening stone; pen & ink.
– *Mate, bombilla & yerba*
– Four notebooks
– Two maps (north & south)
– Fishing tackle
– Hunting knife
– *Tool kit*: pliers; needle-nosed pliers; barbell spanner; Y-spanner; flat spanner; Allen keys; tyre levers; spoke key; screwdriver; puncture repair kit; freewheel remover tool; isolating tape; glue; tent patches; Thermarest patches; oil; spare tyre, inner tube, brake and gear wire; tin opener; bicycle lock.
– *Clothes*: 3 pairs underpants; 3 handkerchiefs; 2 shirts; 3 singlets; 3 pairs shorts; 1 towel; 2 pairs socks; bathing suit; 1 pair long trousers; belt; tennis shoes; *alpargatas*; flip-flops; cotton scarf.
– Hat
– Torch
– Police whistle
– Sunglasses
– Speedometer
– Bicycle pump
– Two litres of water

HER

– Bicycle – Raleigh Lady Granada
– 4 Karrimor Corniche panniers
– Tent poles
– Two Thermarest mats
– Tarpaulin/bicycle cover
– Two Barbour jackets
– Fishing rod
– Rubber bungees
– *First Aid Kit*: bandage; adhesive bandages; disinfectant/antiseptic; burn cream; water purifying tablets; thermometer; vitamins; aspirin; indigestion tablets; liniment; cotton pads; insect repellent.
– Hunting knife
– Wire grille
– Two aluminium plates
– Two enamel cups

– Two spoons & forks
– Salt
– Matches
– Laundry soap (bar)
– One pair rubber gloves
– Ten metres stout string
– *Toiletries*: soap; shampoo; toothpaste; toothbrushes; comb; shaving cream; shaving brush; razor; after-shave; deodorant; dental floss; contact lens solution etc; manicure set.
– *Cosmetics, etc*: night facial cream; eau-de-cologne; body lotion; hand lotion; skin tonic; lipstick; lipstick brush; rouge; ribbons; hair clips; elastic bands; hair brush; sewing kit; pads; alarm clock.
– *Clothes*: 1 pair long trousers; 2 pairs shorts; *smart* overall; 3 pairs underpants; 4 pairs socks; 6 T-shirts; bathing suit; belt; tennis shoes; *alpargatas*; flip-flops.
– Hat
– Police whistle
– Sheet
– Documents
– Bicycle lock
– Bicycle pump
– Two litres of water

BIBLIOGRAPHY

Diccionario Geográfico del Uruguay – Orestes Araújo, Imprenta Artística de Dornaleche y Reyes; Montevideo 1900

Historia de los Charrúas y Demás Tribus Indígenas del Uruguay – Orestes Araújo, J. M. Serrano; Montevideo 1911

Medicina Popular y Folklore Mágico del Uruguay – Idelfonso Pereda Valdés, Galien; Montevideo 1943

Hortus Guaranensis: Fauna Indígena Julio S. Storni, 1940

Journal of A Voyage To The River Plate (Including Observations Made During a Residence in the Republic of Monte Video) – W. Whittle, Bradshaw & Blacklock, London 1846

Pilchas Criollas – Fernando O. Assunção, Impresora Uruguaya Colombino S.A.; Montevideo, 1976

Vocabulario y Refranero Criollo – Tito Saubidet, Editorial Guillermo Kraft, Ltda; Buenos Aires 1943

Artigas y la Emancipación del Uruguay – John Street, Barreiro y Ramos, S.A.; Montevideo (Originally published as Artigas and the Emancipation of Uruguay – John Street; Cambridge University Press 1959)

Cuentos del Uruguay – Editorial Espasa-Calpe S.A.; Buenos Aires 1945

Proceso Histórico del Uruguay – Alberto Zum Felde, ARCA Editorial S.R.L.; Montevideo

Historia Uruguaya, Tomos 1–7 (see detail below)
Ediciones de la Banda Oriental, S.R.L.; Montevideo
Tomo 1: **La Banda Oriental en la Lucha de los Imperios**, José Claudio Williman (h) & Carlos Panizza Pons;

Tomo 2: **Artigas y el Federalismo en el Río de la Plata**, Washington Reyes Abadie

Tomo 3: **La Cisplatina, La Independencia y La República Caudille-sca**, Alfredo Castellanos

Tomo 4: **Apogeo y Crisis del Uruguay Pastoril y Caudillesco**, José Pedro Barrán

Tomo 5: **El Uruguay de la Modernización**, Enrique Mendez Vives

Tomo 6: **La Epoca Batllista**, Benjamín Nahum

Tomo 7: **Crisis Política y Recuperación Económica**, Benjamín Nahum; Angel Cocchi; Ana Frega; Yvette Trochon

Las Décadas Infames – Oscar H. Bruschera, Linardi y Risso; Montevideo 1986

Serie 'Los Departamentos' Editores: Daniel Aljanati; Mario Benedetto; Walter Perdomo, Editorial 'Nuestra Tierra'; Montevideo 1970